ORIGINALISM:
A QUARTER-CENTURY
OF DEBATE

ORIGINALISM:
A QUARTER-CENTURY
OF DEBATE

FOREWORD BY

Justice Antonin Scalia

EDITED BY

Steven G. Calabresi

Since 1947
REGNERY
PUBLISHING, INC.
An Eagle Publishing Company • Washington, DC

Library of Congress Cataloging-in-Publication Data
Originalism: a quarter-century of debate / edited by Steven G. Calabresi.
p. cm.

ISBN 978-1-59698-050-1

1. Constitutional law—United States—Interpretation and construction. 2. Rule of law—United States. I. Calabresi, Steven G.
KF4749.A2R85 2007
342.7302—dc22
2007022100

Published in the United States by
Regnery Publishing, Inc.
One Massachusetts Avenue, NW
Washington, DC 20001
www.regnery.com

Manufactured in the United States of America

10 9 8 7 6 5 4 3 2 1

To Mimi

Contents

Introduction

A CRITICAL INTRODUCTION
TO THE ORIGINALISM DEBATE

by Steven G. Calabresi

T his book commemorates the twenty-fifth anniversary of the founding of the Federalist Society in 1982. For the last quarter century, the Society and many of its members have promoted originalism as the correct philosophy to use in interpreting the Constitution. The originalism debate is of central importance to the Federalist Society's mission of promoting the rule of law, constitutionally limited government, and the separation of powers. We believe that ours should be a government of laws and not one of men or of judges.

Over the last quarter century, originalism has been the subject of much discussion. That debate, which had been proceeding quietly in American law schools, burst into noisy and public view with a speech by then-attorney general Edwin Meese, III, to the American Bar Association on July 9, 1985, which called for a Jurisprudence of Original Intention. Leading Supreme Court Justice William J. Brennan, Jr., entered the fray as did many other famous judges and law professors. General Meese honored the Federalist Society by delivering his response to Justice Brennan in November 1985 to the Federalist Society's Lawyers Division. We think this response and a speech that Gen-

1

eral Meese gave a year later at Tulane University remain among the most enduring statements of the originalist creed.

For that reason, we published a booklet in 1986 entitled "The Great Debate" that contained the key contributions to the originalism debate at that time. We continue to think that the originalism debate is of central importance to the Federalist Society's mission. We therefore chose to celebrate the twentieth anniversary of General Meese's spèech to our Lawyers Division by making originalism the theme of our 2005 National Lawyers Division Convention. With this book, we are now publishing the most important speeches that were given in the Meese-Brennan debate more than twenty years ago and portions of the twenty-year retrospective conference we held in November 2005. This book then contains a quarter-century of writings for and against originalism.

The speeches from our conference show that the issues General Meese raised more than twenty years ago are timeless and are still hotly contested. President George W. Bush's recent appointments of Reagan administration alumni John Roberts to be Chief Justice of the United States and of Samuel Alito to be an Associate Justice have led many Federalists to hope that there may now be four justices sympathetic to originalism on the Supreme Court. Six of the nine current justices are over the age of sixty-five, which used to be the mandatory retirement age in private business. It seems likely therefore that there will be several Supreme Court vacancies in the next six years. This book addresses the question of what judicial philosophy we should look for in picking new members of the Supreme Court. The reader will find in these pages the best and most brilliant defenders and opponents of the originalist creed. We hope this book will inform and shape the ongoing great debate over the merits of constitutional originalism.

The publication of this book comes at a time when three other brilliant originalist books have just been published: Mr. Meese's own *Heritage Guide to the Constitution*; Akhil Reed Amar's *America's Constitution*; and Randy Barnett's *Restoring the Lost Constitution*. Strikingly, the Meese and Amar books both go through the Constitution clause by clause from the Preamble to the Twenty-Seventh Amendment. The Barnett book offers a general originalist theory of constitutional law, which is sound on constitutional theory and enumerated powers, but faulty as to the Fourteenth Amendment. We think this flurry of originalist writing shows the continuing hold that the originalism debate has on the public mind even after a quarter-century.

In the remainder of this introduction, I want to give the reader a critical and opinionated guide to the ideas raised by some of the sources that follow. I will begin with a critical discussion of General Meese's speech to the ABA on July 9, 1985, and will end by very briefly discussing each of the panels and debates reprinted here from our 2005 Lawyers Conference. For each item I discuss, I will offer my own opinionated reading of the texts.

ATTORNEY GENERAL MEESE'S 1985 SPEECH TO THE ABA

The first theme of General Meese's 1985 ABA speech is the primacy of the rule of law. General Meese begins by saying we Americans "pride ourselves on having produced the greatest political wonder of the world—a government of laws and not of men." He goes on to quote Thomas Paine as saying, "America has no monarch: Here the law is king." This emphasis on the rule of law is central to originalism. Originalists believe that the written Constitution is our fundamental law and that it binds all of us—even Supreme Court justices. Those justices who abandon the original meaning of the text of the Constitution invariably end up substituting their own political philosophies for those of the framers. We Americans have to decide whether we want a government of laws or one of judges. Is the constitutional text going to bind the Supreme Court, or will the justices in essence write and rewrite the text? General Meese's ABA speech comes down squarely in favor of the idea "that the Constitution is a limitation on judicial power as well as executive and legislative" power.

The argument for the rule of law is in part that the alternative is to give judges too much discretion, which would produce big swings in constitutional law that would be destabilizing and undemocratic. But there is much more to it than that. There is, in addition, the idea that courts and judges should be able to avoid "the charge of being either too conservative or too liberal." There is no liberal or conservative meaning of the text of the Constitution; there is only a right meaning and a wrong meaning. Those who convert the Constitution into a license for judges to make policy instead of being a limit on the power of judges pervert a document that is supposed to limit power into one that sanctions it. For this reason, General Meese rightly says that "a constitution that is viewed as only what the judges say it is no longer is a constitution in the true sense."

This leads to a second theme of General Meese's ABA speech, which is that the whole idea of constitutionally limited government itself is at stake in the originalism debate. If the original meaning of the text of the Constitution does not bind the Supreme Court, why should it bind the president or the chairman of the joint chiefs of staff? Once we abandon originalism in the Supreme Court why not abandon it everywhere else as well? Such a decision is perverse because, as General Meese points out, judges and Supreme Court justices were supposed to be the "bulwarks of a limited constitution" and not a French Revolutionary-style Committee of Public Safety that would legislate on the most sensitive issues of morality and religion by five-to-four votes without the limitations imposed on the legislature of bicameralism and presentment. Indeed, the only reason judges have power to hold laws unconstitutional is because the Constitution is a higher law that binds legislative and executive officials and that trumps unconstitutional actions those officials might take. But if the Constitution does not bind the justices, why should it bind the president or Congress? Accordingly, abandoning originalism means abandoning the rationale which *Marbury v. Madison* uses to justify judicial review. Without originalism there can be no constitutionally limited government and no judicial review.

Moreover, if we abandon originalism in constitutional interpretation then why not abandon it with respect to interpreting all other legal writings, including statutes, contracts, wills, deeds, and even old

Supreme Court decisions? How many non-originalists would defend the idea that lower federal court judges are not bound by the original meaning of Justice Blackmun's opinion in *Roe v. Wade*, but are free instead to give that opinion a moral reading in light of today's evolving standards of decency? Not many. It is more than slightly ironic that those who favor judicial policy-making by the Supreme Court claim that lower court judges should slavishly follow Supreme Court case law that has been totally made up. If non-originalism is right when it comes to Supreme Court interpretation of the People's Constitution then surely it is right when district judges are applying made-up Supreme Court case law. The right answer on this, as on so many other questions, was long ago expressed by Justice Joseph Story when he said, "The first and fundamental rule in the interpretation of all instruments is, to construe them according to the sense of the terms, and the intention of the parties."

General Meese's ABA speech mentions three areas of Supreme Court case law where he faults the Court for not following original meaning in a way that was producing bad policy consequences. Strikingly, twenty years later all three areas of public policy have been or are about to be transformed.

The first area General Meese mentioned was federalism, where he faulted the Supreme Court for its five-to-four decision in *Garcia v. San Antonio Metropolitan Transit Authority*, which greatly extended the power of the national government. Twenty years later the *Garcia* decision is in essence a dead letter, and there has been a stunning revival of the doctrine of constitutional federalism on the Supreme Court. This revival began with the Court's 1995 decision in *United States v. Lopez* and continued in such cases as *United States v. Morrison, City of Boerne v. Flores, New York v. United States, Printz v. United States, Seminole Tribe v. Florida*, and *Alden v. Maine*. General Meese's 1985 challenge to the Supreme Court's federalism case law was, in retrospect, a rousing success.

A second area of law where General Meese urged change in doctrine was in the field of criminal law. Here Meese noted that the Supreme Court was moving in the right direction, and the Court has continued to be much more sympathetic to law enforcement than it had been in the 1960s and 1970s. The biggest change in criminal law since 1985 has come with the adoption of the Sentencing Reform Act in 1986, which has led to much higher and more certain sentences for those convicted of crimes. The result has been a huge drop in crime rates and a dramatic increase in the number of criminals incarcerated. Here again, General Meese's initiative has carried the day generally, although more remains to be done by the Supreme Court, which ought to get rid of the exclusionary rule altogether.

The third and final area of law where General Meese called for reform in 1985 was in the area of religion, and here there has been little progress as of spring 2007. A key problem was that Reagan Supreme Court appointee Sandra Day O'Connor essentially voted for non-originalist positions in religion clause cases. Justice O'Connor's replacement by Justice Samuel Alito is likely to lead to a big change in the Supreme Court's religion clause case law. How big a change will probably depend less on Justice Alito, who seems to be a firm originalist, and more on Reagan appointee Anthony Kennedy, who is feckless and inconstant. Still, Justice Kennedy has been consistently more originalist on religion clause cases than was Justice O'Connor, so Kennedy's replacement of Justice O'Connor as the swing vote in religion clause cases ought to move the law in the direction General Meese called for in 1985.

In sum, General Meese's ABA speech ended with his statement that it would be the Reagan administration's policy to press for a Jurisprudence of Original Intention in all of its official actions including in the briefs that the Administration filed and the judges it appointed. One can only conclude that, with the hindsight of twenty years, many of the changes General Meese called for ended up being made.

JUSTICE WILLIAM BRENNAN, JR.,'S 1985 SPEECH AT GEORGETOWN UNIVERSITY

The main theme of Justice Brennan's speech in response to Attorney General Meese was to emphasize what he called the "transformative purpose" of the constitutional text, which he argued embodies an "aspiration to social justice, brotherhood, and human dignity that brought this country into being." Justice Brennan argued that General Meese's vision of reading the text in light of its original meaning was "little more than arrogance cloaked as humility" because it was arrogant at our vantage point to claim we could discern how the Framers would apply the moral-philosophic natural law principles he thought they wrote into the Constitution to late twentieth century problems. Brennan added that "We current Justices read the Constitution in the only way we can: as twentieth-century Americans. We look to the history of the time of framing and to the intervening history of interpretation. But the ultimate question must be, what do the words of the text mean in our time? For the genius of the Constitution rests not in any static meaning it might have had in a world that is dead and gone, but in the adaptability of its great principles to cope with current problems and current needs."

To say that the genius of a constitution lies in the fluidity of its meaning is a little bit like saying that the genius of the brakes on your car is the way they can be used for acceleration. The whole point of having a constitution or a bill of rights in the first place is to memorialize and entrench certain fundamental rights so they can prevail in moments of passion when a crazed mob might want to cast them aside. To praise the Constitution primarily for its ability to be adapted to current problems and needs is thus to overlook the very reasons why we entrenched principles in the Constitution in the first place. More fundamentally, there are four specific errors in reasoning that permeate Justice Brennan's speech that deserve elaboration.

The first error is that Justice Brennan would totally cast aside the constitutional idea that it is feasible to have a system of inter-generational lawmaking. The precept that underlies written constitutions is that it is valuable for us to agree to be bound by constitutional rules our great-grandfathers made so that we in turn can adopt new constitutional amendments that will bind our great-grandchildren. Justice Brennan denies that such inter-generational lawmaking is desirable, or indeed that it is even feasible. He thinks the text of the

Constitution is like the text of a poem, to which each generation of readers brings most of the meaning.

The fact of the matter is that there are many circumstances where it is essential that entrenched rules be in place in order for liberty to flourish. Who would go to the trouble of writing a controversial book if he could not know for sure that he would not be imprisoned for it in twenty years, in violation of the First Amendment? Who would work hard to start a business if he could not be certain that it would not be taken from him without just compensation being paid, in violation of the Takings Clause? Without the ability to entrench freedom of speech and of the press, or constitutional protections for private property rights, we would all have less freedom today. Just as contract law empowers private individuals by creating a framework for private ordering, so too does constitutional law empower private individuals by credibly entrenching guarantees of individual freedom. Each generation gives up something by being bound by the rights it's predecessors entrenched, and it gains something by being able to entrench new rights for it's posterity. This system of inter-generational lawmaking would be completely undone if each generation read the Constitution like a poem to which it brought most of the meaning.

This illustrates a broader point which Steven D. Smith of the University of San Diego Law School has written about well, which is that legal texts are just scrawls of markings on a piece of paper if they are separated from the meaning that was given to those scrawls by the Framers who wrote them. Why agree to be bound by the words of the Constitution, the scrawls on a piece of paper, but for the meaning we know the Framers meant those scrawls to have and the authoritative position of the Framers themselves? This is especially so because the constitutional text was not written like a poem to inspire us but as a command about what we should or should not do. The constitutional text is much more like other legal writings such as statutes, wills, contracts, and Supreme Court opinions than it is like a poem. And part of the reason for that is because, at the end of the day, the interpretations we give the constitutional text are enforced at gunpoint, whereas the reading we give a poem is not.

The second error that Justice Brennan makes comes with his dismissive talk about the undesirability of us moderns being bound by "a world that is dead and gone." Non-originalists frequently like to argue that none of us living today should be bound down by "the dead hand of the past," *i.e.* by the Framers' Constitution. To begin with, it might be noted that there is a lot of law by dead people on the books today that non-originalists just assume we must be bound by. No one ever argues that the Social Security laws or the Civil Rights Act of 1964 or the Sixteenth Amendment giving Congress the power to impose an income tax should be ignored because those laws were made by dead people. For that matter, most non-originalists I know would be appalled by the suggestion that district judges should be free not to follow *Roe v. Wade* just because all nine justices who participated in the decision of that case are now dead. Justice Brennan could not possibly have meant by his speech to dismiss all laws enacted mostly by people who are now dead because the result of that would be chaos. What he probably meant was that he and his fellow justices ought to be able to pick and choose which laws written by dead people we were bound by and which ones we were not.

But to say that is to give the current justices on the Supreme Court a license to conduct regular spring cleanings of the Constitution in which they get to throw out some, but not most, of the laws made by the dead. Why on Earth should we trust the justices with that kind of power in a world where we know that power corrupts and absolute power corrupts absolutely? Justice Brennan would have us entrust five out of nine life-tenured justices with the power to erase parts of the Constitution and transformatively construe others. He argues the Framers meant to give five out of nine justices the power to, for example, eliminate the death penalty, even though a bill to deregulate the trucking industry would need to be approved by two houses of Congress, overcome a filibuster, and then be signed by the President, or be passed by two-thirds majorities of both houses over the President's veto, in order to become law. What are the odds that the Framers, who created our cumbersome system for national law-making, meant to give five-to-four majorities of the Supreme Court the power to legislate on the most sensitive issues of morality and religion? Brennan's position is simply not a credible one.

Third, Justice Brennan accuses originalists of practicing "arrogance cloaked as humilty," but, in fact, he is the one whose position is arrogant. Justice Brennan's view is that those of us in the present generation are better than our benighted ancestors. We have exceeded our ancestors not only in technology but also moral worth. With all due respect, it is Justice Brennan's position that is arrogant and not General Meese's. The American Constitution has survived for two centuries, is the oldest and first such document in existence, and has inspired countless spinoffs around the world. Is it not arrogant to dismiss the original meaning of that document lightly as Justice Brennan does? I understand and agree with the argument that we should not engage in ancestor worship, and I agree with President Reagan that America's best days lie ahead. We as a society believe in the progress that has come from and that will come from living the American dream. But the amended Constitution is a good document that has carried us a long way and that makes us still today the freest and most fortunate people on earth—the last best hope of man on earth. It is not arrogant ancestor worship to respect such a text the way children respect their parents. It would, however, be arrogant to discard such a text in the name of instead following the teachings of *Future Shock* or *The Greening of America*.

The final error made by Justice Brennan is that he raises the level of generality of the Constitution in order to justify the left-wing outcomes he wants. He describes the Bill of Rights as protecting human dignity and then asks whether the death penalty, for example, is compatible with human dignity. This is nothing more than the lawyerly sleight of hand used by Justice Douglas in *Griswold v. Connecticut*. The text of the Constitution does not speak vaguely of human dignity; it speaks specifically about freedom of speech and of the press, about unreasonable searches and seizures, and about property not being taken absent the paying of just compensation. At the end of the day, Justice Brennan's primary concern is that the text of the Constitution be construed to produce what he deems to be good consequences.

Doing this makes "the rule of law and not of men" impossible; which leads to very bad long-run consequences. Playing games with the level of generality of the constitutional text to produce good consequences is just as bad as saying that the nine justices have a commission to legislate from the bench. Legislating from the bench turns out to be what Justice Brennan's speech was all about.

ATTORNEY GENERAL MEESE'S 1985 SPEECH TO THE FEDERALIST SOCIETY

The first theme of General Meese's 1985 Federalist Society speech is his emphasis on the accessibility of the historical materials about the framing of the Constitution and its original meaning. General Meese pointed out how incredibly young our country is, how the Founding did not really happen that long ago, how the America of the 1780s was awash in pamphlets, newspapers and books, how much writing was done by Federalists and Anti-Federalists during the ratification debates, and how detailed were the notes James Madison took of the deliberations at the Constitutional Convention. As General Meese claimed, "the Constitution is not buried in the mists of time. We know a tremendous amount of the history of its genesis." It might be added that the most authoritative sources of all for original meaning textualists—dictionaries and grammar books from the 1780s—abound, and can easily be consulted. We also have at our disposal legal textbooks used by the framers, such as Blackstone's *Commentaries*, which shed light on the meaning of legal terms of art in the Constitution. And, for all the information available from the 1780s, even more information is available from the Civil War era when the three critical Reconstruction amendments were adopted. In short, Justice Brennan was simply wrong to the extent that he portrayed the "period surrounding the creation of the Constitution [as if it had been] a dark and mythical realm."

A second theme of General Meese's 1985 Federalist society speech is his close focus on the words of the constitutional text. General Meese repeatedly notes that the text is exactly specific in some places, like requiring that the President be at least thirty-five years old; that it is more general in other places, such as where it empowers Congress to regulate commerce and not merely trade and barter; and that it is still more general than that in clauses like the Fourth Amendment's ban on unreasonable searches and seizures. The speech clearly indicates that it is the original meaning of the words, and not merely the intention of those who wrote them, that is the law. General Meese rightly says that, "Where the language of the Constitution is specific, it must be obeyed. Where there is a demonstrable consensus among the Framers and ratifiers as to a principle stated or implied by the Constitution, it should be followed. Where there is ambiguity as to the precise meaning or reach of a constitutional provision, it should be interpreted and applied in a manner so as to at least not contradict the text of the Constitution itself." Above all, the thing we should note about the Constitution is that we have a written Constitution, unlike the British, and we have always venerated that written document. As General Meese rightly says, "The presumption of a written document is that it conveys meaning."

The point that it is the original meaning of the constitutional text, and not the intentions of the Framers, that is law was made by Justice Scalia in an important speech to the Justice Department in June 1986, just days before his nomination to the Supreme Court, and General Meese subsequently spoke of advocating a jurisprudence of original meaning rather than a jurisprudence of original intention. But General Meese's 1985 Federalist Society speech already clearly recognizes the primacy of the text over the intentions of those who wrote it.

A third theme of General Meese's 1985 Federalist Society speech is that the "undergirding premise [of the Constitution] remains that democratic self-government is subject only to the limits of certain constitutional principles." Part of what is at stake in the originalism debate is the power of cities, states, and Congress to exercise self-government. Representative democracy is one of the prime freedoms the Constitution protects, and a philosophy of constitutional interpretation that fails to protect democracy in its proper sphere is itself unconstitutional. The Constitution imposes very few limits on democratic government, and there are many foolish things that legislatures can do under our Constitution without violating that document at all. One of the chief flaws of Brennan-style non-originalism is that it took hotly contested issues like abortion out of the democratic process in the fifty states, where compromise was possible, and put them under the power of the Supreme Court, which could not produce compromise solutions. The constitutionalizing and nationalizing of the abortion dispute in *Roe v. Wade* has embittered the confirmation process for all federal judges and has roiled our politics for more than thirty years. Whatever ones personal position on the abortion question, I think all Americans should be able to see that the Supreme Court's thirty year effort to write a national abortion code has been a bitter and poisonous mistake.

A fourth and final theme of General Meese's 1985 Federalist Society speech is his point that following Justice Brennan and construing the Constitution in light of evolving standards of human dignity can lead the Court badly astray. We must never forget that *Dred Scott v. Sandford*, *Lochner v. New York*, and *Korematsu v. United States* were all substantive due process decisions where the Court was guided by its own twisted ideas about what "human dignity" required. Another tragedy of constitutional law, *Plessy v. Ferguson*, was, as General Meese argued, a case where the Supreme Court ignored the original meaning of the Fourteenth Amendment in favor of giving weight to Jim-Crow-era evolving standards of human decency. One could make a powerful case that the history of judicial review has been largely one of errors and tragedies. Thus, *Dred Scott* brought on a Civil War, the *Slaughter-House* and *Civil Rights Cases* strangled the Fourteenth Amendment in its crib, *Plessy v. Ferguson* sanctioned an era of state-sponsored segregation, *Lochner v. New York* delayed the implementation of progressive labor laws for thirty years, *Hammer v. Dagenhart* delayed the implementation of laws against child labor for a generation, *Korematsu v. United States* sanctioned government-run, racially discriminatory concentration camps, and *Roe v. Wade* led to the slaughter of more than thirty million innocent human lives. In any rational cost-benefit analysis of the institution of judicial review over the last two hundred years, the tragedy side of the scales of justice is heavily weighed down. There is good reason, in short, to be very skeptical of Supreme Court justices who are promising to promote "human dignity."

JUDGE ROBERT H. BORK'S 1985 SPEECH AT THE UNIVERSITY OF SAN DIEGO LAW SCHOOL

Judge Robert H. Bork is the intellectual godfather of originalism. Judge Bork laid the foundation for originalism in a 1971 *Indiana Law Journal* article, popularized originalism in a series of speeches in the 1970s and 1980s, championed the cause of originalism in his confirmation hearings to be a justice on the U.S. Supreme Court, and then, after he was unjustly denied confirmation, Judge Bork went on to write a definitive defense of originalism in his celebrated book *The Tempting of America*. Much of what Judge Bork addresses in his speech has already been discussed earlier in this introduction, but I do want to call attention to five key points that Judge Bork makes which I have not commented on so far.

First, Judge Bork explains that the "problem for constitutional law always has been and always will be the resolution of the Madisonian dilemma." The dilemma he says "is that neither the majority nor the minority can be trusted to define the proper spheres of democratic authority and individual liberty. The first would court tyranny by the majority; the second tyranny by the minority." Judge Bork argues that the role of one's judicial philosophy is to solve the Madisonian dilemma by setting judicial ground rules on when the majority and the minority respectively ought to rule. He claims that following the intentions of the framers and treating the Constitution like law will satisfy the Madisonian dilemma in a way that constrains judicial discretion. Indeed, he claims the only way of constraining judicial discretion is "if the judges interpret the [Constitution's] words according to the intentions of those who drafted, proposed, and ratified" them.

Judge Bork's argument is powerful, but in my humble opinion it suffers from some imprecision because technically it is the words of the Constitution that are law, and not the intentions of those who wrote the document, that are the supreme law of the land. The original public meaning of the Constitution's words as revealed in old dictionaries is certainly law, but there is no reason to think that the un-enacted, idiosyncratic intentions of particular Framers are law. Certainly the Framers did not think so. That is why James Madison kept his notes of the Constitutional Convention secret for fifty years after the Framing until the time of his death. There is a difference between legislative history and law. Only the constitutional text that was ratified can be called the law.

Judge Bork's second important point is that many of those who try to resolve the Madisonian dilemma do so by seeking guidance from some moral philosophy or from natural law. But Bork argues, "Not only is moral philosophy wholly inadequate to the task but there is no reason for the rest of us, who have our own moral visions, to be governed by the judge's moral predilections." This is a fundamental and profound point. Many of us, myself included, believe in the existence of a divinely prescribed natural law. We think, in the words of the Declaration of Independence, that our Creator has given us inalienable natural rights including the rights to life, liberty, and the pursuit of happiness. But it does not follow from this that courts and judges should protect those rights or enforce natural law. Judges are trained lawyers, so it makes sense to think they would be better than legislators at interpreting texts or summarizing our traditions. But there is no reason at all to think that judges would be better at discerning moral philosophy than are citizens or legislators. In fact, there is reason to think that we might be better governed by nine names chosen at random from the telephone directory than we would be by the Supreme Court.

Judge Bork's third important point is that originalists can easily apply timeless constitutional commands to new technologies, like wiretapping or television broadcasting, and to changed circumstances, like an explosion in costly suits for libel and slander. This negates a standard argument that is often made against originalism. Bork argues that all an originalist "requires is that the text, structure, and history of the Constitution provide him not with a conclusion but with a premise. That premise states a core value that the Framers intended to protect. The intentionalist judge must then supply the minor premise in order to protect the constitutional freedom in circumstances the framers could not foresee." Thus, we can apply the First Amendment to broadcasting and cable television, or the Fourth Amendment to electronic wiretaps. Bork concedes that we may not succeed in deciding all of these cases in the way that the Framers would have done, but "[e]ntire ranges of problems will be placed off-limits to judges, thus preserving democracy in those areas where the framers intended democratic government."

The final important point made in Judge Bork's essay concerns the claims of libertarian scholars that the Constitution protects economic liberty in a way that renders the modern regulatory state constitutionally suspect. Judge Bork is responding here to the theories of the late libertarian scholar Bernard Siegan, but what he says might just as easily be said of libertarian scholar Randy Barnett's recent book. Bork concedes that the text of the Constitution protects economic rights in the Contracts Clause and the Takings Clause and that perhaps those clauses have been under-enforced. He thus acknowledges that it is just as much a violation of originalism to read a clause out of the Constitution as it is for a court to invent a new right like the right to privacy.

Where Bork takes issue with results-oriented libertarians like Siegan is when they claim that the Fourteenth Amendment requires that governments prove to a court that their legislation satisfies important governmental objectives, that their challenged law is substantially related to the achievement of those objectives, and that a similar result cannot be achieved by less drastic means. Siegan's claims in this respect resemble those of Randy Barnett, who argues in his new book that the Constitution creates a presumption of liberty which state and federal governments must overcome to justify any of their laws. Bork says rightly that "[t]here are some general statements by some of the framers of the fourteenth amendment that seem to support a conception of the judicial function like this one. But it does not appear that the idea was widely shared or that it was understood by the states that ratified the amendment. Such a revolutionary alteration in our constitutional arrangements ought to be more clearly shown to have been intended before it is accepted. This version of judicial review would make judges platonic guardians subject to nothing that can properly be called law."

PRESIDENT RONALD REAGAN'S 1986 SPEECH AT THE WHITE HOUSE AT THE INVESTITURE OF CHIEF JUSTICE WILLIAM H. REHNQUIST AND OF JUSTICE ANTONIN SCALIA

President Reagan's remarks at the investiture of Chief Justice Rehnquist and Justice Scalia show him implementing Attorney General Meese's originalist approach to constitutional law in using his appointment power. Reagan makes it clear that he selected Rehnquist and Scalia precisely because of their judicial philosophies. Three themes in Reagan's brief remarks deserve mention and praise.

First, President Reagan's speech, like many others of his speeches, contains exceptionalist rhetoric that claims the United States is a special country, populated by a special people, with a special mission in the world. Reagan quotes Abraham Lincoln as saying that our republic was "the last best hope of man on earth," and he refers to the "inspired wisdom" of our Constitution. He notes that "all of us, as Americans, are joined in a great common enterprise to write the story of freedom—the greatest adventure mankind has ever known and one which we must pass on to our children and their children—remembering that freedom is never more than one generation away from extinction." Reagan concludes by quoting Daniel Webster who essentially believed that our written Constitution is the Ark of the Covenant of the New Israel that is America. Webster said: "Miracles do not cluster. Hold on to the Constitution of the United States and to the Republic for which it stands—what has happened once in 6,000 years may never happen again. Hold on to your Constitution, for if the American Constitution shall fall there will be anarchy throughout the world."

This belief of President Reagan's that America is a special place, with a special people, who have a special role in the world, has direct implications for constitutional interpretation. There is a movement afoot now on the Supreme Court which has at times gathered the votes of as many as six justices to apply foreign constitutional law in resolving interpretive questions under the Constitution. By reminding us of our special destiny as a people and of the miracle that is our Constitution, President Reagan shows the error in most cases of applying foreign constitutional law to the interpretation of our Constitution. It would be wrong for the Supreme Court to apply French, German, or Canadian constitutional rules to us because America is a very different country, and our people are very different from the peoples of France, Germany, and Canada. Americans have always believed that this country is a shining city on a hill—a beacon of liberty to the rest of the world. We are more patriotic, more religious, harder working, more libertarian, and more moralistic than are the other developed countries of the Western world. President Reagan was right to exhort us to "hold on" to the Framers' Constitution because it is a remarkable document for a remarkable country. President Reagan's exceptionalist rhetoric explains why in most cases the Supreme Court should not look for guidance to foreign constitutional law.

Second, President Reagan's speech emphasizes the importance of the fact that our Constitution is one that provides for limited government. He notes that the Framers "settled on a judiciary that would be independent and strong, but one whose power would also, they believed, be confined within the boundaries of a written Constitution and laws." He said that "the Founding Fathers designed a system of checks and balances, and of limited government, because they knew that the great preserver of our freedoms would never be the courts or either of the other branches alone. It would always be the totality of our Constitutional system, with no one part getting the upper hand." Reagan ends by again quoting Lincoln, who asked, "What constitutes the bulwark of our own liberty?" Lincoln's answer: "It is the love of liberty which God has planted in us." And Reagan then says, "Yes, we the people are the ultimate defenders of freedom. We the people created the government and gave it its powers. And our love of liberty, and our spiritual strength, our dedication to the Constitution are what, in the end, preserves our great nation and this great hope for all mankind."

In these comments, President Reagan shows that he firmly understood a point that most constitutional law professors have never understood, which is that the Constitution is enforced by we the people acting through the system of checks and balances, and not by the unilateral actions of the Supreme Court. Moreover, Reagan recognizes that the Constitution limits the Supreme Court, as well as empowering it. The reason restoring respect for the original Constitution promotes the cause of constitutionally limited government is because it is that kind of government which our original Constitution prescribed. Thus, the advocates of the original meaning of the Constitution in the United States are by definition also advocates of limited government.

Third, and finally, President Reagan says that the judicial philosophy he advocates is one of judicial restraint, and he praises Rehnquist and Scalia by saying they are also advocates of judicial restraint in the tradition of Justices Holmes and Frankfurter whom Reagan praises. These passages raise the question of whether originalism and judicial restraint are the same thing or whether Reagan meant to endorse only judges who never strike anything down as being unconstitutional. The answer to this question is revealed by Reagan's discussion mentioned above about how our Constitution provides for limited government and checks and balances both of which he praises. Reagan clearly expects his restrained justices to be faithful to our written Constitution and not to simply defer to actions of the political branches that may violate that Constitution. By calling for judicial restraint therefore, President Reagan was not calling for judicial passivity, but for justices who would follow the written commands of the Constitution in making their decisions. Sometimes the text might render an act of another branch or of a state unconstitutional, and then it would be the duty of the restrained judge to say so. Far more often the constitutional text allows for democratic governance and then it is the task of the restrained judge to uphold the governmental action in question. The point is that judicial restraint means judges following and obeying the supreme law of the Constitution. President Reagan made that clear with his approving quote of Justice Felix Frankfurter's statement that "[t]he highest exercise of judicial duty is to subordinate one's personal will and one's private views to the law."

ATTORNEY GENERAL EDWIN MEESE III'S 1986 SPEECH AT TULANE UNIVERSITY

The first theme of General Meese's path-breaking speech at Tulane University in 1986 was to echo President Reagan's exceptionalist rhetoric upon the appointment of Chief Justice Rehnquist and of Justice Scalia. General Meese quoted Gladstone approvingly as saying that the Constitution is "the most wonderful work ever struck off at a given time by the brain and purpose of man." He goes on to note that "[n]o sooner was the Constitution adopted than it became an object of astonishing reverence." By celebrating the text of our written Constitution, General Meese prepares the ground for a devastating attack on the Supreme Court's decisional case law.

Second, General Meese draws a sharp distinction between the Constitution and constitutional law. The first, he informs us, is the six-thousand-word written text of 1787, as amended. The second are the opinions of the Supreme Court printed in more than five hundred volumes of the U.S. Reports. While the constitutional law opinions of the Court are bulkier than the text, General Meese argues it is the text and only the text which is the supreme law of the land binding forevermore on the political branches of the federal government and the States. General Meese approvingly quotes constitutional historian Charles Warren as saying that "[h]owever the Court may interpret the provisions of the Constitution, it is still the Constitution which is the law and not the decision of the Court." Justice Frankfurter made the same point when he said that "[t]he ultimate touchstone of constitutionality is the Constitution itself and not what we have said about it." Indeed, General Meese notes that if the text of the Constitution were not supreme over the decisions of the Supreme Court that court would not be empowered to overrule itself, as it has done more than one hundred and seventy times in its history. "To confuse the Constitution with judicial pronouncements allows no standard by which to criticize and to seek the overruling of what University of Chicago Law Professor Philip Kurland once called the "derelicts of constitutional law," cases such as *Dred Scott* and *Plessy v. Ferguson.*

Third, General Meese notes that it is only the text of the written Constitution to which we the people of the United States have given our consent. The people have never consented to be governed in a formal way by the five hundred volumes of the U.S. Reports. We know from the Declaration of Independence that a fundamental precept of our constitutional order is that governments are instituted and dissolved by the people and that legitimate government requires the consent of the governed. The American people have consented to be governed by the Constitution, but they have not consented to be governed by the Supreme Court's decisional case law.

Fourth, General Meese discusses the binding qualities of a constitutional decision by the Supreme Court, and he concedes that such decisions bind "the parties in a case and also the executive branch for whatever enforcement is necessary. But such a decision does not establish a supreme law of the land that is binding on all persons and parts of the government henceforth and forevermore." What this means is that, as General Meese said, "Constitutional interpretation is not the business of the Court only, but also properly the business of all branches of government." We the people can react to Supreme Court decisions with which we disagree, and "we can make our response through the presidents, senators, and representatives we elect at the national level." General Meese concludes that: "The Supreme Court, then, is not the only interpreter of the Constitution. Each of the three coordinate branches of government created and empowered by the Constitution—the executive and legislative no less than the judicial—has a duty to interpret the Constitution in the performance of its official functions. In fact, every official takes an oath precisely to that effect."

General Meese essentially here articulates and defends departmentalism, the idea that the Constitution is enforced by all three branches of the federal government acting together as agents of "We the People." This is an idea with an illustrious history, having been previously defended by Thomas Jefferson, James Madison, Andrew Jackson, Abraham Lincoln, Franklin Roosevelt, and Ronald Reagan. Departmentalism is important because it leads directly to judicial restraint, and to the idea that all laws arrive before the courts with a presumption of constitutionality. The reason for this is that departmentalists believe that Congress, when it passes a law, and the President, when he signs and executes it, implicitly make a judgment that the law in question is constitutional as well as being desirable as a policy matter. Since judgments of constitutionality are made by all three branches of the federal government acting together, a law that arrives in court with the *imprimatur* of two of the three branches should be presumed to be constitutional. And, the courts should be restrained in striking down such a law except where it appears by a preponderance of the evidence to conflict with the Constitution. I would not go as far as James Bradley Thayer and invalidate only laws that are clearly and beyond a reasonable doubt unconstitutional. But I do think the burden of proof lies on those who are challenging the constitutionality of a law or of an executive branch action.

The Tulane speech also makes clear that Chief Justice Hughes was wrong when he quipped, "The Constitution is what the judges say it is." It is not. The Constitution is what the text says and what we the people say it is, acting through our agents in all three branches of government over a long period of time. The Constitution is enforced and given meaning not just by the Supreme Court but by the whole Madisonian system of checks and balances.

It follows that for a precedent of constitutional law to become settled it must be the case that all three branches of the federal government must have agreed that a matter is well settled for at least a generation. Thus, the constitutionality of paper money or of the Social Security Act are settled matters in our constitutional system, but *Roe v. Wade* is not. All of this flows inexorably and logically from the statement of the Tulane speech that the Constitution is enforced by all three branches of the federal government acting together.

Those seeking to describe the actual behavior of the Supreme Court without normatively judging that behavior often claim that the Supreme Court follows the election returns. The most famous political scientist to make this claim is Yale's Robert Dahl. Bruce Ackerman makes a similar point when he says that the Supreme Court is the caboose on the train of government, and the President and Senate are the locomotive. There is some truth to this account, which suggests again that the Constitution is not simply enforced by the Supreme Court.

For two reasons, however, it is a mistake to uncritically accept the idea that the Supreme Court mechanically follows the election returns. First, the Court does not follow the election returns as a descriptive matter on issues where elite opinion differs from mass opinion. It follows elite opinion instead. This is vividly illustrated by the Supreme Court's case law opposing prayer in public schools which has been rejected by more than seventy percent of the public in opinion polls taken over a forty-year period of time. Second, vacancies on the Court now occur only on average once every four years, whereas between 1789 and 1970 they occurred on average once every two years. That means it takes twice as long now to get the Supreme Court to follow the election returns as it did a generation ago.

The core insight of the Tulane speech that ultimately we the people are the only legitimate interpreters of the Constitution is dead right, however. The Constitution, federal statutes, and treaties may be the supreme law of the land, but the Supreme Court's case law most definitely is not.

PANEL ON ORIGINALISM AND UNENUMERATED RIGHTS

The first panel discussion in this book discusses whether there is a role for unenumerated rights in constitutional law. Throughout its history, the Court has periodically enforced rights that are not expressly enumerated in the Constitution. In *Dred Scott*, for instance, the Court discovered that the right to bring slaves into a territory was protected by the Due Process Clause of the Fifth Amendment. In the twentieth century, the Court has found the right to abortion in the Due Process Clause of the Fourteenth Amendment. More recently, scholars have referred to the Ninth Amendment of the Bill of Rights as a source of unenumerated rights. Does the Constitution provide any legitimate foundation for the enforcement of unenumerated rights?

The correct answer to that question is the one given by Justice Antonin Scalia in his opinion for the Supreme Court in *Michael H. v. Gerald D.*, and by Chief Justice Rehnquist in an opinion which got five votes, *Washington v. Glucksberg*. The Scalia-Rehnquist position on unenumerated rights is ably defended by Michael McConnell on this panel, and I would refer those who are interested in this question to his speech printed later in this book.

Like McConnell, I think the original meaning of the Privileges or Immunities Clause of the Fourteenth Amendment is that it protects against State infringement a few unenumerated rights that are so deeply rooted in history and tradition that they have been followed since 1868, if not since the days of the American Revolution. Obviously, the so-called right to privacy is not such a right. I agree with McConnell, and disagree with John Harrison, in concluding that the Privileges or Immunities Clause is not only an anti-discrimination clause but is also a clause which protects individual rights from State abridgement. Laws can "abridge" rights by discriminating, as the Fifteenth Amendment shows, or by infringing on individual rights, as the First Amendment shows. The Fifteenth and First Amendments both use the word "abridge" and this leads me to think McConnell is right that that word in the Privileges or Immunities Clause protects against both types of abridgements.

McConnell rightly points out that the rights reserved by the Ninth Amendment against infraction by the Federal Government cannot, by definition, be constitutional rights, but he does not address the question of whether the Federal Government has the enumerated power in the first place to infringe unenumerated rights that are deeply rooted in history and tradition and that go back to 1776. On this issue, I agree with Gary Lawson who has argued that federal laws infringing unenumerated rights that date back to 1776 are not "necessary *and proper*" means for implementing other powers which the Constitution confers. The only unenumerated rights I think are protected against *federal* infringement are those that are so deeply rooted in history and tradition that they date back to 1776. An example of such a right might include the freedom to pick your own health care provider. A federal law that deprived individuals of such a right in the name of creating national health insurance might not be "necessary *and proper*."

PANEL ON ORIGINALISM AND PRAGMATISM

Pragmatic theories of constitutional interpretation have enjoyed renewed interest. Are they necessarily critiques of originalism, or can originalism be defended on pragmatic grounds? More generally, pragmatism asserts that the ultimate defense of constitutional law, like other human institutions, is the good it can do for people now. Can adherence to the original meaning of a two-hundred-year-old document still be defended as beneficial today?

Modern-day advocates of pragmatism as the correct theory of judicial decision-making think judges should give a lot of weight to the consequences their decisions produce. The leading advocates today of such a results-oriented jurisprudence are undoubtedly Justice Stephen Breyer and Judge Richard Posner. Posner defends this approach in a leading book entitled, appropriately enough, *Overcoming Law*. It is accurate to say that Judge Posner favors replacing the rule of law with the rule of judges. This raises the interesting question that I once asked him at a colloquium, which is whether those who read Seventh Circuit or Supreme Court opinions ought to follow those opinions only in so far as doing so led to what they deemed in their personal opinion to be good consequences. He said yes. I then asked him whether citizens filling out their tax returns should follow the Internal Revenue Code only in so far as doing so led to what they deemed in their personal opinion to be good consequences. The judge declined to answer.

There is an obvious problem with pragmatic, results-oriented judging, which is that it produces bad results because it guts the rule of law. Robert's *Rules of Order* informs us that "where there is no law, but every man does what is right in his own eyes, there is the least of real liberty." This statement is indisputably true. A Supreme Court whose justices decide cases in a results oriented way is nothing less than a nine-member French Revolutionary Committee of Public Safety. Why on Earth should the citizens of a democracy allow a committee of superannuated lawyers to make binding rules on the most sensitive issues of morality and religion on a five-to-four vote based on their own personal moral and religious beliefs? Why especially should we combine this with an ordinary lawmaking system in which laws implementing mundane matters like trucking deregulation must pass two houses of Congress, overcome a filibuster in the Senate, and be either signed by the President or repassed by a two-thirds vote of both houses?

Telling judges to be policy makers is itself unpragmatic and will lead to bad results not good ones. Judges are not good at making policy or judging consequences on a case-by-case basis. They have much less information at their disposal than do legislators because they cannot hold hearings, they cannot visit their home districts and talk to constituents, and they cannot engage in *ex parte* contacts with experts. Judges live an insulated existence where they talk mainly to their law clerks and spouses, and the information they get about the real world comes in the highly stylized form of a legal brief or from reading the *New York Times* editorial page. Judges have no incentive to find out and implement the will of the people. Instead, their incentive is to acquire fame by ingratiating themselves to editorial writers.

What judges in theory might be good at is dispassionately interpreting legal texts and the deeply rooted traditions of the American people. They should stick to doing precisely that. Instead of worrying about the result in particular cases, judges should follow the rule of law in thousands of cases because doing so leads to better results than not doing so. The problem with Justice Breyer's and Judge Posner's consequentialism, as they grandly call result-oriented judging, is that it produces bad consequences on a system-wide basis.

PANEL ON ORIGINALISM AND PRECEDENT

Some have argued that precedent is impossible to reconcile with originalism because for originalists only the understanding of the text matters, not prior judicial interpretations of the text. Article VI of the Constitution makes only the Constitution itself "the supreme Law of the land," not Supreme Court case law. On the other hand, jurisprudential giants as diverse as Hamilton, Madison, and Marshall all seemed to put stock in precedent. This panel considers the role precedent ought to play for originalists and whether precedent poses a greater problem for originalism than it does for other theories of constitutional interpretation.

I participated in this panel as both moderator and panelist, and my views are stated in the essay that appears later in this book. Accordingly, I will not restate them here.

THE ORIGINAL MEANING OF THE COMMERCE, SPENDING, AND NECESSARY AND PROPER CLAUSES

This panel applies originalism to the central legal questions of federalism. What commentators have labeled "the modern federalism revolution" began with the Court's construction of the Commerce Clause in *United States v. Lopez*. But recently the Court has upheld federal statutes on the basis of the Spending Clause and the Necessary and Proper Clause. While Justice Thomas has extensively written about the original understanding of the Commerce Clause, the justices in general have not spent much time exploring the original meaning of those clauses. This panel will consider the proper original understanding of all three clauses and whether that understanding can or should be revised to prevent Congress from exercising plenary authority.

The debate between Michael Paulsen and Randy Barnett on this panel is one of the finest debates the Federalist Society has ever sponsored, and I hope it is widely read. I do not, however, find myself in complete agreement with either one of them. I will focus, as they do, on two clauses, the Necessary and Proper Clause, and the Property Clause that Paulsen argues confers the spending power, since I agree with them that all the famous New-Deal-era Supreme Court cases which are thought to be broad readings of the Commerce Clause in fact rest on the Necessary and Proper Clause instead. My understanding of the Necessary and Proper Clause here is shaped by the scholarship of Gary Lawson and Patricia Granger Lawson.

I agree with Justice Scalia and Michael Paulsen that the Necessary and Proper Clause does give Congress the implied power to regulate wholly intrastate activities that substantially affect interstate commerce. I think the New Deal decisions in *United States v. Darby* and in *NLRB v. Jones & Laughlin Steel Corp.* are rightly decided. I disagree with Paulsen, however, to the extent that he implies that *Wickard v. Filburn* and *Raich v. Gonzales* are correct. Like Chief Justice Rehnquist and Justices O'Connor and Thomas, I do not think regulating the growth of small home-grown amounts of wheat or marijuana for personal consumption is a "necessary and proper" means toward the end of regulating interstate commerce. Congress could, in my view, wholly forbid the intrastate sale of wheat or marijuana (a commercial activity) or ban its shipment across state lines (pure interstate commerce). But growing crops at home for one's own consumption, however, is an activity that so thoroughly lacks a nexus to interstate commerce that I do not think Congress has the power to regulate it. This is not to say that Congress cannot, under the Necessary and Proper Clause, regulate the possession of some items. I have no doubt that Congress could outlaw private possession of a home-made nuclear bomb or of some lethal virus or bacterium on the grounds that doing so was "necessary and proper" to carrying out the other enumerated powers.

At this point, Mike Paulsen, Justice Scalia, and Judge Easterbrook would all shout at me that I favor judicial activism because I would let Supreme Court justices substitute their own notion of what laws are "necessary and proper" for Congress's. Paulsen and Scalia, at least, are, however, *estopped* from making this claim against me because they agree that the Gun Free School Zone Act, struck down in *Lopez*, and the Violence Against Women Act, struck down in *Morrison*, were not laws that were "necessary and proper" and that it was not activist for the Supreme Court to so hold.

The solution to the conundrum posed by the Necessary and Proper Clause is to recognize that the meaning of the words "necessary and proper" is not left by the Constitution either to Congress alone or to a five-justice majority of the Supreme Court applying the justices' own personal, idiosyncratic idea of what is "necessary and proper." The meaning of these words and their application to present-day problems depends, in the end, on what the American people think they mean acting over a long period of time through our three branch process of constitutional interpretation. Federal laws barring guns in schools or violence against women, in a world where more than forty of the states already bar those things, hardly seem to be "necessary," much less "proper." The same point might be made more generally to attack the federalization of the criminal law. Why would it be "necessary" and "proper" for Congress to outlaw a lot of things that are already outlawed by almost all of the states? It might be "necessary and proper" to have a federal ban on possession of a nuclear weapon or on criminal civil rights violations, but a federal ban on sexual assaults or bringing a gun within a thousand feet of a school when virtually every state already outlaws those things? That seems like quite a stretch.

A federal law barring the growth for personal consumption of a standard and safe farm commodity like wheat veers so far in the direction of recognizing a new enumerated power to regulate agriculture that it is unlikely most of the American people would have thought such a law to be "necessary and proper." In fact, the reaction of even my most liberal constitutional law students is always to guffaw when we get to *Wickard*. They obviously do not believe the federal law upheld in *Wickard* was "necessary and proper." The same is

true of the Controlled Substances Act to the extent it forbids possession for medical purposes of home-grown marijuana. The fact that a
large number of states and huge majorities of people in national public opinion polls all think that the medicinal use of marijuana is
unthreatening proves this fact. The three dissenting justices in the
Raich case were not thus simply substituting their own personal and
idiosyncratic views of what was "necessary and proper" for Congress's views. They were applying instead the widely-held social
understanding of the American people.

The Court already claims that it looks to that widely held social
understanding when it enforces the Cruel and Unusual Punishment
Clause of the Eighth Amendment by doing a nose count of state laws.
The Necessary and Proper Clause poses exactly the same interpretational conundrum as is posed by the Eighth Amendment. As Justice
Scalia has rightly pointed out, the present Supreme Court is far too
willing to substitute its own view of what is "cruel and unusual" for
the American people's, and, in this respect, the Court is just plain
wrong. But Scalia's Eighth Amendment dissents do not call on his colleagues only to find unconstitutional those punishments that were
thought to be so in the 1790s. Instead, Scalia reads the Amendment
as proscribing punishments that, say, three-fourths of the states (to
borrow a rule from Article V) think are prohibited today.

The Necessary and Proper Clause ought to be interpreted the same
way. In the 1790s laws like those the Court upheld in *Darby* or *Jones*
and *Laughlin Steel* would not have been deemed to be "necessary and
proper," but no one doubts that three-fourths of the states would
deem such laws permissible today. It is far less clear that three-fourths
of the states really believe it is "necessary and proper" to have federal
laws against guns in schools or violence against women. And Justice
Scalia, quite rightly, was not convinced of that either.

The Court ought, as Paulsen claims, to show a lot of deference to
Congress before it strikes down a law as it did in *Lopez* and *Morrison* because it exceeded the scope of the power granted by the Necessary and Proper Clause. It may even be that the Court should strike
down only one egregious such law every ten or twenty years, doing

just enough to prompt Congress to do a better job of policing itself. But when Congress uses the Necessary and Proper Clause to federalize criminal law or regulate what one grows on one's own land, when numerous states would allow that commodity to be grown, Congress has gone too far. At this point, it is appropriate for the Supreme Court to intervene so that Congress does not become the sole judge of the scope of Congress's own powers. Anyone who wants to read more about my views on federalism should consult my *Michigan Law Review* article entitled, "A Government of Limited and Enumerated Powers: In Defense of *United States v. Lopez*."

The other congressional power addressed by this panel is the spending power and here I must disagree with Paulsen, and with David Engdahl, that the spending power flows out of the clause in Article IV that gives Congress "Power to dispose of and make all needful Rules and Regulations respecting the Territory or other Property belonging to the United States." Paulsen argues this is a plenary grant of power, as Alexander Hamilton said, but to read it as the source of the spending power seems a stretch. The more plausible source of the spending power is the Necessary and Proper Clause. Structurally, one would expect to find the spending power in Article I, Section 8 along with the taxing power. The spending power is one of the major powers of Congress so it would be odd for the framers to describe it not in Article I, which is about Congress, but in Article IV, which is largely about the federal government and the states.

This construction is confirmed by the Clause in Article I, Section 9, which provides that: "No Money shall be drawn from the Treasury, but in Consequence of Appropriations made by Law." In general, Article I, Section 9, limits powers granted to Congress by Article I, Section 8. The fact that the Appropriations Clause appears in Article I, Section 9, thus strongly suggests that the Spending Power has already been conferred by Article I, Section 8, rather than anticipating the Property Clause of Article IV.

It is theoretically possible that the Property Clause could be read as the source of the Spending Power as Pauslen and Engdahl claim, but it seems like a stretch. It is far more likely that the property that the Property Clause gives Congress plenary power to dispose of is either real property or the equivalents to tangible personal property, but not all taxpayer money. This suggests that the test for whether spending is permissible under the Constitution is one that calls for determining whether the spending in question is "necessary and proper" to the carrying out of any or all of the enumerated powers of the federal government. This may well lead to a doctrinal test very much like the one the Court adopted in *South Dakota v. Dole.*

DEBATE OVER WHETHER ORIGINALISTS ARE "RADICALS IN ROBES"

This debate between Cass Sunstein and Charles Cooper focuses on the claim made in a recent book by Cass Sunstein that originalists are really "radicals in robes." Sunstein claims that the adoption of originalism would lead to a series of bad consequences including the abandonment of rights for women, the abandonment of the idea that the federal government cannot discriminate on the basis of race, the overturning of the principle of *Brown v. Board of Education,* and the end of the incorporation doctrine. Any theory that would produce such catastrophic results must, in Sunstein's view, be wrong. More broadly, Sunstein accuses originalists of believing that the Constitution implements something suspiciously like the platform of the 2004 National Republican convention that nominated President Bush. This is a serious charge, and it deserves a serious response. I agree with Charles Cooper's comments in rebuttal of Cass Sunstein, and would add the following points.

Sunstein's first claim is that originalism cannot explain why the federal government is forbidden from engaging in race or sex discrimination. I disagree. The first question any originalist must ask in a case challenging a federal law is where did Congress get the power to pass that federal law in the first place. Article I, Section 8, does not give Congress the power to pass laws that discriminate on the basis of race or sex. Thus, for Congress to claim such power, it would have to argue that laws that discriminate on the basis of race or sex are "necessary *and proper*" means for the carrying out of some enumerated end. I think given the passage of the Fourteenth and Nineteenth Amendments it would be impossible to make that case for laws that discriminate on the basis of race and exceedingly difficult to make it for most laws that discriminate on the basis of sex.

The grant of power to Congress to pass "necessary and proper" laws is logically read in light of the prohibitions the text of the Fourteenth Amendment puts on the states. It is more than a little hard to argue that it is "necessary and proper" for Congress to do something which the states are *constitutionally forbidden* from doing unless one can show some reason why the federal government ought to be treated differently from the states. It is a basic principle of textualism that texts should be read holistically so that one portion of the text is synthesized with the rest of the text. The Fourteenth Amendment is every bit as much a part of the Constitution as is the Necessary and Proper Clause and the two texts should be read together. Whatever may have been the case before 1868, I think it would not be reasonable after that date for the Court to uphold as "proper" federal laws designed to create a racial caste system. The same thing applies after the 1920 adoption of the Nineteenth Amendment for laws designed to create a sexual caste system, although it should be noted that there are laws that discriminate on the basis of sex that do not create such a caste system, like the laws providing for separate men's and women's restrooms.

In any event, the burning issue in anti-discrimination law today is not racial or sexual discrimination, which has been forbidden by federal statute since 1964. The real anti-discrimination issue before the Supreme Court today is discrimination on the basis of sexual orientation. Are laws that discriminate on that basis "necessary and proper?" I think the answer is plainly yes. There is no constitutional amendment that bans discrimination on the basis of sexual orientation the way the Fourteenth bans race discrimination and the way the Nineteenth bans sex discrimination as to political rights, which, historically, have been handed out more selectively than civil rights. Given the long history of laws against sodomy, I think Congress could plausibly pass a law to govern the military along the lines of the "Don't ask, don't tell" policy or the Defense of Marriage Act. Interestingly, with all of Sunstein's advocacy of liberal judicial restraint, he is mysteriously quiet about the constitutionality of laws that make distinctions on the basis of sexual orientation. Could it be that Sunstein is not really judicially restrained after all?

Sunstein might respond to my arguments above from the Necessary and Proper Clause by asking how originalists could defend *Bolling v. Sharp*'s holding that Congress lacked the power to run segregated schools in the District of Columbia given its specific power "To exercise Legislation in all cases whatsoever" over the District. The answer is that racially discriminatory acts of Congress are not acts of "Legislation," they are acts of congressional "Adjudication." These acts are ones whereby Congress finds that a certain race of people deserves harsh treatment simply because of who they are and not because of what they have done. Racially discriminatory federal laws are thus not within the grant of power to Congress to pass "Legislation" to govern the District of Columbia. They are also a kind of bill of attainder in that they single out a small group for harsh legal treatment without any judicial finding of guilt. Article I, Section 9, forbids Congress from passing bills of attainder, and a federal law assigning school children on the basis of race to a second class system of schools in the wake of the adoption of the Fourteenth Amendment can only be called a legislative punishment directed against a small group of people for no good reason whatsoever. The separation of powers allows Congress to legislate. It does not allow Congress to punish.

Sunstein's second big claim is to trot out the old canard that originalism cannot justify *Brown v. Board of Education*, which struck down segregation in schools, or *Loving v. Virginia*, which struck down anti-miscegenation laws. This is just plain false. When the Fourteenth Amendment was adopted in 1868 more than three-quarters of the states had provisions in their state constitutions defining a public school education as being a fundamental right. Every state I am aware of in 1868 recognized marriage as being a fundamental right. What this means is that the right to a public school education and to marry were "privileges or immunities" in 1868, as a matter of positive law. And, as John Harrison has conclusively shown, the Fourteenth Amendment was plainly meant at a bare minimum to outlaw racial discrimination as to privileges or immunities. Michael McConnell has confirmed this fact as to segregated schools with a superb article that argues from what is called subsequent legislative history, but one does not need to look to the debates that led up to the passage of the Civil Rights Act of 1875 to see why *Brown* and *Loving* are right. The rights to go to public school and to marry were fundamental rights in 1868, and the Fourteenth Amendment allows no state to discriminate as to fundamental rights on the basis of race.

Sunstein would respond that my argument would have come as news to the people who wrote the Fourteenth Amendment because many of them plainly did not believe that amendment outlawed anti-miscegenation laws much less required integration in public schools. The answer to that is that original meaning textualists have never claimed that Congress understood what it was doing when it passed legal texts. All we have claimed is that those texts are the law and have to be read like laws. Congress frequently passes laws without knowing what is in them, and Congress sometimes passes contradictory laws as it did for years when it spent money both on advertisements against smoking and on tobacco price supports. I do not claim Congress understood what it did when it passed the Fourteenth Amendment. My only claim is about what the original public meaning of the text of the amendment must have been.

Sunstein also claims that it is impossible for originalism to explain how the Fourteenth Amendment outlaws sexual discrimination. This too is wrong. Unlike the Thirteenth and Fifteenth Amendments, which are plainly addressed to the issue of racial discrimination, the Fourteenth Amendment cryptically bans "discrimination" in general without telling us the bases as to which "discrimination" is banned. John Harrison rightly I think reads the ban on discrimination in the Fourteenth Amendment as being a ban on all systems of class legislation—a ban if you will on caste systems in general. Thus, I presume that if a state in this country tried to set up a Hindu style caste system, we would have no trouble recognizing that that effort violated the Fourteenth Amendment. The same thing would be true if a state divided its citizens into nobles and serfs in a medieval-style system of feudalism. I submit that after the passage of the Nineteenth Amendment in 1920 a good case could be made that at least some laws discriminating on the basis of sex became forbidden caste-like laws. If the Nineteenth Amendment gave women the political right to vote, which children and felons lack, then surely it tells us something about whether women enjoy equal civil rights to men which even children and felons have. Obviously, the Nineteenth Amendment does not of its own force give women equal civil rights but surely its adoption affects how we should read the no-caste-based discrimination rule of the Fourteenth.

Does the Fourteenth Amendment forbid discrimination on the basis of sexual orientation as a form of caste-based discrimination? I think not. Gays and lesbians should have to secure passage of a constitutional amendment like the Fourteenth or the Nineteenth before that legal change can occur. Nor does the Fourteenth Amendment ban on caste-based laws render unconstitutional laws against abortion as a form of sex discrimination. Laws against abortion are favored in greater numbers by women than men. If we had a nationwide referendum on abortion in which only women could vote, many restrictions on abortion would pass that the Supreme Court does not allow today, including probably a ban on second trimester abortions. The fact of the matter is that the population group that most strongly backs a woman's right to choose are men between the ages of eighteen and thirty years old. I wonder what explains that?

Sunstein's third big claim is that originalism cannot explain the "one person, one vote" rulings by which the Supreme Court reapportioned the nation. Never, however, does he address Judge Robert Bork's argument in *The Tempting of America* that the heart of those decisions could have been and should have been arrived at by applying the Guarantee Clause of Article IV. I agree with Bork and also think that while a rule of "one person, one vote" is defensible for the House of Representatives and for state houses of representatives. I think it is absurd, however, to argue that "one person, one vote" is required for state senates, given that we do not follow that rule for the U.S. Senate. Whatever one thinks on this latter point, the issue is surely closed at this point as a matter of *stare decisis*.

Sunstein's fourth big claim is that originalism would lead to the de-incorporation of the Establishment Clause and possibly of the entire Bill of Rights. This, too, turns out to be wrong, although the argument as to why is somewhat intricate. To begin with, Akhil Amar has made a powerful case for incorporation in his superb book on *The Bill of Rights*. But even if Amar were wrong that the Privileges or Immunities Clause referred to the rights of national citizenship in the Bill of Rights it would still be the case that privileges or immunities of state citizenship in 1868 were protected against individually targeted abridgements. In 1868, an overwhelming majority of the states had establishment clauses in their own State constitutions. This means the right to be free of a state-established church was a fundamental right in 1868 which the Fourteenth Amendment said could not be abridged.

The same argument undoubtedly applies to many, if not all, of the other rights in the Bill of Rights. I have not had time yet to check on how many states had equivalents to the First Amendment, the Fourth Amendment, the Takings Clause, or the Eighth Amendment in 1868, but I will bet most of them did. If so, then all of these rights are privileges or immunities of state citizenship which are protected against abridgement. At the same time, I will bet that few if any states in 1868 had exclusionary rules or *Miranda* warnings. This would tend to suggest that key Warren Court cases like *Mapp v. Ohio* and *Miranda v. Arizona* were a step too far, which is exactly what General Meese was arguing twenty years ago.

Sunstein's fifth big claim is that the right to privacy and *Griswold v. Connecticut* cannot be justified under originalism. And here, he is right. They cannot be justified. Those decisions should at a minimum not be extended any further, and ideally they should be overruled.

Sunstein's sixth big claim is that the ban on regulatory takings cannot be justified using originalism. This argument proceeds from the premise that regulating property is not the same thing as "taking" it away altogether. Since the Takings Clause only prohibits "takings," Sunstein thinks regulation must be okay. To begin with, one would have to know what the State constitutional law provided in 1868 to know what kind of property rights were privileges or immunities when the Fourteenth Amendment was passed. I simply do not know the answer to that, but it could be that some states forbade things like regulatory takings. Some states probably forbade the taking of the property of A and the giving of it to B. Second, what the Rehnquist Court has done with respect to regulatory takings is functionally indistinguishable from what the Warren Court did in *New York Times v. Sullivan* for libel and slander suits against public officials. In both instances, a new form of government regulation was growing up that threatened a core constitutional value, be it property rights or freedom of speech and of the press. In both instances, the Court acted to protect the core constitutional value from erosion. If *New York Times v. Sullivan* is right, as I think it was, then the Supreme Court's case law limiting regulatory takings must be right as well.

Sunstein's seventh big claim is that originalism would lead to the revival of the non-delegation doctrine and the elimination of independent agencies. The implication is that the regulatory State would come crashing down. This is again not true. A revived non-delegation doctrine would at most threaten a few portions of a few statutes. Congress would be free to re-regulate in these areas so long as it passed more specific laws. And this is assuming that all originalists believe in the non-delegation doctrine (as I do), but many originalists like Justice Scalia do not accept the doctrine.

As to independent agencies, no one really cares whether Federal Trade Commission or Federal Communications Commission commissioners are removable or not. The issue is important only to protect against new congressional incursions on the executive branch like the now-dead independent counsel law. More people might care about the removability of governors of the Federal Reserve Board, but as Alan Greenspan's nearly twenty year tenure as Chairman of the Federal Reserve showed there are powerful political incentives that make it very risky for presidents to play political games with the money supply.

Sunstein's eighth and final big claim is that originalism would lead to the repeal of the New-Deal-era case law upholding broad federal power. Again, this claim is greatly overstated. I argued above that *Darby* and *Jones and Laughlin Steel* were both rightly decided, and I would add to that list *Heart of Atlanta Motel vs. United States* and *Katzenbach v. McClung.* The cases where I have criticized limitless federal power are: *Lopez, Raich,* and *Wickard v. Filburn.* I cannot believe that any reasonable person would conclude the sky was falling if those three cases had come out the other way, or if the Supreme Court were to put the brakes on the federalization of the criminal law. Indeed, I would have thought that the Left might agree with putting the brakes on the federalization of the criminal law or with deciding *Raich* the other way, but who am I to predict what constitutional leftists are going to do?

Sunstein's parade of horribles about the conclusions he says originalism will lead to can be refuted on every point except for his statement that originalism would mean the end of the so-called right to privacy. But before ending let me mention some good consequences that would flow from adopting originalism. This country would be better off with more federalism and more decentralization. We have far too much power concentrated in Washington, D.C., right now. We would be better off with a president who had more power to manage the bureaucracy. We need the unitary executive that the Framers meant us to have, and not rule by life-tenured federal bureaucrats. We would be better off if we did not abort a million babies a year as we have done since 1973. This would make us a more just society as well. We would be better off if students could pray and read the Bible in public school and if the Ten Commandments could be posted in public places. Religion is needed in the public square. We would be better off if citizens could engage in core political speech by contributing whatever they wanted to contribute to candidates for public office. Current contribution limits for candidates for public office are absurdly too low. We would be better off if we could grow wheat on our own farms without federal intrusion. The same thing goes for growing basil in our kitchens. We would be better off if criminals never got out of jail because of the idiocy of the exclusionary rule. Millions of Americans have been victimized by crime thanks to the Warren Court's odd ideas about criminal law enforcement. We would be better off if our homes could not be seized by developers acting in cahoots with state and local government. Private property is a core right of free individuals living in a free society. We would be better off if state governments could not pass laws impairing the obligations of contracts. Freedom of contract is also a core right of free individuals.

In short, Ronald Reagan was right when he urged us all to "hold on to" the amended Constitution of 1787 because it is a miracle the likes of which has not been seen in 6,000 years of world history. The United States is the freest nation on Earth and the arsenal of democracy because we have a better Constitution than does Britain, or France, or Germany, or Canada. Restoring the force of the original Constitution will lead to good consequences, not bad ones.

PART I

Foreword

JUSTICE ANTONIN SCALIA

In introducing this volume devoted to the philosophy of constitutional interpretation known as originalism, it would be foolish to pretend that that philosophy has become (as it once was) the dominant mode of interpretation in the courts, or even that it is the irresistible wave of the future. The interpretive philosophy of the "living Constitution"—a document whose meaning changes to suit the times, as the Supreme Court sees the times—continues to predominate in the courts, and in the law schools. Indeed, it even predominates in the perception of the ordinary citizen, who has come to believe that what he violently abhors must be unconstitutional. It is no easy task to wean the public, the professoriate, and (especially) the judiciary away from such a seductive and judge-empowering philosophy.

But progress has been made. Twenty years ago, when I joined the Supreme Court, I was the only originalist among its numbers. By and large, counsel did not know I was an originalist—and indeed, probably did not know what an originalist was. In their briefs and oral arguments on constitutional issues they generally discussed only the most recent Supreme Court cases and policy considerations; not a word about what the text was thought to mean when the people adopted it.

If any light was to be shed on the latter question, it would be through research by me and my law clerks. Today, the secret is out that I am an originalist, and there is even a second one sitting with me, Justice Clarence Thomas. Rarely, nowadays, does counsel fritter away two out of nine votes by failing to address what Justice Thomas and I consider dispositive. Originalism is in the game, even if it does not always prevail.

Sometimes, moreover, it does prevail, as in *Crawford v. Washington*, a thoroughly originalist Supreme Court opinion that brought the Confrontation Clause back to its moorings after twenty-four years adrift in the Sea of Evolutionism had reduced it to nothing more than a guarantee that hearsay accusations would bear unspecified "indicia of reliability."[1] Or in *Apprendi v. New Jersey*, where fidelity to the original meaning of the Sixth Amendment's jury-trial guarantee put an end to a movement in both state and federal legislation to impose mandatory sentence enhancements (*i.e.,* additional jail time) on the basis of aggravating facts found to be true only by a judge, and by a mere preponderance of the evidence.[2] (Both of these significant cases, by the way, give the lie to the frequently heard contention that originalism is nothing more than a device to further conservative views.) In other cases, even when what I would consider the correct originalist position has not carried the day, the debate between the majority and dissenting opinions has been carried on in originalist terms.[3] Bad originalism is originalism nonetheless, and holds forth the promise of future redemption.

In the law schools as well, originalism has gained a foothold. I used to be able to say, with only mild hyperbole, that one could fire a cannon loaded with grapeshot in the faculty lounge of any major law school in the country and not strike an originalist. That is no longer possible. Even Harvard Law School, the flagship of legal education (I can say that because I am a HLS graduate) has, by my count, no less than three originalists on its faculty (no names, please). Twenty years ago there was none. Not that all law schools, or even a majority of law schools have originalist professors; but being an originalist is no longer regarded as intellectually odd, if not un-intellectual.

To be sure, not all developments have been encouraging. American constitutional evolutionism has, so to speak, metastasized, infecting courts around the world. The American Supreme Court's "living document" now finds its correlative in the Canadian Supreme Court's "living tree," and in the pronouncement of the European Court of Human Rights that the Convention it applies "must be interpreted in light of current conditions." Increasingly, nowadays, foreign courts cite our opinions, and we theirs, because (I fear) judges in all countries believe they are engaged in the very same enterprise: not in determining the original meaning of the unalienable rights approved by the American people or the Canadian people or by the European nations that signed the Convention on Human Rights; nor even in determining what present-day Americans or Canadians or Europeans believe the human-rights provisions *ought* to mean; but in determining *for themselves* the *true* content of human rights, much as judges in common-law jurisdictions once believed they were all pursuing the same "brooding omnipresence" of The Common Law. One might expect this international development to strengthen the conviction of our domestic evolutionary judges that they are on the right track (can we be wrong in pronouncing this new human right when the vast majority of the world's judges agree with us?). It may be, however, that the sheer spectacle of our judges' determining the meaning of the American Constitution by falling into step with the judges of foreign courts will bring home to the American people the profoundly undemocratic nature of the evolutionary enterprise.

In any case, there is reason to be hopeful. The upcoming generation of judges and lawyers will have been exposed to originalist thinking far more than was my own—if not through their law professors then through lectures and symposia sponsored by the Federalist Society; and if through neither of those then at least through the reading of originalist Supreme Court opinions and dissents. It is the very premise of our free system that, in a fair and equal competition of ideas, the truth will prevail. The essays in this volume are directed to that end.

One

SPEECH BEFORE THE
AMERICAN BAR ASSOCIATION

Washington, D.C., July 9, 1985,
Attorney General Edwin Meese, III

Welcome to our Federal City. It is, of course, entirely fitting that we lawyers gather here in this home of our government. We Americans, after all, rightly pride ourselves on having produced the greatest political wonder of the world—a government of laws and not of men. Thomas Paine was right: "America has no monarch: Here the law is king." Perhaps nothing underscores Paine's assessment quite as much as the eager anticipation with which Americans await the conclusion of the term of the Supreme Court. Lawyers and laymen alike regard the Court not so much with awe as with a healthy respect. The law matters here and the business of our highest court—the subject of my remarks today—is crucially important to our political order.

In reviewing a term of the Court, it is important to take a moment and reflect upon the proper role of the Supreme Court in our constitutional system. The intended role of the judiciary generally and the Supreme Court in particular was to serve as the "bulwarks of a limited constitution." The judges, the Founders believed, would not fail to regard the Constitution as "fundamental law" and would "regulate their decisions" by it. As the "faithful guardians of the Constitution," the judges were expected to resist any political effort to depart from the literal provisions of the Constitution. The text of the document and the original intention of those who framed it would be the judicial standard in giving effect to the Constitution.

You will recall that Alexander Hamilton, defending the federal courts to be created by the new Constitution, remarked that the want of a judicial power under the Articles of Confederation had been the crowning defect of that first effort at a national constitution. Ever the consummate lawyer, Hamilton pointed out that "laws are a dead letter without courts to expound and define their true meaning."

The Anti-Federalist Brutus took him to task in the New York press for what the critics of the Constitution considered his naiveté. That prompted Hamilton to write his classic defense of judicial power in *Federalist* 78. An independent judiciary under the Constitution, he said, would prove to be the "citadel of public justice and the public security." Courts were "peculiarly essential in a limited constitution." Without them, there would be no security against "the encroachments and oppressions of the representative body," no protection against "unjust and partial" laws. Hamilton, like his colleague Madison, knew that *all* political power is "of an encroaching nature." In order to keep the powers created by the Constitution within the boundaries marked out by the Constitution, an independent—but constitutionally bound—judiciary was essential. The purpose of the Constitution, after all, was the creation of limited but also energetic government, institutions with the power to govern, but also with structures to keep the power in check. As Madison put it, the Constitution enabled the government to control the governed, but also obliged it to control itself.

But even beyond the institutional role, the Court serves the American republic in yet another, more subtle way. The problem of any popular government, of course, is seeing to it that the people obey the laws. There are but two ways: either by physical force or by moral force. In many ways the Court remains the primary moral force in American politics. De Tocqueville put it best:

> The great object of justice is to substitute the idea of right for that of violence, to put intermediaries between the government and the use of its physical force . . . .
>
> It is something astonishing what authority is accorded to the intervention of a court of justice by the general opinion of mankind . . . .
>
> The moral force in which tribunals are clothed makes the use of physical force infinitely rarer, for in most cases it takes its place; and when finally physical force is required, its power is doubled by his moral authority.

By fulfilling its proper function, the Supreme Court contributes both to institutional checks and balances and to the moral under-girding of the entire constitutional edifice. For the Supreme Court is the only national institution that daily grapples with the most fundamental political questions—and defends them with written expositions. Nothing less would serve to perpetuate the sanctity of the rule of law so effectively.

But that is not to suggest that the justices are a body of Platonic guardians. Far from it. The Court is what it was understood to be when the Constitution was framed–a political body. The judicial process is, at its most fundamental level, a political process. While not a partisan political process, it is political in the truest sense of that word. It is a process wherein public deliberations occur over what constitutes the common good under the terms of a written constitution.

As a result, as Benjamin Cardozo pointed out, "the greatest tides and currents which engulf the rest of men do not turn aside in their course and pass the judges by." Granting that, de Tocqueville knew what was required. As he wrote:

> The federal judges therefore must not only be good citizens and men of education and integrity . . . [they] must also be statesmen; they must know how to understand the spirit of the age, to confront those obstacles that can be overcome,

and to steer out of the current when the tide threatens to carry them away, and with them the sovereignty of the union and obedience to its laws.

On that confident note, let us consider the Court's work this past year. As has been generally true in recent years, the 1984 term did not yield a coherent set of decisions. Rather, it seemed to produce what one commentator has called a "jurisprudence of idiosyncrasy." Taken as a whole, the work of the term defies analysis by any strict standard. It is neither simply liberal nor simply conservative; neither simply activist nor simply restrained; neither simply principled nor simply partisan. The Court this term continued to roam at large in a veritable constitutional forest.

I believe, however, that there are at least three general areas that merit close scrutiny: federalism, criminal law, and freedom of religion.

FEDERALISM

In *Garcia v. San Antonio Metropolitan Transit Authority*, the Court displayed what was in the view of this Administration an inaccurate reading of the text of the Constitution and a disregard for the Framers' intention that state and local governments be a buffer against the centralizing tendencies of the national Leviathan.[1] Specifically, five Justices denied that the Tenth Amendment protects states from federal laws regulating the wages and hours of state or local employees. Thus the Court overruled—but barely—a contrary holding in *National League of Cities v. Usery*.[2] We hope for a day when the Court returns to the basic principles of the Constitution as expressed in *Usery;* such instability in decisions concerning the fundamental principle of federalism does our Constitution no service....

Our view is that federalism is one of the most basic principles of our Constitution. By allowing the states sovereignty sufficient to govern, we better secure our ultimate goal of political liberty through decentralized government. We do not advocate states' rights; we advocate states' responsibilities. We need to remember that state and local governments are not inevitably abusive of rights. It was, after all, at the turn of the century the states that were the laboratories of social and economic progress—and the federal courts that blocked their way. We believe that there is a proper constitutional sphere for state governance under our scheme of limited, popular government.

CRIMINAL LAW

Recognizing, perhaps, that the nation is in the throes of a drug epidemic which has severely increased the burden borne by law enforcement officers, the Court took a more progressive stance on the Fourth Amendment, undoing some of the damage previously done by its piecemeal incorporation through the Fourteenth Amendment. Advancing from its landmark *United States v. Leon*, which created a good-faith exception to the Exclusionary Rule when a flawed warrant is obtained by police, the Court permitted warrantless searches under certain limited circumstances.... [3]

Similarly, the Court took steps this term to place the *Miranda v. Arizona* ruling in proper perspective, stressing its origin in the Court rather than in the Constitution.[4] In *Oregon v. Elstad*, the Court held that failure to administer *Miranda* warnings and the consequent receipt of a confession ordinarily will not taint a second confession after *Miranda* warnings are received.[5]

The enforcement of criminal law remains one of our most important efforts. It is crucial that the state and local authorities—from the police to the prosecutors—be able to combat the growing tide of crime effectively. Toward that end we advocate a due regard for the rights of the accused—but also a due regard for the keeping of the public peace and the safety and happiness of the people. We will continue to press for a proper scope for the rules of exclusion, lest truth in the fact-finding process be allowed to suffer.

I have mentioned the areas of federalism and criminal law, now I will turn to the religion cases.

RELIGION

Most probably, this term will be best remembered for the decisions concerning the Establishment Clause of the First Amendment. The Court continued to apply its standard three-pronged test. . . .

In trying to make sense of the religion cases—from whichever side—it is important to remember how this body of tangled case law came about. Most Americans forget that it was not until 1925, in *Gitlow v. New York*, that *any* provision of the Bill of Rights was applied to the states.[6] Nor was it until 1947 that the Establishment Clause was made applicable to the states through the Fourteenth Amendment. This is striking because the Bill of Rights, as debated, created and ratified was designed to apply *only* to the national government. . . .

The point, of course, is that the Establishment Clause of the First Amendment was designed to prohibit Congress from establishing a national church. The belief was that the Constitution should not allow Congress to designate a particular faith or sect as politically above the rest. But to argue, as is popular today, that the Amendment demands strict neutrality between religion and irreligion would have struck the founding generation as bizarre. The purpose was to prohibit religious tyranny, not to undermine religion generally.

In considering these areas of adjudication—federalism, criminal law, and religion—it seems fair to conclude that far too many of the Court's opinions were, on the whole, more policy choices than articulations of constitutional principle. The voting blocs, the arguments, all reveal a greater allegiance to what the Court thinks constitutes sound public policy, rather than deference to what the Constitution—its text and intention—may demand. It is also safe to say that until there emerges a coherent jurisprudential stance, the work of the Court will continue in this ad hoc fashion. But that is not to argue for *any* jurisprudence. In my opinion a drift back toward the radical egalitarianism and expansive civil libertarianism of the Warren Court would once again be a threat to the notion of limited but energetic government.

What, then, should a constitutional jurisprudence actually be? It should be a jurisprudence of original intention. By seeking to judge policies in light of principles, rather than remold principles in light of policies, the Court could avoid both the charge of incoherence *and* the charge of being either too conservative or too liberal.

A jurisprudence seriously aimed at the explication of original intention would produce defensible principles of government that would not be tainted by ideological predilection. This belief in a jurisprudence of original intention also reflects a deeply rooted commitment to the idea of democracy. The Constitution represents the consent of the governed to the structures and powers of the government. The Constitution is the fundamental will of the people; that is why it is the fundamental law. To allow the courts to govern simply by what it views at the time as fair and decent is a scheme of government no longer popular; the idea of democracy has suffered. The permanence of the Constitution has been weakened. A constitution that is viewed as only what the judges say it is no longer is a constitution in the true sense.

Those who framed the Constitution chose their words carefully; they debated at great length the minutest points. The language they chose meant something. It is incumbent upon the Court to determine what that meaning was. This is not a shockingly new theory; nor is it arcane or archaic.

Joseph Story, who was in a way a lawyer's Everyman—lawyer, justice, and teacher of law—had a theory of judging that merits reconsideration. Though speaking specifically of the Constitution, his logic reaches to statutory construction as well.

> In construing the Constitution of the United States, we are in the first instance to consider, what are its nature and objects, its scope and design, as apparent from the structure of the instrument, viewed as a whole and also viewed in its component parts. Where its words are plain, clear and determinate, they require no interpretation....Where the words admit of two senses, each of which is conformable to general usage, that sense is to be adopted, which without departing from the literal import of the words, best harmonizes with the nature and objects, the

scope and design of the instrument.

A jurisprudence of original intention would take seriously the admonition of Justice Story's friend and colleague, John Marshall, in *Marbury* that the Constitution is a limitation on judicial power as well as executive and legislative. That is what Chief Justice Marshall meant in *McCulloch* when he cautioned judges never to forget it is a constitution they are expounding.

It has been and will continue to be the policy of this administration to press for a jurisprudence of original intention. In the cases we file and those we join as *amicus,* we will endeavor to resurrect the original meaning of constitutional provisions and statutes as the only reliable guide for judgment.

We will pursue our agenda within the context of our written Constitution of limited yet energetic powers. Our guide in every case will be the sanctity of the rule of law and the proper limits of governmental power.

It is our belief that only "the sense in which the Constitution was accepted and ratified by the nation," and only the sense in which laws were drafted and passed, provide a solid foundation for adjudication. Any other standard suffers the defect of pouring new meaning into old words, thus creating new powers and new rights totally at odds with the logic of our Constitution and its commitment to the rule of law.

Two

SPEECH TO THE TEXT AND TEACHING SYMPOSIUM

Georgetown University, Washington, D.C.
October 12, 1985
Justice William J. Brennan, Jr.

I am deeply grateful for the invitation to participate in the Text and Teaching Symposium. This rare opportunity to explore classic texts with participants of such wisdom, acumen and insight as those who have preceded and will follow me to this podium is indeed exhilarating. But it is also humbling. Even to approximate the standards of excellence of these vigorous and graceful intellects is a daunting task. I am honored that you have afforded me this opportunity to try.

It will perhaps not surprise you that the text I have chosen for exploration is the amended Constitution of the United States, which, of course, entrenches the Bill of Rights and the Civil War amendments, and draws sustenance from the bedrock principles of another great text, the Magna Carta. So fashioned, the Constitution embodies the aspiration to social justice, brotherhood, and human dignity that brought this nation into being. The Declaration of Independence, the Constitution, and the Bill of Rights solemnly committed the United States to be a country where the dignity and rights of all persons were equal before all authority. In candor, we must concede that part of this egalitarianism in America has been more pretension than realized fact. But we are an aspiring people, a people with faith in progress. Our amended Constitution is the lodestar for our aspirations. Like every text worth reading, it is not crystalline. The phrasing is broad and the limitations of its provisions are not clearly marked. Its majestic generalities and ennobling pronouncements are both luminous and obscure. This ambiguity of course calls forth interpretation, the interaction of reader and text. The encounter with the constitutional text has been, in many senses, my life's work.

My approach to this text may differ from the approach of other participants in this symposium to their texts. Yet such differences may themselves stimulate reflection about what it is we do when we "interpret" a text. Thus I will attempt to elucidate my approach to the text as well as my substantive interpretation.

Perhaps the foremost difference is the fact that my encounters with the constitutional text are not purely or even primarily introspective; the Constitution cannot be for me simply a contemplative haven for private moral reflection. My relation to this great text is inescapably public. That is not to say that my reading of the text is not a personal reading, only that the personal reading perforce occurs in a public context and is open to critical scrutiny from all quarters.

The Constitution is fundamentally a public text—the monumental charter of a government and a people—and a Justice of the Supreme Court must apply it to resolve public controversies. For, from our beginnings, a most important consequence of the constitutionally created separation of powers has been the American habit, extraordinary to other democracies, of casting social, economic, philosophical, and political questions in the form of law suits, in an attempt to secure ultimate resolution by the Supreme Court. In this way, important aspects of the most fundamental issues confronting our democracy may finally arrive in the Supreme Court for judicial determination. Not infrequently, these are the issues upon which contemporary society is most deeply divided. They arouse our deepest emotions. The main burden of my twenty-nine terms on the Supreme Court has thus been to wrestle with the Constitution in this heightened public context, to draw meaning from the text in order to resolve public controversies.

Two other aspects of my relation to this text warrant mention. First, constitutional interpretation for a federal judge is, for the most part, obligatory. When litigants approach the bar of court to adjudicate a constitutional dispute, they may justifiably demand an answer. Judges cannot avoid a definitive interpretation because they feel unable to, or would prefer not to, penetrate to the full meaning of the Constitution's provisions. Unlike literary critics, judges cannot merely savor the tensions or revel in the ambiguities inhering in the text—judges must resolve them.

Second, consequences flow from a justice's interpretation in a direct and immediate way. A judicial decision respecting the incompatibility of Jim Crow with a constitutional guarantee of equality is not simply a contemplative exercise in defining the shape of a just society. It is an order, supported by the full coercive power of the State, for the present society to change in a fundamental aspect. Under such circumstances the process of deciding can be a lonely, troubling experience for fallible human beings conscious that their best may not be adequate to the challenge. We Justices are certainly aware that we are not final because we are infallible; we know that we are infallible only because we final. One does not forget how much may depend on the decision. More than the litigants may be affected. The course of vital social, economic, and political currents may be directed.

These three defining characteristics of my relation to the constitutional text—its public nature, obligatory character, and consequentialist aspect—cannot help but influence the way I read that text. When Justices interpret the Constitution they speak for their community, not for themselves alone. The act of interpretation must be undertaken with full consciousness that it is, in a very real sense, the community's interpretation that is sought. Justices are not platonic guardians appointed to wield authority according to their personal moral predilections. Precisely because coercive force must attend any judicial decision to countermand the will of a contemporary majority, the Justices must render constitutional interpretations that are received as legitimate. The source of legitimacy is, of course, a wellspring of controversy in legal and political circles. At the core of the debate is what the late Yale Law School professor Alexander Bickel labeled "the counter-majoritarian difficulty." Our commitment to self-governance in a representative democracy must be reconciled with vesting in electorally unaccountable Justices the power to invalidate the expressed desires of representative bodies on the ground of inconsistency with higher law. Because judicial power resides in the authority to give meaning to the Constitution, the debate is really a debate about how to read the text, about constraints on what is legitimate interpretation.

There are those who find legitimacy in fidelity to what they call "the intentions of the Framers." In its most doctrinaire incarnation, this view demands that Justices discern exactly what the Framers thought about the question under consideration and simply follow that intention in resolving the case before them. It is a view that feigns self-effacing deference to the specific judgments of those who forged our original social compact. But in truth it is little more than arrogance cloaked as humility. It is arrogant to pretend that from our vantage we can gauge accurately the intent of the Framers on application of principle to specific, contemporary questions. All too often, sources of potential enlightenment such as records of the ratification debates provide sparse or ambiguous evidence of the original intention. Typically, all that can be gleaned is that the Framers themselves did not agree about the application or meaning of particular constitutional provisions, and hid their differences in cloaks of generality. Indeed, it is far from clear whose intention is relevant—that of the drafters, the congressional disputants, or the ratifiers in the states? Or even whether the idea of an original intention is a coherent way of thinking about a jointly drafted document drawing its authority from a general assent of the states. And apart from the problematic nature of the sources, our distance of two centuries cannot but work as a prism refracting all we perceive. One cannot help but speculate that the chorus of lamentations calling for interpretation faithful to "original intention"—and proposing nullification of interpretations that fail this quick litmus test—must inevitably come from persons who have no familiarity with the historical record.

Perhaps most importantly, while proponents of this facile histori-cism justify it as a de-politicization of the judiciary, the political underpinnings of such a choice should not escape notice. A position that upholds constitutional claims only if they were within the spe-cific contemplation of the Framers in effect establishes a presumption of resolving textual ambiguities against the claim of constitutional right. It is far from clear what justifies such a presumption against claims of right. Nothing intrinsic in the nature of interpretation—if there is such a thing as the "nature" of interpretation—commands such a passive approach to ambiguity. This is a choice no less politi-cal than any other; it expresses antipathy to claims of the minority rights against the majority. Those who would restrict claims of right to the values of 1789 specifically articulated in the Constitution turn a blind eye to social progress and eschew adaptation of overarching principles to changes of social circumstance.

Another, perhaps more sophisticated, response to the potential power of judicial interpretation stresses democratic theory: because ours is a government of the people's elected representatives, substan-tive value choices should by and large be left to them. This view emphasizes not the transcendent historical authority of the framers but the predominant contemporary authority of the elected branches of government. Yet it has similar consequences for the nature of proper judicial interpretation. Faith in the majoritarian process coun-sels restraint. Even under more expansive formulations of this approach, judicial review is appropriate only to the extent of ensur-ing that our democratic process functions smoothly. Thus, for exam-ple, we would protect freedom of speech merely to ensure that the people are heard by their representatives, rather than as a separate, substantive value. When, by contrast, society tosses up to the Supreme Court a dispute that would require invalidation of a legislature's sub-stantive policy choice, the Court generally would stay its hand because the Constitution was meant as a plan of government and not as an embodiment of fundamental substantive values.

The view that all matters of substantive policy should be resolved through the majoritarian process has appeal under some circumstances, but I think it ultimately will not do. Unabashed enshrinement of majority would permit the imposition of a social caste system or wholesale confiscation of property so long as a majority of the authorized legislative body, fairly elected, approved. Our Constitution could not abide such a situation. It is the very purpose of a Constitution—and particularly of the Bill of Rights—to declare certain values transcendent, beyond the reach of temporary political majorities. The majoritarian process cannot be expected to rectify claims of minority right that arise as a response to the outcomes of that very majoritarian process. As James Madison put it:

> The prescriptions in favor of liberty ought to be leveled against that quarter where the greatest danger lies, namely, that which possesses the highest prerogative of power. But this is not found in either the Executive or Legislative departments of Government, but in the body of the people, operating by the majority against the minority. (I Annals 437)

Faith in democracy is one thing, blind faith quite another. Those who drafted our Constitution understood the difference. One cannot read the text without admitting that it embodies substantive value choices; it places certain values beyond the power of any legislature. Obvious are the separation of powers; the privilege of the Writ of Habeas Corpus; prohibition of Bills of Attainder and *ex post facto* laws; prohibition of cruel and unusual punishments; the requirement of just compensation for official taking of property; the prohibition of laws tending to establish religion or enjoining the free exercise of religion; and, since the Civil War, the banishment of slavery and official race discrimination. With respect to at least such principles, we simply have not constituted ourselves as strict utilitarians. While the Constitution may be amended, such amendments require an immense effort by the People as a whole.

To remain faithful to the content of the Constitution, therefore, an approach to interpreting the text must account for the existence of these substantive value choices, and must accept the ambiguity inherent in the effort to apply them to modern circumstances. The Framers discerned fundamental principles through struggles against particular malefactions of the Crown; the struggle shapes the particular contours of the articulated principles. But our acceptance of the fundamental principles has not and should not bind us to those precise, at times anachronistic, contours. Successive generations of Americans have continued to respect these fundamental choices and adopt them as their own guide to evaluating quite different historical practices. Each generation has the choice to overrule or add to the fundamental principles enunciated by the Framers; the Constitution can be amended or it can be ignored. Yet with respect to its fundamental principles, the text has suffered neither fate. Thus, if I may borrow the words of an esteemed predecessor, Justice Robert Jackson, the burden of judicial interpretation is to translate "the majestic generalities of the Bill of Rights, conceived as part of the pattern of liberal government in the eighteenth century, into concrete restraints on officials dealing with the problems of the twentieth century."[1]

We current Justices read the Constitution in the only way that we can: as twentieth century Americans. We look to the history of the time of framing and to the intervening history of interpretation. But the ultimate question must be: What do the words of the text mean in our time? For the genius of the Constitution rests not in any static meaning it might have had in a world that is dead and gone, but in the adaptability of its great principles to cope with current problems and current needs. What the constitutional fundamentals meant to the wisdom of other times cannot be their measure to the vision of our time. Similarly, what those fundamentals mean for us, our descendants will learn, cannot be the measure to the vision of their time. This realization is not, I assure you, a novel one of my own creation. Permit me to quote from one of the opinions of our Court, *Weems v. United States,* written nearly a century ago:[2]

> Time works changes, brings into existence new conditions and purposes. Therefore, a principle to be vital must be capable of wider application than the mischief which gave

it birth. This is peculiarly true of constitutions. They are not ephemeral enactments, designed to meet passing occasions. They are, to use the words of Chief Justice John Marshall, "designed to approach immortality as nearly as human institutions can approach it." The future is their care and provision or events of good and bad tendencies of which no prophesy can be made. In the application of a constitution, therefore, our contemplation cannot be only of what has been, but of what may be.

Interpretation must account for the transformative purpose of the text. Our Constitution was not intended to preserve a preexisting society but to make a new one, to put in place new principles that the prior political community had not sufficiently recognized. Thus, for example, when we interpret the Civil War Amendments to the charter—abolishing slavery, guaranteeing blacks equality under law, and guaranteeing blacks the right to vote—we must remember that those who put them in place had no desire to enshrine the status quo. Their goal was to make over their world, to eliminate all vestige of slave caste.

Having discussed at some length how I, as a Supreme Court Justice, interact with this text, I think it time to turn to the fruits of this discourse. For the Constitution is a sublime oration on the dignity of man, a bold commitment by a people to the ideal of libertarian dignity protected through law. Some reflection is perhaps required before this can be seen.

The Constitution on its face is, in large measure, a structuring text, a blueprint for government. And when the text is not prescribing the form of government it is limiting the powers of that government. The original document, before addition of any of the amendments, does not speak primarily of the rights of man, but of the abilities and disabilities of government. When one reflects upon the text's preoccupation with the scope of government as well as its shape, however, one comes to understand that what this text is about is the relationship of the individual and the state. The text marks the metes and bounds of official authority and individual autonomy. When one studies the boundary that the text marks out, one gets a sense of the vision of the individual embodied in the Constitution.

As augmented by the Bill of Rights and the Civil War Amendments, this text is a sparkling vision of the supremacy of the human dignity of every individual. This vision is reflected in the very choice of democratic self-governance: the supreme value of a democracy is the presumed worth of each individual. And this vision manifests itself most dramatically in the specific prohibitions of the Bill of Rights, a term which I henceforth will apply to describe not only the original first eight amendments, but the Civil War amendments as well. It is a vision that has guided us as a people throughout our history, although the precise rules by which we have protected fundamental human dignity have been transformed over time in response to both transformations of social condition and evolution of our concepts of human dignity.

Until the end of the nineteenth century, freedom and dignity in our country found meaningful protection in the institution of real property. In a society still largely agricultural, a piece of land provided men not just with sustenance but with the means of economic independence, a necessary precondition of political independence and expression. Not surprisingly, property relationships formed the heart of litigation and of legal practice, and lawyers and judges tended to think stable property relationships the highest aim of the law.

But the days when common law property relationships dominated litigation and legal practice are past. To a growing extent economic existence now depends on less certain relationships with government—licenses, employment, contracts, subsidies, unemployment benefits, tax exemptions, welfare and the like. Government participation in the economic existence of individuals is pervasive and deep. Administrative matters and other dealings with government are at the epicenter of the exploding law. We turn to government and to the law for controls which would never have been expected or tolerated before this century, when a man's answer to economic oppression or difficulty was to move two hundred miles west. Now hundreds of thousands of Americans live entire lives without any real prospect of the dignity and autonomy that ownership of real property could confer. Protection of the human dignity of such citizens requires a much modified view of the proper relationship of individual and State.

In general, problems of the relationship of the citizen with government have multiplied and thus have engendered some of the most important constitutional issues of the day. As government acts ever more deeply upon those areas of our lives once marked "private," there is an even greater need to see that individual rights are not curtailed or cheapened in the interest of what may temporarily appear to be the "public good." And as government continues in its role of provider for so many of our disadvantaged citizens, there is an even greater need to ensure that government act with integrity and consistency in its dealings with these citizens. To put it another way, the possibilities for collision between government activity and individual rights will increase as the power and authority of government itself expands, and this growth, in turn, heightens the need for constant vigilance at the collision points. If our free society is to endure, those who govern must recognize human dignity and accept the enforcement of constitutional limitations on their power conceived by the Framers to be necessary to preserve that dignity and the air of freedom which is our proudest heritage. Such recognition will not come from a technical understanding of the organs of government, or the new forms of wealth they administer. It requires something different, something deeper—a personal confrontation with the well-springs of our society. Solutions of constitutional questions from that perspective have become the great challenge of the modern era. All the talk in the last half-decade about shrinking the government does not alter this reality or the challenge it imposes. The modern activist state is a concomitant of the complexity of modern society; it is inevitably with us. We must meet the challenge rather than wish it were not before us.

The challenge is essentially, of course, one to the capacity of our constitutional structure to foster and protect the freedom, the dignity, and the rights of all persons within our borders, which it is the great design of the Constitution to secure. During the time of my public service this challenge has largely taken shape within the confines of the interpretive question whether the specific guarantees of the Bill of Rights operate as restraints on the power of state government. We recognize the Bill of Rights as the primary source of express information as to what is meant by constitutional liberty. The safeguards enshrined in it are deeply etched in the foundation of America's freedoms. Each is a protection with centuries of history behind it, often dearly bought with the blood and lives of people determined to prevent oppression by their rulers. The first eight Amendments, however, were added to the Constitution to operate solely against federal power. It was not until the Thirteenth and Fourteenth Amendments were added, in 1865 and 1868, in response to a demand for national protection against abuses of state power, that the Constitution could be interpreted to require application of the first eight amendments to the states.

It was in particular the Fourteenth Amendment's guarantee that no person be deprived of life, liberty, or property without process of law that led us to apply many of the specific guarantees of the Bill of Rights to the states. In my judgment, Justice Cardozo best captured the reasoning that brought us to such decisions when he described what the Court has done as a process by which the guarantees "have been taken over from the earlier articles of the federal bill of rights and brought within the Fourteenth Amendment by a process of absorption...[that] has had its source in the belief that neither liberty nor justice would exist if [those guarantees]...were sacrificed."[3] But this process of absorption was neither swift nor steady. As late as 1922 only the Fifth Amendment guarantee of just compensation for official taking of property had been given force against the states. Between then and 1956 only the First Amendment guarantees of speech and conscience and the Fourth Amendment ban of unreasonable searches and seizures had been incorporated—the latter, however, without the exclusionary rule to give it force. As late as 1961, I could stand before a distinguished assemblage of the bar at New York University's James Madison Lecture and list the following as guarantees that had not been thought to be sufficiently fundamental to the protection of human dignity so as to be enforced against the states: the prohibition of cruel and unusual punishments, the right against self-incrimination, the right to assistance of counsel in a criminal trial, the right to confront witnesses, the right to compulsory process, the right not to be placed in jeopardy of life or limb more than once upon accusation of a crime, the right not to have illegally obtained evidence introduced at a criminal trial, and the right to a jury of one's peers.

The history of the quarter-century following that Madison Lecture need not be told in great detail. Suffice it to say that each of the guarantees listed above has been recognized as a fundamental aspect of ordered liberty. Of course, the above catalogue encompasses only the rights of the criminally accused, those caught, rightly or wrongly, in the maw of the criminal justice system. But it has been well said that there is no better test of a society than how it treats those accused of transgressing against it. Indeed, it is because we recognize that incarceration strips a man of his dignity that we demand strict adherence to fair procedure and proof of guilt beyond a reasonable doubt before taking such a drastic step. These requirements are, as Justice Harlan once said, "bottomed on a fundamental value determination of our society that it is far worse to convict an innocent man than to let a guilty man go free."[4] There is no worse injustice than wrongly to strip a man of his dignity. And our adherence to the constitutional vision of human dignity is so strict that even after convicting a person according to these stringent standards, we demand that his dignity be infringed only to the extent appropriate to the crime and never by means of wanton infliction of pain or deprivation. I interpret the Constitution plainly to embody these fundamental values.

Of course the constitutional vision of human dignity has, in this past quarter-century, infused far more than our decisions about the criminal process. Recognition of the principle of "one person, one vote" as a constitutional one redeems the promise of self-governance by affirming the essential dignity of every citizen in the right to equal participation in the democratic process. Recognition of so-called "new property" rights in those receiving government entitlements affirms the essential dignity of the least fortunate among us by demanding that government treat with decency, integrity and consistency those dependent on its benefits for their very survival. After all, a legislative majority initially decides to create governmental entitlements; the Constitution's Due Process clause merely provides protection for entitlements thought necessary by society as a whole. Such due process rights prohibit government from imposing the devil's bargain of bartering away human dignity in exchange for human sustenance. Likewise, recognition of full equality for women—equal protection of the laws—ensures that gender has no bearing on claims to human dignity.

Recognition of broad and deep rights of expression and conscience reaffirms the vision of human dignity in many ways. They too redeem the promise of self-governance by facilitating—indeed demanding—robust, uninhibited, and wide-open debate on issues of public importance. Such public debate is of course vital to the development and dissemination of political ideas. As importantly, robust public discussion is the crucible in which personal political convictions are forged. In our democracy, such discussion is a political duty; it is the essence of self-government. The constitutional vision of human dignity rejects the possibility of political orthodoxy imposed from above; it respects the right of each individual to form and to express political judgments, however far they may deviate from the mainstream and however unsettling they might be to the powerful or the elite. Recognition of these rights of expression and conscience also frees up the private space for both intellectual and spiritual development free of government dominance, either blatant or subtle. Justice Brandeis put it so well sixty years ago when he wrote: "Those who won our independence believed that the final end of the State was to make men free to develop their faculties; and that in its government the deliberative forces should prevail over the arbitrary. They valued liberty both as an end and as a means."[5]

I do not mean to suggest that we have in the last quarter-century achieved a comprehensive definition of the constitutional ideal of human dignity. We are still striving toward that goal, and doubtless it will be an eternal quest. For if the interaction of this Justice and the constitutional text over the years confirms any single proposition, it is that the demands of human dignity will never cease to evolve.

Indeed, I cannot in good conscience refrain from mention of one grave and crucial respect in which we continue, in my judgment, to fall short of the constitutional vision of human dignity. It is in our continued tolerance of State-administered execution as a form of punishment. I make it a practice not to comment on the constitutional issues that come before the Court, but my position on this issue, of course, has been for some time fixed and immutable. I think I can venture some thoughts on this particular subject without transgressing my usual guideline too severely.

As I interpret the Constitution, capital punishment is under all circumstances cruel and unusual punishment prohibited by the Eighth and Fourteenth Amendments. This is a position of which I imagine you are not unaware. Much discussion of the merits of capital punishment has in recent years focused on the potential arbitrariness that attends its administration, and I have no doubt that such arbitrariness is a grave wrong. But for me, the wrong of capital punishment transcends such procedural issues. As I have said in my opinions, I view the Eighth Amendment's prohibition of cruel and unusual punishments as embodying to unique degree moral principles that substantively restrain the punishments our civilized society may impose on those persons who transgress its laws. Foremost among the moral principles recognized in our cases and inherent in the prohibition is the primary principle that the State, even as it punishes, must treat its citizens in a manner consistent with their intrinsic worth as human beings. A punishment must not be so severe as to be utterly and irreversibly degrading to the very essence of human dignity. Death for whatever crime and under all circumstances is a truly awesome punishment. The calculated killing of a human being by the State involves, by its very nature, an absolute denial of the executed person's humanity. The vilest murder does not, in my view, release the State from constitutional restraints on the destruction of human dignity. Yet an executed person has lost the very right to have rights, now or ever. For me, then, the fatal constitutional infirmity of capital punishment is that it treats members of the human race as nonhumans, as objects to be toyed with and discarded. It is, indeed, "cruel and unusual." It is thus inconsistent with the fundamental premise of the Clause that even the basest criminal remains a human being possessed of some potential, at least, for common human dignity.

This is an interpretation to which a majority of my fellow Justices—not to mention, it would seem, a majority of my fellow countrymen—does not subscribe. Perhaps you find my adherence to it, and my recurrent publication of it, simply contrary, tiresome, or quixotic. Or perhaps you see in it a refusal to abide by the judicial principle of *stare decisis,* obedience to precedent. In my judgment, however, the unique interpretive role of the Supreme Court with respect to the Constitution demands some flexibility with respect to the call of *stare decisis.* Because we are the last word on the meaning of the Constitution, our views must be subject to revision over time, or the Constitution falls captive, again, to the anachronistic views of long-gone generations. I mentioned earlier the judge's role in seeking out the community's interpretation of the Constitutional text. Yet, again in my judgment, when a Justice perceives an interpretation of the text to have departed so far from its essential meaning, that Justice is bound, by a larger constitutional duty to the community, to expose the departure and point toward a different path. On this issue, the death penalty, I hope to embody a community striving for human dignity for all, although perhaps not yet arrived.

You have doubtless observed that this description of my personal encounter with the constitutional text has in large portion been a discussion of public developments in constitutional doctrine over the last century. That, as I suggested at the outset, is inevitable because my interpretive career has demanded a public reading of the text. This public encounter with the text, however, has been a profound source of personal inspiration. The vision of human dignity embodied there is deeply moving. It is timeless. It has inspired Americans for two centuries and it will continue to inspire as it continues to evolve. That evolutionary process is inevitable, and, indeed, it is the true interpretive genius of the text.

If we are to be as a shining city upon a hill, it will be because of our ceaseless pursuit of the constitutional ideal of human dignity. For the political and legal ideals that form the foundation of much that is best in American institutions—ideals jealously preserved and guarded throughout our history—still form the vital force in creative political thought and activity within the nation today. As we adapt our institutions to the ever-changing conditions of national and international life, those ideals of human dignity—liberty and justice for all individuals—will continue to inspire and guide us because they are entrenched in our Constitution. The Constitution with its Bill of Rights thus has a bright future, as well as a glorious past, for its spirit is inherent in the aspirations of our people.

Three

SPEECH BEFORE THE D.C. CHAPTER OF THE FEDERALIST SOCIETY LAWYERS DIVISION

Washington, D.C., November 15, 1985
Attorney General Edwin Meese, III

A large part of American history has been the history of Constitutional debate. From the Federalists and the Anti-Federalists, to Webster and Calhoun, to Lincoln and Douglas, we find many examples. Now, as we approach the bicentennial of the framing of the Constitution, we are witnessing another debate concerning our fundamental law. It is not simply a ceremonial debate, but one that promises to have a profound impact on the future of our Republic.

The current debate is a sign of a healthy nation. Unlike people of many other countries, we are free both to discover the defects of our laws and our government through open discussion and to correct them through our political system.

This debate on the Constitution involves great and fundamental issues. It invites the participation of the best minds the bar, the academy, and the bench have to offer. In recent weeks there have been important new contributions to this debate from some of the most distinguished scholars and jurists in the land. Representatives of the three branches of the federal government have entered the debate; journalistic commentators, too.

A great deal has already been said, much of it of merit and on point. But occasionally there has been confusion. There has been some misunderstanding, some perhaps on purpose. Caricatures and straw men, as one customarily finds even in the greatest debates, have made appearances. Still, whatever the differences, most participants are agreed about the same high objective: fidelity to our fundamental law.

Today I would like to discuss further the meaning of constitutional fidelity. In particular, I would like to describe in more detail this administration's approach.

Before doing so, I would like to make a few commonplace observations about the original document itself. It is easy to forget what a young country America really is. The bicentennial of our independence was just a few years ago; that of the Constitution still two years off. The period surrounding the creation of the Constitution is not a dark and mythical realm. The young America of the 1780s and '90s was a vibrant place, alive with pamphlets, newspapers, and books chronicling and commenting upon the great issues of the day. We know how the Founding Fathers lived and much of what they read, thought, and believed. The disputes and compromises of the Constitutional Convention were carefully recorded. The minutes of the Convention are a matter of public record. Several of the most important participants—including James Madison, the "father" of the Constitution—wrote comprehensive accounts of the convention. Others, Federalists and Anti-Federalists alike, committed their arguments for and against ratification, as well as their understandings of the constitution, to paper, so that their ideas and conclusions could be widely circulated, read, and understood.

In short, the Constitution is not buried in the mists of time. We know a tremendous amount of the history of its genesis. The Bicentennial is encouraging even more scholarship about its origins. We know who did what, when, and many times why. One can talk intelligently about a "founding generation."

With these thoughts in mind, I would like to discuss the administration's approach to constitutional interpretation. But to begin, it may be useful to say what it is not.

Our approach does not view the Constitution as some kind of super-municipal code, designed to address merely the problems of a particular era—whether those of 1787, 1789, or 1868. There is no question that the Constitutional Convention grew out of widespread dissatisfaction with the Articles of Confederation. But the delegates at Philadelphia moved beyond the job of patching that document to write a *Constitution*. Their intention was to write a document not just for their times but for posterity.

The language they employed clearly reflects this. For example, they addressed *commerce*, not simply shipping or barter. Later the Bill of Rights spoke, through the Fourth Amendment, to "unreasonable searches and seizures," not merely the regulation of specific law enforcement practices of 1789. Still later, the framers of the Fourteenth Amendment were concerned not simply about the rights of black citizens to personal security, but also about the equal protection of the law for all persons within the states. The Constitution is not a legislative code bound to the time in which it was written. Neither, however, is it a mirror that simply reflects the thoughts and ideas of those who stand before it.

Our approach to constitutional interpretation begins with the document itself. The plain fact is it exists. It is something that has been written down. Walter Berns of the American Enterprise Institute has noted that the central object of American constitutionalism was "the effort" of the Founders "to express fundamental governmental arrangements in a legal document—to 'get it in writing'." Indeed, judicial review has been grounded in the fact that the Constitution is a written, as opposed to an unwritten, document. In *Marbury v. Madison,* John Marshall rested his rationale for judicial review on the fact that we have a written constitution with meaning that is binding upon judges. "[I]t is apparent," he wrote, "that the framers of the Constitution contemplated that instrument as a rule for the government of *courts*, as well as of the legislature. Why otherwise does it direct the judges to take an oath to support it?"

The presumption of a written document is that it conveys meaning. As Thomas Gray of the Stanford Law School has said, it makes "relatively definite and explicit what otherwise would be relatively indefinite and tacit."

We know that those who framed the Constitution chose their words carefully. They debated at great length the minutest points. The language they chose meant something. They proposed, they substituted, they edited, and they carefully revised. Their words were studied with equal care by state ratifying conventions. This is not to suggest that there was unanimity among the Framers and ratifiers on all points. The Constitution and the Bill of Rights, and some of the subsequent amendments, emerged after protracted debate. Nobody got everything they wanted. What's more, the Framers were not clairvoyants—they could not foresee every issue that would be submitted for judicial review. Nor could they predict how all foreseeable disputes would be resolved under the Constitution. But the point is the meaning of the Constitution can be known.

What does this written Constitution mean? In places it is exactingly specific. Where it says the president of the United States must be at least thirty-five years of age it means exactly that. (I have not heard of any claim that thirty-five means thirty or twenty-five or twenty.) Where it specifies how the House and Senate are to be organized, it means what it says.

The Constitution also expresses particular principles. One is the right to be free of an unreasonable search and seizure. Another concerns religious liberty. Another is the right to equal protection of the laws.

Those who framed these principles meant something by them. And the meanings can be found. The Constitution itself is also an expression of certain general principles. These principles reflect the deepest purpose of the Constitution—that of establishing a political system through which Americans can best govern themselves consistent with the goal of securing liberty.

The text and structure of the Constitution is instructive. It contains very little in the way of specific political solutions. It speaks volumes on how problems should be approached, and by *whom*. For example, the first three articles set out clearly the scope and limits of three distinct branches of national government; the powers of each being carefully and specifically enumerated. In this scheme it is no accident to find the legislative branch described first, as the Framers had fought and sacrificed to secure the right of democratic self-governance. Naturally, this faith in republicanism was not unbounded, as the next two articles make clear.

Yet the Constitution remains a document of powers and principles. And its undergirding premise remains that democratic self-government is subject only to the limits of certain constitutional principles. This respect of the political process was made explicit early on. When John Marshall upheld the Act of Congress chartering a national bank in *McCulloch v. Mayland*, he wrote: "The Constitution [was] intended to endure for ages to come, and, consequently, to be adapted to the various crises of human affairs."[1] But to use *McCulloch*, as some have tried, as support for the idea that the Constitution is a protean, changeable thing is to stand history on its head. Marshall was keeping faith with the original intention that Congress be free to elaborate and apply constitutional powers and principles. He was not saying that the Court must invent some new constitutional value in order to keep pace with the times. In Walter Berns' words, "Marshall's meaning is not that the Constitution may be adapted to the 'various crises of human affairs,' but that the legislative powers granted by the Constitution are adaptable to meet these crises."

The approach this administration advocates is rooted in the text of the Constitution as illuminated by those who drafted, proposed, and ratified it. In his famous commentary on the Constitution of the United States, Justice Joseph Story explained that: "The first and fundamental rule in the interpretation of all instruments is, to construe them according to the sense of the terms, and the intention of the parties."

Our approach understands the significance of a written document and seeks to discern the particular and general principles it expresses. It recognizes that there may be debate at times over the application of these principles. But it does not mean these principles cannot be identified.

Constitutional adjudication is obviously not a mechanical process. It requires an appeal to reason and discretion. The text and intention of the Constitution must be understood to constitute the banks within which constitutional interpretation must flow. As James Madison said, if "the sense in which the Constitution was accepted and ratified by the nation...be not the guide in expounding it, there can be no security for a consistent and stable government, more than for a faithful exercise of its powers."

Thomas Jefferson, so often cited incorrectly as a framer of the Constitution, in fact shared Madison's view: "Our peculiar security is in the possession of a written Constitution. Let us not make it a blank paper by construction." Jefferson was even more explicit in his personal correspondence:

> On every question of construction [we should] carry ourselves back to the time, when the Constitution was adopted; recollect the spirit manifested in the debates; and instead of trying [to find], what meaning may be squeezed out of the text, or invented against it, conform to the probable one, in which it passed.

In the main, jurisprudence that seeks to be faithful to our Constitution—a jurisprudence of original intention, as I have called it—is not difficult to describe. Where the language of the Constitution is specific, it must be obeyed. Where there is a demonstrable consensus among the Framers and ratifiers as to a principle stated or implied by the Constitution, it should be followed. Where there is ambiguity as to the precise meaning or reach of a constitutional provision, it should be interpreted and applied in a manner so as to at least not contradict the text of the Constitution itself.

Sadly, while almost every one participating in the current constitutional debate would give assent to these propositions, the techniques and conclusions of some of the debaters do violence to them. What is the source of this violence? In large part I believe that it is the misuse of history stemming from the neglect of the idea of a written constitution.

There is a frank proclamation by some judges and commentators that what matters most about the Constitution is, not its words, but its so-called "spirit." These individuals focus less on the language of specific provisions than on what they describe as the "vision" or "concepts of human dignity" they find embodied in the Constitution. This approach to jurisprudence has led to some remarkable and tragic conclusions.

In the 1850s, the Supreme Court under Chief Justice Roger B. Taney read blacks out of the Constitution in order to invalidate Congress' attempt to limit the spread of slavery. The *Dred Scott* decision, famously described as a judicial "self-inflicted wound," helped bring on the Civil War. There is a lesson in this history. There is danger in seeing the Constitution as an empty vessel into which each generation may pour its passion and prejudice.

Our own time has its own fashions and passions. In recent decades many have come to view the Constitution—more accurately, part of the Constitution, provisions of the Bill of Rights and the Fourteenth Amendment—as a charter for judicial activism on behalf of various constituencies. Those who hold this view often have lacked demonstrable textual or historical support for their conclusions. Instead they have "grounded" their rulings in appeals to social theories, to moral philosophies or personal notions of human dignity, or to "penumbras," somehow emanating ghostlike from various provisions—identified and not identified—in the Bill of Rights. The problem with this approach is that, as John Hart Ely, Dean of the Stanford Law School, has observed with respect to one such decision, is not that it is bad constitutional law, but that it is not constitutional law in any meaningful sense at all.

Despite this fact, the perceived popularity of some results in particular cases has encouraged some observers to believe that any critique of the methodology of those decisions is an attack on the results. This perception is sufficiently widespread that it deserves an answer. My answer is to look at history.

When the Supreme Court sounded the death knell for official segregation in the country in *Brown v. Board of Education*, it earned all the plaudits it received. But the Supreme Court in that case was not giving new life to old words, or adapting a "living," "flexible"

Constitution to new reality.[2] It was restoring the original principle of the Constitution to constitutional law. The *Brown* Court was correcting the damage done fifty years earlier, when in *Plessy v. Ferguson*, an earlier Supreme Court had disregarded the clear intent of the framers of the Civil War Amendments to eliminate the legal degradation of blacks, and had contrived a theory of the Constitution to support the charade of "separate but equal" discrimination.

Similarly, the decisions of the New Deal and beyond that freed Congress to regulate commerce and enact a plethora of social legislation were not judicial adaptations of the Constitution to new realities. They were in fact removals of encrustations of earlier courts that had strayed from the original intent of the Framers regarding the power of the legislature to make policy.

It is amazing how so much of what passes for social and political progress is really the undoing of old judicial mistakes. Mistakes occur when the principles of specific constitutional provisions—such as those contained in the Bill of Rights—are taken by some as invitations to read into the Constitution values that contradict the clear language of other provisions.

Acceptances to this illusory invitation have proliferated in recent decades. One Supreme Court justice identified the proper judicial standard as asking "what's best for this country." Another said it is important to "keep the Court out in front" of the general society. Various academic commentators have poured rhetorical grease on this judicial fire, suggesting that constitutional interpretation appropriately be guided by such standards as whether a public policy "personifies justice," or "comports with the notion of moral evolution," or confers "an identity" upon our society, or was consistent with "natural ethical law," or was consistent with some "right of equal citizenship."

Unfortunately, as I've noted, navigation by such lodestars has in the past given us questionable economics, governmental disorder, and racism—all in the guise of constitutional law. Recently one of the distinguished judges of one of our federal appeals courts got it about right when he wrote: "The truth is that the judge who looks outside the Constitution always looks inside himself and nowhere else."[3] Or, as we recently put it before the Supreme Court in an important brief: "The further afield interpretation travels from its point of departure in the text, the greater the danger that constitutional adjudication will be like a picnic to which the framers bring the words and the judges the meaning."[4]

In the *Osborne v. Bank of the United States* decision twenty-one years after *Marbury*, Chief Justice Marshall further elaborated his view of the relationship between the judge and the law, be it statutory or constitutional:

> Judicial power, as contradistinguished from the power of the laws, has no existence. Courts are the mere instruments of the law, and can will nothing. When they are said to exercise a discretion, it is a mere legal discretion, a discretion to be exercised in discerning the courts prescribed by law; and, when that is discerned, it is the duty of the Court to follow it.[5]

Any true approach to constitutional interpretation must respect the document in all its parts and be faithful to the Constitution in its entirety. What must be remembered in the current debate is that interpretation does not imply results. The Framers were not trying to anticipate every answer. They were trying to create a tripartite national government, within a federal system, that would have the flexibility to adapt to face new exigencies—as it did, for example, in chartering a national bank. Their great interest was in the distribution of power and responsibility in order to secure the great goal of liberty for all.

A jurisprudence that seeks fidelity to the Constitution—a jurisprudence of original intention—is not a jurisprudence of political results. It is very much concerned with process, and it is a jurisprudence that in our day seeks to de-politicize the law. The great genius of the constitutional blueprint is found in its creation and respect for spheres of authority and the limits it places on governmental power. In this scheme the Framers did not see the courts as the exclusive custodians

of the Constitution. Indeed, because the document posits so few conclusions it leaves to the more political branches the matter of adapting and vivifying its principles in each generation. It also leaves to the
people of the states, in the Tenth Amendment, those responsibilities
and rights not committed to federal care. The power to declare acts
of Congress and laws of the states null and void is truly awesome.
This power must be used when the Constitution clearly speaks. It
should not be used when the Constitution does not.

In *Marbury v. Madison*, at the same time he vindicated the concept of judicial review, Marshall wrote that the "principles" of the
Constitution "are deemed fundamental and permanent," and, except
for formal amendment, "unchangeable." If we want a change in our
Constitution or in our laws we must seek it through the formal mech-
anisms presented in that organizing document of our government.

In summary, I would emphasize that what is at issue here is not an
agenda of issues or a menu of results. At issue is a way of government.
A jurisprudence based on first principles is neither conservative nor liberal, neither right nor left. It is a jurisprudence that cares about com-
mitting and limiting to each organ of government the proper ambit of
its responsibilities. It is a jurisprudence faithful to our Constitution.

By the same token, an activist jurisprudence, one which anchors
the Constitution only in the consciences of jurists, is a chameleon
jurisprudence, changing color and form in each era. The same
activism hailed today may threaten the capacity for decision through
democratic consensus tomorrow, as it has in many yesterdays. Ultimately, as the early democrats wrote into the Massachusetts State
Constitution, the best defense of our liberties is a government of laws
and not men. On this point it is helpful to recall the words of the late
Justice Frankfurter. As he wrote:

> [T]here is not under our Constitution a judicial remedy for
> every political mischief, for every undesirable exercise of
> legislative power. The Framers carefully and with deliber-
> ate forethought refused so to enthrone the judiciary. In this
> situation, as in others of like nature, appeal for relief does

not belong here. Appeal must be to an informed, civically militant electorate.

I am afraid that I have gone on somewhat too long. I realize that these occasions of your Society are usually reserved for brief remarks. But if I have imposed upon your patience, I hope it has been for a good end. Given the timeliness of this issue, and the interest of this distinguished organization, it has seemed an appropriate forum to share these thoughts.

I close, unsurprisingly, by returning a last time to the period of the Constitution's birth. As students of the Constitution are aware, the struggle for ratification was protracted and bitter. Essential to the success of the campaign was the outcome of the debate in the two most significant states: Virginia and New York. In New York the battle between Federalist and Anti-Federalist forces was particularly hard.

Both sides eagerly awaited the outcome in Virginia, which was sure to have a profound effect on the struggle in the Empire State. When news that Virginia had voted to ratify came, it was a particularly bitter blow to the Anti-Federalist side. Yet on the evening the message reached New York an event took place that speaks volumes about the character of early America. The losing side, instead of grousing, feted the Federalist leaders in the taverns and inns of the city. There followed a night of drinking, good fellowship, and mutual toasting. When the effects of the good cheer wore off, the two sides returned to their inkwells and presses, and the debate resumed.

There is a great temptation among those who view this debate form the outside to see in it a clash of personalities, a bitter exchange. But you and I, and the other participants in this dialogue, know better. We and our distinguished opponents carry on the old tradition of free, uninhibited, and vigorous debate. Out of such arguments come no losers, only truth. It's the American way. And the Founders would not want it any other way.

Four

Speech at the University of San Diego Law School

November 18, 1985
Judge Robert H. Bork
(Reprinted originally in the University of San Diego Law Review)

To approach the subject of economic rights it is necessary to state a general theory about how a judge should deal with the Constitution of the United States in adjudication that brings that document before the court. More specifically, I intend to speak to the question of whether a judge should consider himself or herself bound by the original intentions of those who framed, proposed, and ratified the Constitution. I think the judge is so bound. I want to demonstrate that original intent is the only legitimate basis for constitutional decision and I wish to meet objections that have been made to that proposition.

This has been a topic of fierce debate in the law schools for the past thirty years. The controversy shows no sign of subsiding. To the contrary, the torrent of words is freshening.

It is odd that the one group whose members rarely discuss the intellectual framework within which they decide cases is the federal judiciary. Judges, by and large, are not much attracted to theory. That is unfortunate, and perhaps it is changing. There are several reasons why it should change.

Law is an intellectual system. It progresses, if at all, through continual intellectual exchanges. There is no reason why members of the judiciary should not engage in such discussion and, since theirs is the ultimate responsibility, every reason why they should.

Moreover, the only real control the American people have over their judges is that of criticism that ought to be informed and to focus not upon the congeniality of political results but upon the judges' faithfulness to their assigned role.

Finally, we appear to be at a tipping point in the relationship of judicial power to democracy. The opposing philosophies about the role of judges are being articulated more clearly. Those who argue that original intention is crucial do so in order to draw a sharp line between judicial power and democratic authority. Their philosophy is called intentionalism or interpretivism. Those who would assign an ever increasing role to judges are called non-intentionalist or non-interpretivist. The future role of the American judiciary will be decided by the victory of one set of ideas or the other.

I want to stress that I did not come here to enter into political controversy. This is a subject I have been teaching and writing about for twenty years, most of that time as a professor. I have been arguing with professors and that is what I will be doing tonight. In these remarks I am not concerned to prove that any particular decision or doctrine is wrong. I am concerned with the method of reasoning by which constitutional argument should proceed.

The problem for constitutional law always has been and always will be the resolution of what has been called the Madisonian dilemma. The United States was founded as what we now call a Madisonian system, one which allows majorities to rule in wide areas of life simply because they are majorities, but which also holds that individuals have some freedoms that must be exempt from majority control. The dilemma is that neither the majority nor the minority can be trusted to define the proper spheres of democratic authority and individual liberty. The first would court tyranny by the majority; the second tyranny by the minority.

Over time it came to be thought that the resolution of the Madisonian problem—the definition of majority power and minority freedom—was primarily the function of the judiciary and, most especially, the function of the Supreme Court. That understanding, which now seems a permanent feature of our political arrangements, creates the need for constitutional theory. The courts must be energetic to protect the rights of individuals, but they must also be scrupulous not to deny the majority's legitimate right to govern. How can that be done?

Any intelligible view of constitutional adjudication starts from the proposition that the Constitution is law. That may sound obvious but in a moment you will see that it is not obvious to a great many law professors. What does it mean to say that the words in a document are law? One of the things it means is that the words constrain judgment. They control judges every bit as much as they control legislators, executives, and citizens.

The provisions of the Bill of Rights and the Civil War Amendments not only have contents that protect individual liberties, they also have limits. They do not cover all possible or even all desirable liberties. Freedom of speech covers speech, not sexual conduct. Freedom from unreasonable searches and seizures does not protect the power of businesses to set prices. The fact of limits means that the judge's authority has limits and outside the designated areas democratic institutions govern.

If this were not so, if judges could govern areas not committed to them by specific clauses of the Constitution, then there would be no law other than the will of the judge. It is common ground that such a situation is not legitimate in a democracy. Justice Brennan recently put the point well: "Justices are not platonic guardians appointed to wield authority according to their personal moral predilections." This means that any defensible theory of constitutional interpretation must demonstrate that it has the capacity to control judges. An observer must be able to say whether or not the judge's result follows fairly from the premises and is not merely a question of taste or opinion.

There are those in the academic world, professors at very prestigious institutions, who deny that the Constitution is law. I will not rehearse their arguments here or rebut them in detail. I note merely that that there is one question they do not address. If the Constitution is not law, law that, with the usual areas of ambiguity at the edges, nevertheless tolerably tells judges what to do and what not to do—if the Constitution is not law in that sense, what authorizes judges to set at naught the majority judgment of the representatives of the American people?

If the Constitution is not law, if, as yet another professor put it, it is of "questionable authority," why is the judge's authority superior to that of the president, the Congress, the armed forces, the departments and agencies, the governors and legislatures of the states, and that of everyone else in the nation? No answer exists.

The answer that is attempted is usually that the judge must be guided by some form of moral philosophy. Not only is moral philosophy wholly inadequate to the task, but there is no reason for the rest of us, who have our own moral visions, to be governed by the judge's moral predilections.

Those academics who think the Constitution is not law ought to draw the only conclusion that intellectual honesty leaves to them: that judges must abandon the function of constitutional review. I have yet to hear that suggested. The only way in which the Constitution can constrain judges is if the judges interpret the document's words according to the intentions of those who drafted, proposed, and ratified its provisions and its various amendments.

It is important to be plain at the outset what intentionalism means. It is not the notion that judges may apply a constitutional provision only to circumstances specifically contemplated by the Framers. In so narrow a form the philosophy is useless. Since we cannot know how the Framers would vote on specific cases today, in a very different world from the one they knew, no intentionalist of any sophistication employs the narrow version just described.

There is a version that is adequate to the task. Dean John Hart Ely has described it:

What distinguishes interpretivism (or intentionalism) from its opposite is its insistence that the work of the political branches is to be invalidated only in accord with an inference whose starting point, whose underlying premise, is fairly discoverable in the Constitution. That the complete inference will not be found there—because the situation is not likely to have been foreseen—is generally common ground.

In short, all an intentionalist requires is that the text, structure, and history of the Constitution provide him not with a conclusion but with a premise. That premise states a core value that the Framers intended to protect. The intentionalist judge must then supply the minor premise in order to protect the constitutional freedom in circumstances the Framers could not foresee. Courts perform this function all of the time. Indeed, it is the same function they perform when they apply a statute, a contract, a will, or indeed a Supreme Court opinion to a situation the framers of those documents did not foresee.

Thus, we are usually able to understand the liberties that were intended to be protected. We are able to apply the First Amendment's Free Press Clause to the electronic media and to the changing impact of libel litigation upon all the media; we are able to apply the Fourth Amendment's prohibition on unreasonable searches and seizures to electronic surveillance; we apply the Commerce Clause to state regulations of interstate trucking.

Does this version of intentionalism mean that judges will invariably decide cases the way the Framers would if they were here today? Of course not. But many cases will be decided that way and, at the very least, judges will confine themselves to the principles the Framers put into the Constitution. Entire ranges of problems will be placed off-limits to judges, thus preserving democracy in those areas where the Framers intended democratic government. That is better than any non-intentionalist theory can do. If it is not good enough, judicial review under the Constitution cannot be legitimate. I think it is good enough.

There is one objection to intentionalism that is particularly tiresome. Whenever I speak on the subject someone invariably asks, "But
why should we be ruled by men long dead?" The question is never
asked about the main body of the Constitution where we really are
ruled by men long dead in such matters as the powers of Congress,
the president, and the Judiciary. It is asked about the Amendments
that guarantee individual freedoms. The answer as to those is that we
are not governed by men long dead unless we wish to cut back those
freedoms, which the questioner never does. We are entirely free to create all the additional freedoms we wish by legislation, and the nation
has done that frequently. What the questioner is really driving at is
why judges, not the public, but judges, should be bound to protect
only those freedoms actually specified by the Constitution. The objection underlying the question is not to the rule of dead men but to the
rule of living majorities.

Moreover, when we understand that the Bill of Rights gives us
major premises and not specific conclusions, the document is not at
all anachronistic. The major values specified in the Bill of Rights are
timeless in the sense that they must be preserved by any government
we would regard as free. For that reason, courts must not hesitate to
apply old values to new circumstances. A judge who refuses to deal
with unforeseen threats to an established constitutional value, and
hence provides a crabbed interpretation that robs a provision of its
full, fair, and reasonable meaning, fails in his judicial duty.

But there is the opposite danger. Obviously, values and principles
can be stated at different levels of abstraction. In stating the value that
is to be protected, the judge must not state it with so much generality
that he transforms it. When that happens the judge improperly
deprives the democratic majority of its freedom. The difficulty in
choosing the proper level of generality has led some to claim that
intentionalism is impossible.

Thus, in speaking about my view of the Fourteenth Amendment's
Equal Protection Clause as requiring black equality, Professor Paul
Brest of Stanford said:

The very adoption of such a principle, however, demands an arbitrary choice among levels of abstraction. Just what *is* "the general principle of equality that applies to all cases?" Is it the "core idea of *black* equality" that Bork finds in the original understanding (in which case Alan Bakke did not state a constitutionally cognizable claim), or a broader principle of "*racial* equality" (so that, depending on the precise content of the principle, Bakke might have a case after all), or is it a still broader principle of equality that encompasses discrimination on the basis of gender (or sexual orientation) as well? ...

The fact is that all adjudication requires making choices among levels of generality on which to articulate principles, and all such choices are inherently non-neutral. No form of constitutional decision-making can be salvaged if its legitimacy depends on satisfying Bork's requirements that principles be "neutrally derived, defined and applied."

I think that is wrong and that an intentionalist can do what Brest says he cannot. Let me use Brest's example as a hypothetical—I am making no statement about the truth of the matter. Assume for the sake of the argument that a judge's study of the evidence shows that both black and general racial equality were clearly intended, but that equality on matters such as sexual orientation was not under discussion.

The intentionalist may conclude that he can enforce black and racial equality but that he had no guidance at all about any higher level of generality. He has, therefore, no warrant to displace a legislative choice that prohibits certain forms of sexual behavior. That result follows from the principle of acceptance of democratic choice where the Constitution is silent. In short, the problem of levels of generality is solved by choosing no level of generality higher than that which interpretation of the words, structure, and history of the Constitution fairly support.

The power of extreme generalization was demonstrated by Justice William O. Douglas in *Griswold v. Connecticut*.[1] In that case the

Court struck down that state's anti-contraception statute. Justice Douglas created a constitutional right of privacy that invalidated the state's law against the use of contraceptives. He observed that many provisions of the Bill of Rights could be viewed as protections of aspects of personal privacy. He then generalized these particulars into an overall right of privacy that applies even where no provision of the Bill of Rights does. By choosing that level of abstraction, the Bill of Rights was expanded beyond the known intentions of the Framers. Since there is no constitutional text or history to define the right, privacy becomes an unstructured source of judicial power. I am not now arguing that any of the privacy cases were wrongly decided. My point is simply that the level of abstraction chosen makes a generalized right of privacy unpredictable in its application.

A concept of original intent, one that focuses on each specific provision of the Constitution rather than upon generalized values, is essential to prevent courts from invading the proper domain of democratic government.

That proposition is directly relevant to the subject of economic rights and the Constitution. Article I, Section 10, provides that no state shall pass any law impairing the obligations of contracts. The Fifth and Fourteenth Amendments between them prevent either the federal or any state government from taking private property for public use without paying just compensation.

The intention underlying these clauses has been a matter of dispute and perhaps they have not been given their proper force. But that is not my concern here because few deny that original intention should govern the application of these particular clauses.

My concern is with the contention that a more general spirit of libertarianism pervades the original intention underlying the Fourteenth Amendment so that courts may review virtually all regulations of human behavior under the Due Process clause of that amendment. This would include judicial review of economic regulations. The burden of justification would be placed on the government so that all such regulations would start with a presumption of unconstitutionality. Viewed from the standpoint of economic philosophy and of individual freedom the idea has many attractions. But viewed from the standpoint of constitutional structures the idea works a massive shift away from democracy and toward judicial rule.

Professor Siegan has explained what is involved:

> In suits challenging the validity of restraints, the government could have the burden of persuading a court...first, that the legislation serves important government objectives; second, the restraint imposed by government is substantially related to the achievement of these objectives, that is...the fit between means and ends must be close; and third, that a similar result cannot be achieved by a less drastic means.

This method of review is familiar to us from case law. It has merit where the court is examining legislation that appears to threaten a right or a value specified by a provision of the Constitution. But when employed as a formula for the general review of all restrictions on human freedom without guidance from the interpreted Constitution, the court is cut loose from any external moorings and required to perform tasks that are not only beyond its competence but beyond any function that can conceivably be called judicial. That assertion is true, I submit, with respect to each of the three steps of the process described.

The first task assigned the government's lawyers is that of carrying the burden of persuading a court that the "legislation serves important governmental objectives." That means, of course, objectives the court regards as important, and importance also connotes legitimacy. It is well to be clear about the stupendous nature of the function that is thus assigned the judiciary. That function is nothing less than working out a complete and coherent philosophy of the proper and improper ends of government with respect to all human activities and relationships. This philosophy must cover all questions social, economic, sexual, familial, political, etc.

It must be so detailed and well-articulated, all the major and minor premises in place, that it allows judges to decide infinite numbers of concrete disputes. It must also rest upon more than individual preferences of judges in order not only that internal inconsistency be avoided but also that the legitimacy of forcing the chosen ends of government upon elected representatives, who have other ends in mind, can be justified. No theory of the proper ends of government that possesses all of these characteristics is even conceivable. Yet, to satisfy the requirements of adjudication and the premise that a judge may not override democratic choice without an authority other than his own will, each of those qualities is essential.

Suppose that in meeting a challenge to a federal minimum wage law the government's counsel stated that the statute was the outcome of interest group politics, or that it was thought best to moderate the speed of the migration of industry form the North to the South, or that it was part of a policy to aid unions in collective bargaining. How is a court to demonstrate that none of those objectives is important and legitimate? Or, suppose that the lawyer for Connecticut in *Griswold v. Connecticut*, the decision striking down the state's law against the use of contraceptives, stated that a majority, or even a politically influential minority, regarded it as morally abhorrent that couples capable of procreation should copulate without the intention, or at least the possibility, of conception. Can the court demonstrate that moral abhorrence is not an important and legitimate ground for legislation? I think the answer is that the court can make no such demonstration in either of the supposed cases. And, though it may be only a confession of my own limitations, I have not the remotest idea of how one would go about constructing the philosophy that would give the necessary answers—for judges. I am quite clear how I would vote as a citizen or a legislator on each of these statutes.

This brings me to the second stage of review, in which the government bears the burden of persuading the court that the challenged law is "substantially related to the achievement of [its] objectives." In the case of most laws about which there is likely to be controversy, the social sciences are simply not up to the task assigned. Should the government insist upon arguing that a minimum wage law is designed to improve the lot of workers generally, microeconomic theory and empirical investigation may be adequate to show that the means do not produce the ends. The requisite demonstration will become more complex and eventually impossible as the economic analyses grow more involved. It is well to remember, too, that judge-made economics has not been universally admirable. Much that has been laid down under the antitrust laws testifies to that.

Moreover, microeconomics is the best, the most powerful, and the most precise of the social sciences. What is the court to do when told that a ban on the use of contraceptives in fact reduces the amount of adultery in the population? Or if it is told that slowing the migration of industry to the Sun Belt is good because it is more painful to lose jobs than not to get new jobs? (The substantive due process formulation does not directly address cost-benefit analysis, but one might suppose a court employing this kind of review would also ask whether the benefits achieved were worth the costs incurred. Perhaps that is included in the concept of a substantial relationship between ends and means. If so, that introduces into the calculus yet another judgment that can only be legislative and impressionistic.)

The third step—that the government must show that a "similar result cannot be achieved by a less drastic means"—is loaded with ambiguities and disguised tradeoff decisions. A "similar" result may be one along the same lines but not the full result desired by the government. Usually, a lesser, though "similar," result can be achieved by a lesser amount of coercion. A court undertaking to judge such matters will have no guidance other than its own sense of legislative prudence about whether the greater result is or is not worth the greater degree of restriction.

There are some general statements by some framers of the Fourteenth Amendment that seem to support a conception of the judicial function like this one. But it does not appear that the idea was widely shared or that it was understood by the states that ratified the amendment. Such a revolutionary alteration in our constitutional arrangements ought to be more clearly shown to have been intended before it is accepted. This version of judicial review would make judges platonic guardians subject to nothing that can properly be called law.

The conclusion, I think, must be that only by limiting themselves to the historic intentions underlying each clause of the Constitution can judges avoid becoming legislators, avoid enforcing their own moral predilections, and ensure the Constitution is law.

Five

THE INVESTITURE OF CHIEF JUSTICE WILLIAM H. REHNQUIST AND ASSOCIATE JUSTICE ANTONIN SCALIA AT THE WHITE HOUSE

Washington, D.C., September 26, 1986,
President Ronald Reagan

Mr. Chief Justice Burger, Mr. Chief Justice Rehnquist, members of the Court, and ladies and gentlemen:

Today we mark one of those moments of passage and renewal that has kept our Republic alive and strong—as Lincoln called it, the last, best hope of man on Earth—for all the years since its founding. One Chief Justice of our Supreme Court has stepped down, and together with a new Associate Justice, another has taken his place. As the Constitution requires, they've been nominated by the president, confirmed by the Senate, and they have taken the oath of office that is required by the Constitution itself—the oath "to support and defend the Constitution of the United States . . . so help me God."

With these two outstanding men taking their new positions, this is, as I said, a time of renewal in the great constitutional system that our forefathers gave us—a good time to reflect on the inspired wisdom we call our Constitution, a time to remember that the Founding Fathers gave careful thought to the role of the Supreme Court. In a small room in Philadelphia in the summer of 1787, they debated whether the Justices should have life terms or not, whether they should be part of one or the other branches or not, and whether they should have the right to declare acts of the other branches of government unconstitutional or not.

They settled on a judiciary that would be independent and strong, but one whose power would also, they believed, be confined within the boundaries of a written Constitution and laws. In the convention and during the debates on ratification, some said that there was a danger of the courts making laws rather than interpreting them. The framers of our Constitution believed, however, that the judiciary they envisioned would be "the least dangerous" branch of the government, because, as Alexander Hamilton wrote in the *Federalist Papers*, it had "neither force nor will, but merely judgment." The judicial branch interprets the laws, while the power to make and execute those laws is balanced in the two elected branches. And this was one thing that Americans of all persuasions supported.

Hamilton and Thomas Jefferson, for example, disagreed on most of the great issues of their day, just as many have disagreed in ours. They helped begin our long tradition of loyal opposition, of standing on opposite sides of almost every question while still working together for the good of the country. And yet for all their differences, they both agreed—as should be—on the importance of judicial restraint. "Our peculiar security," Jefferson warned, "is in the possession of a written Constitution." And he made this appeal: "Let us not make it a blank paper by construction." Hamilton, Jefferson, and all the Founding Fathers recognized that the Constitution is the supreme and ultimate expression of the will of the American people. They saw that no one in office could remain above it, if freedom were to survive through the ages. They understood that, in the words of James Madison, if "the sense in which the Constitution was accepted and ratified by the nation is not the guide to expounding it, there can be no security for a faithful exercise of its powers."

The Founding Fathers were clear on this issue. For them, the question involved in judicial restraint was not—as it is not—will we have liberal or conservative courts? They knew that the courts, like the Constitution itself, must not be liberal or conservative. The question was and is: Will we have government by the people? And this is why the principle of judicial restraint has had an honored place in our tradition. Progressive, as well as conservative, judges have insisted on its importance—Justice Holmes, for example, and Justice Felix Frankfurter, who once said, "The highest exercise of judicial duty is to subordinate one's personal pulls and one's private views to the law."

Chief Justice Rehnquist and Justice Scalia have demonstrated in their opinions that they stand with Holmes and Frankfurter on this question. I nominated them with this principle very much in mind. And Chief Justice Burger, in his opinions, was also a champion of restraint. All three men understand that the Founding Fathers designed a system of checks and balances, and of limited government, because they knew that the great preserver of our freedoms would never be the courts or either of the other branches alone. It would always be the totality of our constitutional system, with no one part getting the upper hand. And that's why the judiciary must be independent. And that is why it must exercise restraint.

So, our protection is in the constitutional system; and one other place as well. Lincoln asked, "What constitutes the bulwark of our own liberty?" And he answered, "It is in the love of liberty which God has planted in us." Yes, we the people are the ultimate defenders of freedom. We the people created the government and gave it its powers. And our love of liberty and our spiritual strength, our dedication to the Constitution, are what, in the end, preserves our great nation and this great hope for all mankind. All of us, as Americans, are joined in a great common enterprise to write the story of freedom—the greatest adventure mankind has ever known and one we must pass on to our children and their children—remembering that freedom is never more than one generation away from extinction.

The warning, more than a century ago, attributed to Daniel Webster, remains as timeless as the document he revered. "Miracles do not cluster," he said, "Hold on to the Constitution of the United States of America and to the Republic for which it stands—what has happened once in 6,000 years may never happen again. Hold on to your Constitution, for if the American Constitution shall fall there will be anarchy throughout the world."

Six

"THE LAW OF THE CONSTITUTION"

Tulane University, October 21, 1986
Attorney General Edwin Meese III

As you know, recently, in the East Room of the White House, a new Chief Justice and a new Justice of the Supreme Court were sworn in—William Rehnquist and Antonin Scalia, respectively. After both men had taken their oaths to support the Constitution, President Reagan reflected on what he called the "inspired wisdom" of our Constitution:

> Hamilton, Jefferson and all the Founding Fathers recognized that the Constitution is the supreme and ultimate expression of the will of the American people. They saw that no one in office could remain above it, if freedom were to survive through the ages. They understood that, in the words of James Madison, if "the sense in which the Constitution was accepted and ratified by the nation...[is] not the guide in expounding it, there can be no security for a... faithful exercise of its powers."[1]

In concluding, the president repeated a warning given by Daniel Webster more than a century ago. It is a thought especially worth remembering as we approach the bicentennial anniversary of our Constitution:

> Miracles do not cluster....Hold on to the Constitution of the United States of America and to the Republic for which it stands—what has happened once in 6,000 years may never happen again. Hold on to your Constitution, for if the American Constitution shall fall there will be anarchy throughout the world.[2]

For nearly two hundred years, the Constitution, which Gladstone pronounced "the most wonderful work ever struck off at a given time by the brain and purpose of man," has been reflected upon; argued about from many perspectives by great men and lesser ones.[3] The scrutiny has not always been friendly. The debates over ratification, for example, were often rancorous, and scorn was poured on many of the constitutional provisions devised by the Federal Convention in 1787. The Federalists and the Anti-Federalists were, to say the very least, in notable disagreement. Richard Henry Lee of Virginia, a leading Anti-Federalist, was convinced, for example, that the new Constitution was "in its first principles, [most] highly and dangerously oligarchic."[4] He feared, as did a good many others, for the fate of democratic government under so powerful an instrument. Still others thought it unlikely that so large a nation could survive without explicit provision for cultivating civic virtue among the citizens. The critics of the proposed Constitution had serious reservations about this new enterprise in popular government; an effort even the friends of the Constitution conceded was a novel experiment.

No sooner was the Constitution adopted than it became an object of astonishing reverence. The losers in the great ratification debates pitched in to make the new government work. Indeed, so vast was the public enthusiasm that one Senator complained that, in praising the new government, "declamatory gentlemen" were painting "the state of the country under the old congress"—that is, under the Articles of

Confederation—"as if neither wood grew nor water ran in America before the happy adoption of the new Constitution."[5]

It has not all been easy going, of course. There has been some pretty rough sailing during the nearly two hundred years under the Constitution. In fact, the greatest political tragedy in American history was played out in terms of the principles of the Constitution. The debate over nationalism versus confederalism which had first so divided the Federal Convention and later inflamed the animosities of Federalists and Anti-Federalists lingered on. Its final resolution was a terrible and bloody one—the War Between the States. And in the war's wake, the once giddy, almost unqualified adoration of the Constitution subsided into realism.

Today our great charter is once again under close scrutiny. Once again it is grist for the editorial mills of our nation's newspapers and news magazines. And while the attention is generally respectful, it is, to be sure, not uncritical. This attitude I think befits both the subject and our times. It shows better than anything else the continuing health of our republic and the vigor of our politics.

Since becoming Attorney General, I have had the pleasure to speak about the Constitution on several occasions. I have tried to examine it from many angles. I have discussed its moral foundations. I have also addressed on separate occasions its great structural principles—federalism and separation of powers. Tonight I would like to look at it from yet another perspective and try to develop further some of the views that I have already expressed. Specifically, I would like to consider a distinction that is essential to maintaining our limited form of government. This is the necessary distinction between the Constitution and constitutional law. The two are not synonymous. What, then, is this distinction?

The Constitution is—to put it simply but one hopes not simplistically—the Constitution. It is a document of our most fundamental law. It begins "We the People of the United States, in Order to form a more perfect Union..." and ends up, some six thousand words later, with the Twenty-Sixth Amendment.[6] It creates the institutions of our government, it enumerates the powers those institutions may wield, and it cordons off certain areas into which government may not enter. It prohibits the national authority, for example, from passing *ex post facto* laws while it prohibits the states from violating the obligations of contracts.

The Constitution is, in brief, the instrument by which the consent of the governed—the fundamental requirement of any legitimate government—is transformed into a government complete with the powers to act and a structure designed to make it act wisely or responsibly. Among its various internal contrivances (as James Madison called them) we find federalism, separation of powers, bicameralism, representation, an extended commercial republic, an energetic executive, and an independent judiciary. Together, these devices form the machinery of our popular form of government and secure the rights of the people. The Constitution, then, is the Constitution, and as such it is, in its own words, "the supreme Law of the Land."

Constitutional law, on the other hand, is that body of law that has resulted from the Supreme Court's adjudications involving disputes over constitutional provisions or doctrines. To put it a bit more simply, constitutional law is what the Supreme Court says about the Constitution in its decisions resolving the cases and controversies that come before it.

In its limited role of offering judgment, the Court has had a great deal to say. In almost two hundred years, it has produced nearly five hundred volumes of reports of cases. While not all these opinions deal with constitutional questions, of course, a good many do. This stands in marked contrast to the few, slim paragraphs that have been added to the original Constitution as amendments. So, in terms of sheer bulk, constitutional law greatly overwhelms the Constitution. But in substance, it is meant to support and not overwhelm the Constitution from which it is derived.

This body of law, this judicial handiwork, is in a fundamental way unique in our scheme. For the Court is the only branch of our government that routinely, day in and day out, is charged with the awesome task of addressing the most basic, the most enduring, political

questions: What is due process of law? How does the idea of separation of powers affect the Congress in certain circumstances? And so
forth. The answers the Court gives are very important to the stability
of the law so necessary for good government. Yet as constitutional
historian Charles Warren once noted, what's most important to
remember is that "[h]owever the Court may interpret the provisions
of the Constitution, it is still the Constitution which is the law and not
the decisions of the Court."[7]

By this, of course, Charles Warren did not mean that a constitutional decision by the Supreme Court lacks the character of law. Obviously it does have binding quality: it binds the parties in a case and
also the executive branch for whatever enforcement is necessary. But
such a decision does not establish a supreme law of the land that is
binding on all persons and parts of government henceforth and
forevermore.[8]

This point should seem so obvious as not to need elaboration.
Consider its necessity in particular reference to the Court's own work.
The Supreme Court would face quite a dilemma if its own constitutional decisions really were the supreme law of the land, binding on
all persons and governmental entities, including the Court itself, for
then the Court would not be able to change its mind. It could not
overrule itself in a constitutional case. Yet we know that the Court has
done so on numerous occasions. I do not have to remind a New
Orleans audience of the fate of *Plessy v. Ferguson,* the infamous case
involving a Louisiana railcar law, which in 1896 established the legal
doctrine of "separate but equal."[9] It finally and fortunately was struck
down in 1954, in *Brown v. Board of Education.*[10] Just this past term,
the Court overruled itself in *Batson v. Kentucky*[11] by reversing a 1965
decision that had made preemptory challenges to persons on the basis
of race virtually un-reviewable under the Constitution.[12]

These and other examples teach effectively the point that constitutional law and the Constitution are not the same thing. Even so,
although the point may seem obvious, there have been those throughout our history—and especially, it seems, in our own time—who have
denied the distinction between the Constitution and constitutional

law. Such denial usually has gone hand in hand with an affirmation that constitutional decisions are on a par with the Constitution in the sense that they too are the supreme law of the land, from which there is no appeal.

Perhaps the most well-known instance of this denial occurred during the most important crisis in our political history. In 1857, in the *Dred Scott* case, the Supreme Court struck down the Missouri Compromise by declaring that Congress could not prevent the extension of slavery into the territories and that blacks could not be citizens and thus eligible to enjoy the constitutional privileges of citizenship.[13] This was a constitutional decision, for the Court said that the right of whites to possess slaves was a property right affirmed in the Constitution.

This decision sparked the greatest political debate in our history. In the 1858 Senate campaign in Illinois, Stephen Douglas went so far in his defense of *Dred Scott* as to equate the decision with the Constitution. In his third debate with his opponent, Abraham Lincoln, he said:

> It is the fundamental principle of the judiciary that its decisions are final. It is created for that purpose so that when you cannot agree among yourselves on a disputed point you appeal to the judicial tribunal which steps in and decides for you, and that decision is binding on every good citizen.[14]

Furthermore, he later said, "The Constitution has created that Court to decide all Constitutional questions in the last resort, and when such decisions have been made, they become the law of the land."[15] It plainly was Douglas's view that constitutional decisions by the Court were authoritative, controlling, and final, binding on all persons and parts of government the instant they are made—from then on.

Lincoln, of course, disagreed. In his response to Douglas we can see the nuances and subtleties and the correctness of the position that makes most sense in a constitutional democracy like ours—a position that seeks to maintain the important function of judicial review while at the same time upholding the right of the people to govern themselves through the democratic branches of government.

Lincoln said that insofar as the Court "decided in favor of Dred Scott's master and against Dred Scott and his family"—the actual parties in the case—he did not propose to resist the decision.[16] But Lincoln went on to say:

> We nevertheless do oppose *[Dred Scott]*...as a political rule which shall be binding on the voter, to vote for nobody who thinks it wrong, which shall be binding on the members of Congress or the President to favor no measure that does not actually concur with the principles of that decision.[17]

I have provided this example, not only because it comes from a well-known episode in our history, but also because it helps us understand the implications of this important distinction. If a constitutional decision is not the same as the Constitution itself, if it is not binding in the same way that the Constitution is, we as citizens may respond to a decision with which we disagree. As Lincoln in effect pointed out, we can make our responses through the presidents, the senators, and the representatives we elect at the national level. We can also make them through those we elect at the state and local levels. Thus, not only can the Supreme Court respond to its previous constitutional decisions and change them, as it did in *Brown* and has done on many other occasions, but so can the other branches of government, and through them, the American people. As we know, Lincoln himself worked to overturn *Dred Scott* through the executive branch. The Congress joined him in this effort. Fortunately, *Dred Scott*—the case—lived a very short life.

Once we understand the distinction between constitutional law and the Constitution, once we see that constitutional decisions need not be seen as the last words in constitutional construction, once we comprehend that these decisions do not necessarily determine future public policy, once we see all of this, we can grasp a correlative point: constitutional interpretation is not the business of the Court only, but also properly the business of all branches of government.

The Supreme Court, then, is not the only interpreter of the Constitution. Each of the three coordinate branches of government created and empowered by the Constitution—the executive and legislative no less than the judicial—has a duty to interpret the Constitution in the performance of its official functions. In fact, every official takes an oath precisely to that effect.

For the same reason that the Constitution cannot be reduced to constitutional law, the Constitution cannot simply be reduced to what Congress or the President say it is, either. Quite the contrary. The Constitution, the original document of 1787 plus its amendments, is and must be understood to be the standard against which all laws, policies, and interpretations must be measured. It is the consent of the governed with which the actions of the governors must be squared. And this also applies to the power of judicial review. For as Felix Frankfurter once said, "[t]he ultimate touchstone of constitutionality is the Constitution itself and not what we have said about it."[18]

Judicial review of congressional and executive actions for their constitutionality has played a major role throughout our political history. The exercise of this power produces constitutional law. In this task even the courts themselves have on occasion been tempted to think that the law of their decisions is on a par with the Constitution.

Some thirty years ago, in the midst of great racial turmoil, our highest Court seemed to succumb to this very temptation. By a flawed reading of our Constitution and *Marbury v. Madison*,[19] and an even faultier syllogism of legal reasoning, the Court in a 1958 case called *Cooper v. Aaron*[20] appeared to arrive at conclusions about its own power that would have shocked men like John Marshall and Joseph Story.[21]

In this case, in dictum, the Court characterized one of its constitutional decisions as nothing less than "the supreme law of the land."[22] Obviously constitutional decisions are binding on the parties to a case; but the implication of the dictum that everyone should accept constitutional decisions uncritically, that they are judgments from which there is no appeal, was astonishing; the language recalled what Stephen Douglas said about *Dred Scott*.[23] In one fell swoop, the

Court seemed to reduce the Constitution to the status of ordinary constitutional law, and to equate the judge with the lawgiver. Such logic assumes, as Charles Evans Hughes once quipped, that the Constitution is "what the judges say it is."[24] The logic of the dictum in *Cooper v. Aaron* was, and is, at war with the Constitution, at war with the basic principles of democratic government, and at war with the very meaning of the rule of law.[25]

Just as *Dred Scott* had its partisans a century ago, so does the dictum of *Cooper v. Aaron* today. For example, a United States senator criticized a recent judicial nominee of the president for his sponsorship, while a state legislator, of a bill that responded to a Supreme Court decision with which the nominee disagreed. The decision was *Stone v. Graham,* a 1980 case in which the Court held unconstitutional a Kentucky statute that required the posting of the Ten Commandments in the schools of that state.[26] The bill, cosponsored by the judicial nominee—which, by the way, passed his state's Senate by a vote of 39 to 9—would have permitted the posting of the Ten Commandments in the schools of his state. The nominee was acting on the principle Lincoln well understood—that legislators have an independent duty to consider the constitutionality of proposed legislation. Nonetheless, the nominee was faulted for not appreciating that, under *Cooper v. Aaron,* Supreme Court decisions are the supreme law of the land—just like the Constitution. He was faulted, in other words, for failing to agree with an idea that would put the Court's constitutional interpretations in the unique position of meaning the same as the Constitution itself.

My message today is that such interpretations are not and must not be placed in such a position. To understand the distinction between the Constitution and constitutional law is to grasp, as John Marshall observed in *Marbury,* "that the framers of the constitution contemplated that instrument as a *rule for the government of courts, as well as of the legislature.*"[27] This was the reason, in Marshall's view, that a written Constitution is "the greatest improvement on political institutions."[28]

Likewise, James Madison, expressing his mature view of the subject, wrote that as the three branches of government are co-ordinate and equally bound to support the Constitution, "each must in the exercise of its functions be guided by the text of the Constitution according to its own interpretation of it."[29] And, as his lifelong friend and collaborator, Jefferson, once said, the written Constitution is "our peculiar security."[30]

Perhaps no one has ever put it better than did Abraham Lincoln, seeking to keep the lamp of freedom burning bright in the dark moral shadows cast by the Court in the *Dred Scott* case. Recognizing that Justice Taney, in his opinion in that case, had done great violence not only to the text of the Constitution but to the intentions of those who had written, proposed, and ratified it, Lincoln argued that if the policy of government upon vital questions affecting the whole people is to be irrevocably fixed by decisions of the Supreme Court the instant they are made, in ordinary litigation between parties, in personal actions, the people will have ceased to be their own rulers, having to that extent, practically resigned their government into the hands of that emminent tribunal.[31]

Once again, we must understand that the Constitution is and must be understood to be superior to ordinary constitutional law. This distinction must be respected. To confuse the Constitution with judicial pronouncements allows no standard by which to criticize and to seek the overruling of what University of Chicago Law Professor Philip Kurland once called the "derelicts of constitutional law"—cases such as *Dred Scott* and *Plessy v. Ferguson*.[32] To do otherwise, as Lincoln said, is to submit to government by judiciary. But such a state could never be consistent with the principles of our Constitution. Indeed, it would be utterly inconsistent with the very idea of the rule of law to which we, as a people, have always subscribed.

We are the heirs to a long Western tradition of the rule of law. Some 2,000 years ago, for example, the great statesman of the ancient Roman Republic, Cicero, observed, "We are in bondage to the law in order that we may be free."[33] Today, the rule of law is still the very fundament of our civilization, and the American Constitution remains its crowning glory.

Yet if law, as Thomas Paine once said, is to remain "King" in America, we must insist that every department of our government, every official, and every citizen be bound by the Constitution. That is what it means to be "a nation of laws, not of men." As Jefferson once said:

> It is jealousy and not confidence which prescribes limited constitutions to bind down those whom we are obliged to trust with power....In questions of power, then, let no more be said of confidence in man, but bind him down from mischief by the chains of the Constitution.[34]

Again, thank all of you for the honor of addressing you this evening. In closing, let me urge you again to consider Daniel Webster's words: "Hold on to the Constitution...and the Republic for which it stands—what has happened once in 6,000 years may never happen again. Hold on to your Constitution."

PART II

Seven

PANEL ON ORIGINALISM AND UNENUMERATED CONSTITUTIONAL RIGHTS

Suzanna Sherry

Thank you. I am delighted to be here and especially to be on such a distinguished panel.

The question I want to answer this morning briefly is whether Americans of the Founding generation believed that unenumerated rights existed and should be protected by the judiciary. Now very few historical questions have unequivocal answers, and this is one that comes about as close as one can find to an unequivocal yes. The Founding generation of Americans did believe in judicially enforceable unenumerated rights.

The way I am going to answer this question is to discuss very briefly what the founding generation thought, what that generation said, and what that generation did regarding unenumerated rights. I am going to try and give just an illustrative example in each case.

What did the Founding generation of Americans think? Well, they were very concerned about losing their liberty. They did not trust the government. And they did not trust majorities. James Madison provides the most famous example, but he is not the only example. I am sure you are all familiar with *Federalist* 10, where Madison talked about the problem of factions and worried about the tyranny of the majority.

But you may be somewhat less familiar with an earlier version of the same idea. In the Federal Convention in Philadelphia, which drafted the Constitution, James Madison described the purposes of a deliberative senate. It was, he said, to first protect the people against their rulers; secondly, to protect the people against the "transient impressions into which they themselves might be led." Again: worry about the government, worry about the majority.

Anti-Federalists also worried about liberty and encroachments on it. They criticized the Constitution mercilessly for its lack of a Bill of Rights. So we know that the Founders worried about liberty. They saw the Constitution as creating "islands of government in a sea of liberty," rather than islands of liberty in a sea of government.

But that does not tell us very much about what kind of liberty they thought about, what kind of rights they were concerned about. In particular, the fact that they were concerned about rights and liberty does not tell us very much about whether they were thinking about judicial enforcement of unenumerated rights.

So, for that, I want to turn to what the Founding generation of Americans said, especially in the context of the adoption of the Bill of Rights. Even before that, even before the Declaration of Independence, there was a lot of talk about inalienable natural rights. You can see it in political tracts; you can see it in sermons; you can see it in newspapers; you can even see it in arguments in court. Many state constitutions, including many that were written before the federal Constitution, included declarations of rights. They were not called *bills* of rights; they were called *declarations* of rights.

What did they do? They simply declared the lists of rights the citizens already had. They were not establishing rights. They were declaring pre-existing rights. The most interesting evidence, though, comes from the ratification debates over the Constitution. As I said, the Anti-Federalists kept criticizing the Constitution for not having a Bill of Rights. They kept asking, "Why didn't you give us a Bill of Rights?"

The Federalist response was consistent each time. The Federalists always gave the same two-fold answer to the question of why the proposed Constitution did not have a Bill of Rights. First, they said, we do not need a Bill of Rights because those rights exist. Natural rights exist whether they are enumerated or not. Second, they said, a Bill of Rights would be dangerous because it would imply that the list was exhaustive. It would imply that the listed rights were the only rights of Americans.

Here I want to quote from James Iredell in the North Carolina Ratifying Convention. His was a typical Federalist response to this question. He said: "It would be not only useless but dangerous to enumerate a number of rights which are not intended to be given up, because it would be implying in the strongest manner that every right not included in the exception might be impaired by the government without usurpation. And it would be impossible to enumerate every one. Let anyone make what collection or enumeration of rights he pleases, I will immediately mention twenty or thirty more rights not contained in it."

James Madison, who of course wrote the first draft of the Bill of Rights and presented it to Congress, agreed with Iredell and the other Federalists on this point. When he presented his draft of the Bill of Rights to Congress, he explicitly acknowledged the danger, calling it "one of the most plausible arguments I have ever heard urged against the admission of a Bill of Rights into this system." But, he said, he had guarded against it by including what later became the Ninth Amendment: "The enumeration in the Constitution of certain rights shall not be construed to deny or disparage others retained by the people."

So all of the evidence in the debates over the Constitution and all of the evidence in the debates over the Bill of Rights beyond what I have just read to you, all of that evidence suggests that the Ninth Amendment was deliberately designed to prevent any interpretation of the Constitution that might eliminate unenumerated rights.

Finally, let us look at what is probably the least familiar part of this story. That is what the Founding generation—and many generations after them—actually did. Before the Constitution was adopted, and for as long as sixty years after the Constitution was adopted, state and federal court judges invalidated legislative acts that infringed unenumerated rights. They did so explicitly and unabashedly.

Let me repeat that. For sixty years, courts struck down statutes that violated no written constitutional provision simply because those statutes violated natural or unenumerated rights. In case after case, judges invalidated these laws and used language such as "natural rights," "the inheritance of every individual citizen," "fundamental principles of society," the "dictates of moral reason," and "immutable principles of justice." All of these phrases were used to strike down laws enacted by legislatures.

One court said that a particular statute was in violation of natural rights, and "if it is not in violation of the letter of the Constitution, it is of its spirit and cannot be supported." Another, in a different state, said laws not specifically prohibited by written constitutions, but which are "repugnant to reason" and "subvert clearly vested rights" are invalid and must be declared so by the judiciary.

Again, these are just two very typical examples. There are many more like them. I think what this evidence demonstrates quite clearly is that the founding generation for some sixty years believed in the judicial enforcement of unenumerated rights.

So in short, you can support the idea of unenumerated rights without being an originalist, because there may be other reasons to do so. But you cannot be an originalist without supporting unenumerated rights, because a belief in the existence of unenumerated rights was part of the original understanding of the Constitution. Or, in the political language of today, if strict constructionist judges are those who adhere to the Constitution's original meaning, and activist judges are those who protect rights that are not expressly listed in the Constitution, then all strict constructionists should be activists.

Thank you.

✁

Professor Walter Dellinger

There are arguments against judges articulating non-specific unenumerated rights and applying those to set aside the judgments of the politically elected branches of government. But they are not arguments that sound in originalism or fidelity to the text of the Constitution. As I think Suzanna has said, there is ample evidence that the Framers understood that there was a relatively open-ended set of unenumerated rights; and by the time of the Fourteenth Amendment, even more clearly than in 1787, judicially enforceable unenumerated rights.

Following Attorney General Meese's provocative July 9, 1985 speech, there was a great deal of attention paid to the concept of original intention as the legitimate guide to constitutional interpretation. I am persuaded that that is essentially correct; that judges' authority to invalidate acts of popularly elected branches of the government has to flow from some external source. It has to flow from the Constitution. The text of the Constitution has meaning only if it is the meaning that those supermajorities would have adopted. You cannot take the language and play linguistic games with it. It may be fun for a linguist to make something different out of a phrase in the Constitution. But unless it is the meaning that those who marshaled the support of three-fourths of the states and supermajorities in Congress for adoption, then judges have no warrant imposing it. So I do not understand how there can be any non-originalist constitutionalism that is worthy of the name.

But, if you actually go back and look at the original understanding, you do not necessarily find that the original understanding was that those applying the clauses of the Constitution should limit themselves to a very specific set of rights. Let me add one example to those that Suzanna Sherry mentioned.

Following General Meese's talk, I decided it was time to really learn the debates in the Constitutional Convention. So for the ensuing seven years I taught a seminar at Duke where we read the debates at Philadelphia from the first day, May 25, through and up to September 17, 1787; line by line, every word of the debates; and then the debates in the First Congress over the adoption of the Bill of Rights.

One of the things that is most startling for the students comes at the point in the Convention where James Madison is arguing for the establishment of lower federal courts, and Luther Martin of Maryland is arguing that the state courts can be the lower courts for federal cases with Supreme Court review. Madison says that if we do not have federal courts, how will the national government vindicate its interests in the case where local courts would invalidate a criminal conviction under the national laws out of hostility to the national government—because in that case, double jeopardy would prevent the government from taking the case up to the United States Supreme Court.

Several delegates agreed that is right, that double jeopardy would prohibit an appeal from an acquittal in a lower state court. I say to my class, what double jeopardy clause are they talking about? This is 1787. The Fifth Amendment's Double Jeopardy Clause was not even proposed until the First Congress. Well, they are assuming that any law or provision that places someone twice in jeopardy would be void and would be declared so by courts, without the necessity of a constitutional provision precisely on that point. So, there was this sense, and the debates are replete with other examples, that there were judicially enforceable unenumerated rights.

One pragmatic point: the precise question asked is, for this panel, "Does the Constitution provide any legitimate foundation for the enforcement of unenumerated rights?" If the answer to that question is no, the consequences are extraordinarily radical, and would eliminate bases for the protection of personal liberties and economic rights so sweeping that I think you would find it breathtaking. For example, if there were no basis for the enforcement of unenumerated rights, then the governor of New Hampshire could order the state troopers in to close down the *Dartmouth Review*. The Oregon legislature could provide that all oceanfront property shall be seized from its owners and redistributed to those with less income. Because you can look at the Constitution of the United States—and I actually found this week, Hugo Black's bench copy—there is no enumerated right to be free of state government interference with one's freedom of speech; there is nothing enumerated in the Constitution that protects one's property from being seized by the state and redistributed without compensation.

The First Amendment says, you will recall, *Congress* shall pass no law. The Fifth Amendment says that property shall not be taken. But, as John Marshall correctly noted in *Barron v. The City of Baltimore*, the Bill of Rights only applies to the federal government. Ah, you say, but the Fourteenth Amendment incorporated those rights. Well, no. *Adamson v. California* rejected the notion that the Due Process and Privileges and Immunities Clauses of the Fourteenth Amendment were intended to incorporate by reference the Bill of Rights, something that the framers of the Fourteenth Amendment could easily have chosen to do had they chosen to say so.

Indeed, General Meese recognized that it was simply illegitimate to apply these rights against the states as rights of the national Constitution. So applying the First Amendment against the states, or applying the Takings Clause against the states, is to apply and enforce unenumerated rights.

Now a judge feels very comfortable articulating as unenumerated rights those rights that the Bill of Rights enumerates as against the national government. The Supreme Court clearly felt comfortable in doing this in 1925 when it said the freedom of speech is part of the liberty protected by the Fourteenth Amendment. Judges feel comfortable because the first founding generation imposed those restraints on the national government. So, judges do not feel like they are being idiosyncratic when they impose the same rights as against the states.

But that was by no means the limit of what the founding generation thought. At the time we come to the Due Process Clause of the Fourteenth Amendment, there is a lively debate about whether all those unenumerated rights referred to in the Ninth Amendment were intended to be judicially enforceable or whether the people acting politically would be the source of implementing unenumerated rights. By the time of the Fourteenth Amendment, which is the source of most of our controversial unenumerated rights decisions—whether it is contraception or abortion, freedom from excessive punitive damages, freedom from the retroactive imposition of massive liability—whether it is any of those things, the framers of the Fourteenth Amendment were in a very different position than the framers of the original Constitution, because we know what the Fourteenth Amendment framers understood about judicial enforceability and broad construction of the Constitution.

In the fifty years that preceded the adoption of the Fourteenth Amendment, we had, as both the framers and ratifiers were fully familiar with, decisions such as *Marbury v. Madison*. Every right deserves a judicial remedy. *Gibbons v. Ogden, McCulloch v. Maryland, Swift v. Tyson, Fletcher v. Peck, Dred Scott v. Sandford*. Those are all shorthand for cases involving latitude in making phrases of the Constitution, judicially enforceable.

Fletcher v. Peck enforced and expanded a very limited set of clauses—no state shall enact any *ex post facto* law, bill of attainder, or law impairing the obligation of contracts. This is the language John Marshall uses to invalidate a massive seizure of private property by the Georgia legislature. He says it is not really any of these things, but the whole spirit of these clauses, and his concurring justice says natural principles of justice would invalidate Georgia's massive seizure of private property.

So I think you can be an originalist and not rule out the use of unenumerated rights. Indeed, originalism anticipates unenumerated rights. Those rights, I believe, are both economic and personal. I gave the Simon Lecture at the Cato Institute two years ago following the Inaugural Lecture by Judge Douglas Ginsburg. My thesis was that the disparagement by many liberal scholars and jurists of the judicial protection of economic rights has weakened the constitutional foundations for personal liberty. Conversely, the disparagement by some conservative jurists and scholars of unenumerated personal liberties has weakened the foundation for the protection of rights and property, contract and occupational freedom.

The hard questions are the restraint with which a judge ought to exercise those rights. I do think it is legitimate both to limit punitive damages (the taking the property of A and giving it to B when it does not serve a public purpose) and invalidate restraints on personal liberty and I believe that those are one and the same.

If you read Justice Kennedy's two opinions from one term, in the *State Farm v. Campbell* case putting limits on punitive damages, and his opinion in the same term in *Lawrence v. Texas* striking down the Texas homosexual law, they read like one opinion. Both Kennedy opinions impose non-specific unenumerated rights. I think they stand or fall together.

Restraint may well be called for, but so is fidelity to original intent. As Justice Powell and Justice Harlan said the language of the Fourteenth Amendment can not be a null set. Those rights should be found with caution and restraint and with respect for democratic governments, but they should not be abandoned.

At the end of the day there has to be an exercise of judgment. One impoverished notion that what we should do is to look for what specific rights the framers of the Bill of Rights or of the Fourteenth Amendment *would have included had they chosen* to include a specific list must be rejected. The short answer to that is that the Framers did not so choose. They did not leave us with only textually enumerated rights. They chose instead by text and original intent to pass the responsibility to protect unenumerated rights on to us, to be exercised with caution and restraint, but never to be abandoned.

Thank you.

John Harrison

Thank you. I believe that I can demonstrate that we have no rights, enumerated or otherwise, because if we had any, we would not be here at nine in the morning.

Having said that, I suppose I could sit down, but instead I am going to say a little bit more about unenumerated rights. That is not the best of all possible labels, at least if we are talking about provisions like the Ninth Amendment, because in a sense anything that is referred to in the Constitution is a little bit enumerated I am going to say something about the topic as it has come to be called, first, with respect to the Framing and early practice, and then a little bit more with respect to the Fourteenth Amendment.

As to the Framing, I want to stress something about the story that Suzanna Sherry was telling, which is that the Federalists were at pains to emphasize the importance of the principle of enumerated powers, the principle that the federal government had only the powers that had been given to it by the Constitution. There are two ways, if you want to have a government of limited powers, to have it.

One way is to list only certain powers and say the government can not do anything else. The liberty of the people then will be unimpaired where the powers do not reach. Notice the complementary relationship between power and liberty. The other way to do it would be to list the things the government can not do to infringe on liberty and say that the government has the power to do anything else.

The danger with the latter, as Iredell pointed out, is that it is really hard to list all the things that the government should not be able to do. So the primary approach that the federal convention took was the first: list what the government could do and leave as the residuum the retained rights of the people—that is to say, the rights that were not surrendered by granting a power to the government. You can make either one the figure and either one the ground, but there is a lot to be said for making the enumeration of powers the figure and leaving the rights of the people as the ground.

If the primary mechanism that the Constitution uses to protect rights is the principle of enumeration, that then creates a problem if you bring a little bit of the other approach into the Constitution. If you have both the principle of enumeration and some affirmative restrictions listing specific things the government cannot do in the Constitution, how do you make sense of those two? That was something that the Federalists were concerned about. They said, indeed, that a danger of enumeration of rights is that it will create confusion as to whether we have retained the principle of enumerated powers.

So, the more modest reading of the Ninth Amendment in particular is that it emphasizes, no, the primary protection for liberty, the primary protection for retained rights—those that have not been given up—remains the principle of enumerated powers and no one should think from the list of specific exceptions that the government can do everything that is not excepted. We have not switched over to the other way of limiting government, which is listing the exceptions.

So the really hard case for someone who wants to say that there is a strong federal principle of enumerated rights would be one in which Congress wanted to do something that was clearly within an enumerated power, and the objection was that we know that the enumeration reaches what Congress wants to do, but despite that Congress cannot do it, because we know Congress can not do that sort of thing.

I also want to say something about the early practice that Suzanna talked about. I can not address everything she touched on, but I can say something in particular about the Marshall Court and about the invocations of general principles of natural right in the Marshall Court (the Marshall Court as opposed to the very first Supreme Court). This is something very interesting that my colleague Ted White discovered about the Marshall Court. It is true that there are a number of cases that invoke general principles and in particular, of course, the great general principle of American constitutional law in the nineteenth century, which is that the government may not take the property of A and give it to B, because this is America.

If you look at those cases, like for example *Fletcher v. Peck*, you will find that all the invocations of great general principles of the social contract and natural rights, as opposed to specific constitutional provisions like the Contracts Clause, appeared in cases that came from the lower federal courts, where those courts had been exercising their diversity jurisdiction. In diversity cases the federal courts, lower and Supreme, believed themselves authorized to look to all possible sources of law, including law that was neither state nor federal, but just general law, like the general principles of contract and commercial law that were invoked in *Swift v. Tyson*. General law, the Marshall Court's opinions indicate, included general constitutional law, which in turn included great principles of natural rights and the social contract. But the Court distinguished between those principles and the actual limitations contained in the Constitution. It looked to general constitutional law only in cases from lower federal courts under the diversity jurisdiction, and did not do so in cases that came to it from state courts under Section 25 of the Judiciary Act of 1789. It did so because the jurisdiction under Section 25 was limited to claims of error with respect to federal law, including the Constitution, by the state courts, and did not extend to general principles. So the Marshall Court distinguished between those great big principles of the social contract and the actual limitations imposed on the states by the Constitution.

I also want to say a little bit about the Fourteenth Amendment. I want to set out the reading of all three of its primary clauses in the second sentence of Section 1 that does not include any unenumerated rights. This is a reading according to which both the Privileges or Immunities Clause and the Equal Protection Clause are protections of equality, designed to accomplish the great goal of the first section of the Fourteenth Amendment, which was to put into the Constitution the rule of the Civil Rights Act of 1866. The rule of the Civil Rights Act of 1866 was that there was to be no race discrimination with respect to civil rights, rights of contract and property and so forth.

Under that reading, a correct paraphrase of the Privileges or Immunities Clause would be "all citizens shall have the same privileges or immunities," which means all citizens shall have the same civil rights. An abridgment under this reading, the equality based reading, means taking away from one group of citizens' rights that are enjoyed by other groups of citizens under the positive law, so that the baseline of rights that are not to be abridged is the body of rights created by the law of the state. That creates a close similarity between the Fourteenth Amendment Privileges or Immunities Clause and Article IV's Privileges and Immunities Clause.

On a similar reading the Equal Protection Clause establishes universal equality with respect to the protection of the laws. Everybody, all people now and not just all citizens, shall have the same version of a different body of rights (different from the privileges and immunities of citizens) created by the positive law: those rights involving the protection of the laws. This may not be the best defined body of rights, but the important point is that the drafters had in mind some set of entitlements created by the existing law.

The Due Process Clause was primarily understood as being about the means by which things happen under the law. Notice I said the means by which things happen. I did not say procedure, because the distinction between procedural and substantive due process is an anachronism. The concept of substantive due process is not mentioned by the Supreme Court of the United States until some time, I think, in the 1950s.

The primary manifestation of what we would now call substantive due process that was well known to the framers of the Fourteenth Amendment was this: they may well have believed the Due Process Clause of the Fourteenth Amendment would forbid, of course, since this was nineteenth century America, taking the property of A and giving it to B. That was the one thing a legislature could not do.

The reason a legislature could not do that under a Due Process Clause in those days was because legislatures, through the legislative power, could not deprive people of their rights. You could call that principle procedural. It would be more accurate to call it structural. It was a separation of powers concept according to which some kinds of statutes, quintessentially those that took the property of A and gave it to B, constituted deprivations of property. The due process of law constituted what courts did, not what legislatures did. And, therefore, legislatures could not take the property of A and give it to B because they were legislatures, and deprivations of property could be done only through due process of law, which was the process used by courts, not legislatures. That is to say, the due process principle reiterated what they understood as a principle of separation of powers.

The great example of this is, of course, *Dred Scott v. Sandford*, in which members of the Supreme Court asserted that the right of a slave owner to the slave could not be taken away by a piece of legislation, because pieces of legislation are not judicial procedure and are not due process of law.

The last thing I want to say is that I actually think that the best argument in favor of unenumerated rights, as that concept is normally understood, does not arise from the text of the Constitution. It arises from the fact that for a long time, despite what the text might lead you to believe, American judges have, for various reasons and under various rubrics, been imposing limitations that are difficult in fact to square with the text. Nevertheless they have been doing it.

That creates a genuine problem, because the ultimate question always in a legal system, as Professor Hart said, is what is the rule of recognition? What is the actual practice that constitutes the law? You can maintain that the actual practice is not strict adherence to the text of the Constitution, that the actual practice includes extra-textual judicial protection of rights.

I do not think that is true. I think, in fact, that American political behavior, especially in moments of crisis, like the impeachment of President Clinton in 1998, shows that the real rule of recognition is to look at the Constitution and do nothing else. One of the interesting things about the Clinton impeachment was that it produced a sudden attack of originalism and textualism, a recurrence to the Constitution.

So if you think, like I do, that the real rule of recognition is do what the text says and forget everything else, then you will think that anything else is not part of the relevant tradition, but an illegitimate exercise of power. Those, of course, can happen too.

Finally, if you are the kind of originalist I am, a textualist, you will be less concerned with the subjective expectations of the people who participated in framing either the Constitution or the Fourteenth Amendment, and more concerned with what they actually said.

⚜

Lino A. Graglia

The question we are asked to answer "Is there a role for unenumerated rights in constitutional law?" is similar to the question "What is the best fuel for UFOs?" If one responded to this second question by saying that he doubts there are UFOs, he would obviously disqualify himself from a discussion of the best fuel. Similarly, if one responded to the first question by saying he doubts that the Constitution does grant some rights that, nonetheless, it neglects to mention, he would disqualify himself from a discussion as to their proper role. In fact, he would probably thereby establish that he is not a constitutional scholar qualified to participate in any constitutional law discussion.

As I happen to be among the non-believers in unenumerated constitutional rights and other metaphysical entities, I probably should leave the podium at this point and not get in the way of what might be a rich and interesting discussion among believers. That discussion, however, like a discussion of UFOs, would most fittingly take place in the rabbit hole mentioned in *Alice in Wonderland*, and at a meeting chaired by the Red Queen, who could believe three impossible things before breakfast and would therefore have made an excellent constitutional scholar.

Nonetheless, fortunately for you, I have decided to remain in order to point out that a discussion of unenumerated constitutional rights illustrates nicely the only point worth making about constitutional law, namely, that it is a fraud, a product of pretense, the purpose and effect of which is to remove policymaking power from the hands of the American people and transfer it to Supreme Court justices, mirrors and mouthpieces of a cultural elite. How is it possible, outside of the rabbit hole and among grown-ups, to claim that the Constitution authorizes judges to overturn the results of the ordinary political process on the basis of restrictions that do not appear in the Constitution? George Orwell famously noted that there are some ideas so preposterous that only the highly educated can believe them. I would add that there are also some ideas so even more preposterous that only lawyers, professionally trained in blurring the distinction between fact and fiction and inured to the unembarrassed assertion of the preposterous, can believe them.

To begin at the beginning, constitutionalism itself presents problems. It makes sense for the ruled to seek to limit the ruler by agreement, as the barons limited King John in 1215 with the Magna Carta. But why, in a democracy, would a people who are themselves the rulers want to limit their own, or worse, their successors' policy choices? We all agree, I take it, that in a secular society there is no authority or source of wisdom higher than the people. The usual justification for judicially enforced constitutionalism, that it is actually consistent with democracy because it merely keeps people from making mistakes they would later regret, has neither plausibility nor empirical support. Chief Justice Harlan Fiske Stone told us that "it permits appeal from the people drunk to the people sober," but he did not tell us what happens if it is not the people but, as is far more likely, the judges who imbibe? I doubt that you can think of an example of a ruling of unconstitutionality as to which the people later said, "Boy, we sure are glad that those good and wise judges kept us from making that mistake." I never heard anyone say, for example, "If it wasn't for the judges I would have foolishly had my kids go to a neighborhood school instead of being bused across town because of their race." Further, if the people are in fact sovereign, a majority should be able to overcome constitutional limitations at any time, just as the framers of the Constitution overcame the Articles of Confederation. Constitutionalism is an attempt to have the living governed by the dead, but the dead, fortunately, lack means of enforcement.

Whatever the merits of judicially enforced constitutionalism, it has little to do with our topic because judicially enforced constitutionalism, after all, assumes a Constitution. If not based on specific constitutional restrictions, judicial review is not constitutionalism at all, but simply a cover for rule by judges. The problem presented by the notion of judicially enforceable unenumerated constitutional rights is not rule by the dead, but rule by judges who are all too much alive. The argument that, in the absence of specific constitutional restrictions, judges enforce fundamental principles, natural law, tradition, or anything other than their personal political preferences, is an argument best made to the Red Queen.

The question "Does the Constitution provide any legitimate foundation for the enforcement of unenumerated rights?" could not be more misguided. The three pillars of the Constitution are democracy or republicanism—representative self-government through elected legislatures; Federalism—decentralized government with most social policy decisions made at the state level; and separation of powers with legislators making and judges only applying the law. The notion of unenumerated rights is simply a ruse for policymaking by the

Supreme Court—by majority vote of a committee of nine lawyers, unelected and holding office for life, making policy for the nation as a whole from Washington D.C. It is the antithesis of the constitutional system, totally undemocratic and totally centralized, with the judiciary performing the legislative function. It is not enforcement, it is perversion of the Constitution, a means not of protecting our rights but of depriving us of our most important constitutional right, the right of self-government through elected representatives in a federalist system.

The argument that the Ninth Amendment or the Privileges or Immunities Clause of the Fourteenth Amendment authorizes judges to enforce unenumerated rights is academic lawyerism at its worst. Everyone except constitutional law scholars understands that such authority would do nothing but make the judges the final lawmakers on any issue they choose to remove from the ordinary political process and assign to themselves for decision. It is not politically possible to argue openly in this country that rule by majority vote of nine electorally unaccountable lawyers in robes is an improvement on the system of government created by the Constitution; yet that, incredibly enough, is the system we now have. It is a system similar to Iran's. There, too, people get to vote and elect legislators, and the legislators pass laws. But the laws are permitted to operate only if not disapproved of by the Grand Council of Ayatollahs. Here the Supreme Court performs that function.

In order to support and defend this system, liberal constitutional scholars must concoct such fantasies as "unenumerated constitutional rights" and attempt to convince the American people that the result is something other than rule by judges. There is no mystery as to the origin and purpose of the Fourteenth Amendment. As the Supreme Court correctly pointed out in the *Slaughter-House Cases*, it would not even have been suggested except for the need to guarantee basic constitutional rights to blacks, and was not meant to make Supreme Court justices "the perpetual censors" of all state laws. Similarly, it is clear that the Ninth Amendment was adopted for the specific and very limited purpose of countering the argument that a bill of rights could operate to expand, rather than restrict, the national government's power by implying the nonexistence of other rights. It was meant, as it plainly states, to preclude the argument that it abrogates rights, not to authorize judges to create or discover rights. A recent excellent study by Professor Kurt Lash effectively reaffirms that as the Tenth Amendment was meant to limit Congress to its enumerated powers, the Ninth was meant to prevent it from expanding the scope of those powers by liberal construction.

Finally, it may surprise you to learn that I am a believer in "the living Constitution," but only as long as it is the people or their elected representatives who make it live by *reducing* constitutional restrictions on popular government, not when it means as it usually does, the creation of additional restrictions by the Supreme Court. If democracy is the norm, as it should be, constitutional restrictions should be heavily disfavored; new ones should not be created and existing ones should be held to their core meaning, the result of which would be very few rulings of unconstitutionality. If there is any doubt as to the meaning of the Privileges or Immunities Clause or the Ninth Amendment, it should be resolved so as to favor policymaking by elected legislators rather than unelected judges.

Distrust of the American people is the defining characteristic and motivating force of the liberal constitutional scholar. The American people, after all, favor capital punishment, prayer in the schools, restrictions on abortion and pornography, neighborhood schools, a ban on flag burning, and so on. How would it be possible for a liberal intellectual to live in a country like that? The defect of democracy, as they see it, is that people with such unenlightened views get to vote. Unenumerated constitutional rights are their means of correcting that defect. I, on the other hand, oppose unenumerated rights because I agree with Churchill that democracy, with all its shortcomings, is the best form of government available to us. Whatever may be the best form of government, government by majority vote of nine electorally unaccountable lawyers pretending to be enforcing the Constitution must be one of the worst.

Judge Michael W. McConnell

Some might think it imprudent for a sitting federal judge to speak on the contentious topic of unenumerated rights, especially one such as myself, who as an academic wrote and spoke in strong opposition to the legitimacy of the general doctrine and of many of its specific applications, including *Roe v. Wade*.

I have not changed my mind about that. So I feel it necessary to make clear at the beginning that I am not speaking here in my capacity as a court of appeals judge. In that capacity, I have no choice but to recognize *Roe v. Wade*, at least in its modified *Casey* form, as authoritative and binding. It has been affirmed and reaffirmed by Justices appointed by presidents from Nixon to Clinton. From the vantage point of a court of appeals judge, short of a constitutional amendment, and unless or until the Supreme Court changes its collective mind, the question of a constitutional right to abortion is as settled as anything in current constitutional law.

Of course, the same is not true for the Supreme Court itself, which is always free to decide when to reconsider its precedents, in accordance (I hope) with a principled *and consistent* understanding of *stare decisis*. It cannot be right that decisions that one side approves of—such as *Bowers v. Hardwick* or *United States v. Morrison*—are always up for grabs, while decisions favored by the other side are set in concrete. I predict the issue of unenumerated rights, and especially the right to abortion, will continue to divide the nation for some time to come, as it continues to divide the Supreme Court itself, for the very good reason that it goes to the heart of our character as a self-governing nation.

Two answers have dominated this debate. The first is that in the absence of a constitutional norm derived from the text of the Constitution, or perhaps from longstanding experience and tradition, courts have no authority to displace the decisions of the representatives of the people.

At the opposite extreme are those who maintain that the open-ended language of the Constitution is an invitation to judges to decide, on the basis of their "own views about political morality," (quoting Professor Ronald Dworkin), what liberties Americans should enjoy. This makes judging an application of moral philosophy, and for that reason I will call it the "moral philosophic" approach.

The conveners of this panel ask us which approach is most consistent with the original understanding of the Constitution. That requires us to take up the various arguments and sources of authority most often invoked in support of the moral-philosophic approach. I will take them up in order, from least to most plausible.

It is sometimes argued that the Constitutional system has within it an "unwritten constitution," which implicitly recognizes some set of natural rights. We might call this natural law. Now, I believe in natural law, at least at some level, and suspect most of us do. But the notion that natural law can be brought to bear in specified cases, and allowed to trump positive law, is quite foreign to the legal system established by the framers.

We need not look any further than the Tenth Amendment. It provides that the powers not delegated to the United States by the Constitution, *nor prohibited by it to the States*, are reserved to the States respectively, or to the people." In other words, limitations of the powers of the States are not implicit or unwritten. If a limitation on state power is not found in the Constitution, it is not a legal limitation.

But what, you may be thinking, of the Ninth Amendment, a second and more popular putative source of the power of moral philosophic judging? The Ninth, after all, provides that the "enumeration in the Constitution, of certain rights, shall not be construed to deny or disparage others retained by the people."

Some have interpreted this to mean that there really do exist unwritten constitutional rights. But that is not what the Ninth Amendment says. The principal word in the Amendment, "rights," is not the same as our modern term "constitutional rights." It must be remembered that at the time of the framing of the Ninth Amendment, there was no Bill of Rights, and virtually no *constitutional* rights at all. The rights "retained by the people" must have been rights the people then had: such rights as common law rights of property, personal liberty, protection of the person, and contract, statutory rights, rights established by charter, or by custom, or by ordinance.

The most natural reading of the Ninth Amendment, and the one confirmed by the history of its drafting, is that the enumeration of rights in a Bill of Rights was not intended to have any negative implication for any of the many other rights enjoyed by the People. It did not create any power in the judiciary to treat their own moral judgments as trumping positive law.

We move on to the granddaddy of putative sources of authority for moral philosophic judging: substantive due process. This has been the Supreme Court's chosen instrument for finding unenumerated constitutional rights and using them to trump laws enacted by Congress and the legislatures, from *Dred Scott v. Sandford*, the first appearance of the doctrine in the Supreme Court, through *Lochner v. New York*, to *Planned Parenthood v. Casey* and *Lawrence v. Texas*.

One might think that the text of the Due Process Clause contains a sufficient refutation of the doctrine. After all, when it provides that "no state shall deprive any person of life liberty or property without due process of law," it would seem to make clear that the State does have the power to deprive liberty and property, and even life, *with* due process of law, that is, by enforcement of properly enacted laws through proper procedures. No talk on the notion of substantive due process would be complete without quoting Professor John Hart Ely's observation that substantive due process is an oxymoron, on the order of "green pastel redness."

But if mere text does not suffice as an answer, there is more. When Congressman John Bingham, principal author of the Fourteenth Amendment, was asked on the floor of the 39th Congress what was meant by "due process of law," he responded: "I reply to the gentleman, the courts have settled that long ago, and the gentleman can go and read their decisions." The leading case interpreting the Fifth Amendment Due Process Clause prior to the Civil War was

Murray's Lessee v. Hoboken Land & Improvement Co. I am sure you remember it.

In that case, Justice Benjamin Curtis (later to be the leading dissenter in *Dred Scott*) offered the following methodology for determining what "due process" entails in any particular case:

We must examine the constitution itself, to see whether this process be in conflict with any of its provisions. If not found to be so, we must look to those settled usages and modes of proceeding existing in the common and statute law of England, before the emigration of our ancestors, and which are shown not to have been unsuited to their civil and political constitution by having been acted on by them after the settlement of this country.

In other words, the subject of due process, not surprisingly, is "process," which the Court also called "modes of proceeding." The content of due process, moreover, is determined 1) by constitutional language and 2) by "settled usages and modes of proceeding": in other words, by text and longstanding tradition.

There is a fourth possible source of authority, which is the least implausible of the four but, interestingly, has not been invoked by the Supreme Court: the Privileges or Immunities Clause of the Fourteenth Amendment. It has the signal advantages of being found in the written text of the Constitution, and it is directed to the question of substantive rights. It reads: "No State shall make or enforce any law which shall abridge the privileges or immunities of citizens of the United States."

But before devotees of the moral philosophic approach get too excited about this, they should look, as Bingham said we should look, at the cases—in this instance, the cases interpreting the privileges and immunities protected under Article IV.

Time does not permit a thorough examination, but the bottom line is this: at its most expansive, the privilege or immunities clause goes no further than to protect rights "which have, at all times, been enjoyed by the citizens of the several states which compose this Union, from the time of their becoming free, independent, and sovereign." (Quoting from the principal case, *Corfield v. Coryell*.) In other words, rights firmly established by longstanding custom and tradition. These are legal and historical, not moral or philosophical judgments, and one finds such rights only by looking to positive law, not deep within ourselves, or to the mysteries of the universe.

Thus, the privileges or immunities clause, were the Supreme Court to consult it, might provide some support for the unenumerated rights methodology employed by Chief Justice Rehnquist in *Washington v. Glucksberg*, or by Justice Scalia in *Michael H. v. Gerald D.* In these cases, the Court held that it would subject democratically enacted laws to heightened scrutiny where—and only where—claimed rights are "objectively, deeply rooted in this Nation's history and tradition."

Such an approach certainly provides no warrant to striking down laws based on the Justices' own desire to promote social change.

Discussion: Originalism and Unenumerated Constitutional Rights Moderated by Judge Diane P. Wood

JUDGE WOOD: Well, you were promised a lively set of presentations, and I think you certainly got one. What I would like to do to begin with is to return to our panelists and pose a couple of questions. Then we will invite you to make any questions, observations, comments, or other interventions that you would like. So let me begin by asking Suzanna Sherry whether your theory of unenumerated rights means that it has to be Article III federal judges who are some how using these rights as a way to limit legislative authority, either from the Congress of the United States itself, or from the state legislatures?

PROFESSOR SHERRY: No, it certainly does not have to be federal judges. It can also be state judges. It also should be (but less and less is) legislatures. One of the things that we have not talked about is the idea that the Constitution does bind legislatures as well and that they should be looking to it when they are enacting laws.

I think one implication of Professor Graglia's position is that even enumerated rights are not enforceable. That is, his position seems to be that only the legislature may judge the constitutionality of its own actions, because democracy is a master norm.

The problem with that is that democracy is not our only norm. Liberty is at least one of our other norms. That is where judges come in, when the legislature, as the sovereign—as the representative of the people—oversteps the bounds of liberty. The hard questions, of course, are determining when those boundaries have been overstepped.

JUDGE WOOD: Walter, can you think of any cases that might satisfy the Graglia popularity test, instances in which the Supreme Court has limited a piece of legislation and people afterwards say that was a good idea?

MR. DELLINGER: Sure. Take for example *Moore v. City of East Cleveland,* where a woman gets ground up in the machinery of the bureaucracy under a zoning ordinance that tells her that the only family that can occupy a dwelling is one where she cannot take in her two parentless grandchildren who are cousins of each other. The court demands a reason, and finds none that would justify a state restriction. I believe people would approve of the court's decision.

Professor Graglia, always engaging, makes a powerful argument against judicial review from a policy democratic perspective. I do not think, however, that his position is based in the text of the Constitution or its understanding. I think we quickly have come to understand that the Fourteenth Amendment limitations on state excesses is certainly founded in the Constitution. Whether it is valuable or not is a non-originalist, non-textual, non-constitutional policy argument about living in a more pure democracy.

Professor Graglia mentions the fact that Oregon—we do not have to worry about the fact that under his view, and under the view that no enumerated rights are protected, that there is no restriction on what Oregon would do about freedom of speech, freedom of the press, or freedom of religion, because Oregon is not, in fact, going to make the Moonies the state religion.

I would not be so comfortable with the assumption that Oregon is not going to take beach front property and redistribute it to those who have less of it. Nor would I be comfortable in thinking that a state like Nebraska is not going to pass at points in its history any anti-German legislation to prohibit the teaching of German, or that in a similar case in the 1920s any anti-Catholic majorities in the state are going to prohibit the sending of children to parochial schools or to private schools. In these cases the court articulates a notion that part of due process is that a law must satisfy a public purpose. Taking the property of A and giving it to B does not meet that requirement. Nor, as the Supreme Court said in 1874, does just telling A that he must be married to B rather than to C satisfy that judgment.

PROFESSOR GRAGLIA: The problem with saying that law must serve a "public purpose" is that the Constitution might as well say, let all laws be "just," or let all things be "for the best." The problem, of course, is that that simply is not a legal provision or restriction. It is simply a transference of decision-making power from the policy-making branches of government to the courts. Could the state say all beach front property gets redistributed? Well, if a state says that, I am not sure it is wrong. I think private property is very important, but if in a state somehow the situation is such that they want to redistribute, who am I to say that is wrong? That is one of the things they might do.

Indeed, Connecticut might take private property and turn it over to an industry, which they did to the outrage of many conservatives. It seems to me that the people of Connecticut thought that creating three thousand jobs and reviving the economy of New London was more important than protecting private property rights. I do not think that that policy judgment is precluded to them by the Constitution.

In terms of what Suzanna Sherry said, that I would challenge even enforcing enumerated rights, what I said is, yes, constitutionalism presents its problems, but that is not our problem on this panel today. I mean, thanks to the Constitution we cannot have, for example, Arnold Schwarzenegger or the governor of Michigan, Jennifer Granholm, as president. Is that not wonderful the Constitution does that? Is that not nice? What is it doing for us but creating problems? But, it's not my problem....

JUDGE WOOD: Professor Graglia, we need to give Professor Harrison a shot at this as well. I think your position is that there is, in fact, no anti-majoritarian principle in the Constitution, that there is nothing that limits legislative powers.

PROFESSOR GRAGLIA: No, no, the Constitution is anti-majoritarian. I say that. There is a question whether that is desirable. But making up new unenumerated rights is far worse.

JUDGE WOOD: Is there ever a statute, then, that should be struck down? Do you think every case that the Supreme Court has decided, striking down legislation, such as for example, the *Morrison* case or the *Lopez* case, is incorrectly decided?

PROFESSOR GRAGLIA: Those cases are incorrectly decided. If I had to stretch for a case holding something unconstitutional that was correctly decided, it would be more difficult. I think some of the cases disallowing or invalidating restrictions on black voting were correctly decided. The Fifteenth Amendment is clear; you can not deny the vote on grounds of race, and there were some cases striking down bans on African Americans voting that were correctly decided. Interestingly, in my view, the most unconstitutional law the Court ever saw was in the *Blaisdell* Minnesota mortgage moratorium case abridging the freedom of contracts. It was the most unconstitutional law they ever confronted, and they upheld it. They blew their one real shot.

JUDGE WOOD: Let's ask Professor Harrison....

PROFESSOR GRAGLIA: Overturning *Roe v. Wade* is not activism. That is unactivism. That is doing in activism.

JUDGE WOOD: Perhaps so, but let me ask Professor Harrison what he thinks about textual provisions in the Constitution that are themselves rather broadly worded, like the use of the word "liberty" in the due Process Clauses, or like the words "cruel and unusual punishments" in the Eighth Amendment? Also, given your commitment to the Constitution's textual ways of resolving problems, for which you cited the Clinton impeachment proceedings, can I take it from that that you think *Bush v. Gore* was wrongly decided?

PROFESSOR HARRISON: As to the last one, in fact, I think that *Bush v. Gore* was wrongly decided, for a couple of reasons. To begin with, and this one went completely past the Supreme Court, they did not have jurisdiction in that case, because the decision by the Supreme Court of Florida was not final yet. The Supreme Court of Florida had remanded the case to a lower federal court and had not entered a final judgment. Sometimes these things get missed.

It is also true that if you are a serious textualist and also even an original intention person about the Equal Protection Clause; that Clause does not extend to the right to vote. The right to vote is not part of the bundle of legal advantages called the protection of the laws. So a whole lot of cases, including the equal protection aspect of *Bush v. Gore* are incorrect for that reason if you are a textualist.

As for the first part of your question, what to do with the broader provisions of the Constitution, I do not think that the reference to liberty in the Due Process Clause is one of the broader provisions of the Constitution. I think the reference to liberty in the Due Process Clause refers to natural liberty. That is to say to not being physically confined.

There are some hard ones. The ban on cruel and unusual punishment I think is a difficult problem. I do not have a straightforward answer as to what to do with the provision about cruel and unusual punishments for the following reason I will get to in just a second. My general principle is some provisions that are thought to be broad and hard to understand actually are not. That I do need to say. I do need to say that about the Due Process Clause. I do need to say, possibly disagreeing with Judge McConnell about that, about the Privileges or Immunities Clause of the Fourteenth Amendment. But as for, for example, interpreting the ban on cruel and unusual punishments that is genuinely difficult. I think it is difficult because; it forces judges to decide whether, in dealing with a morally drenched concept like that, like cruel and unusual punishment, they have to attempt to answer questions of morality themselves, or look to what they regard as moral conventions adopted by the American people generally. I do not have an answer to that question, but I think the question is confined, that particular one, to the Cruel and Unusual Punishment Clause and a few others like it. There are a few other examples like it. But, again, my general answer is there are not nearly as many general clauses as people think.

JUDGE WOOD: Let me ask Judge McConnell how you would think the Supreme Court should approach the following hypothetical. Suppose Oregon decides that they have been too modest in their end-of-life legislation, so instead they decide to go the Netherlands route and authorize active euthanasia, under whatever procedures they decide to outline—two doctors ascertain that the person is capable is really just a candidate for this—is there any federal constitutional limitation that you would find on that, or would you say that Oregon's decision, legislatively, to authorize active euthanasia should be respected?

JUDGE MCCONNELL: Let me instead attack Lino Graglia.

JUDGE WOOD: I will let you do that for the moment, but then I am going to come back to this while you think about it.

JUDGE MCCONNELL: I do want to strongly disagree with his view that the most unconstitutional law ever before the Supreme Court was the one in the *Blaisdell* case. Surely it was the one in *Jews for Jesus v. Los Angeles Airport,* where the ordinance was that no First Amendment activities are permitted in the airport, which I take it means you can do anything you want to in the airport unless it is a constitutionally protected activity.

Judge Wood asks a much harder question with respect to euthanasia. I would want to know what the law in question actually provides. By "active euthanasia" I assume you mean it is not a case in which an individual in advance has directed that euthanasia be performed but that some other private persons have been delegated the authority to make the decision to end the life of this person?

JUDGE WOOD: Right, that is what I am hypothesizing.

JUDGE MCCONNELL: I have not given this a lot of thought, but there might indeed be some kind of a due process problem with the state delegating such a power to private persons, probably interested in the case, by the way, possibly heirs, possibly people with financial concerns, and possibly people who are professionally involved with the person whose life might be ended. If the state delegates to such persons the decision to end some other person's life, I think that there might well be a constitutional problem with that.

JUDGE WOOD: So what would you say then if the state responding to your scholarly article said, "We are going to establish a board of state officials who will make that final decision whenever the case is submitted to them"?

JUDGE MCCONNELL: Is there going to be a follow-up to this question?

JUDGE WOOD: I just want to know how far you are going to go with this argument that there is no federal constitutional limitation? Perhaps the answer is there is no such limitation, and you have to trust to the legislative judgment of the people of Oregon?

JUDGE MCCONNELL: There are several things about that. First of all, we are talking about life here. There is no question that the right to life is protected under the Due Process Clause, with due process. So one would want to ask the question, what are the settled usages and modes of proceeding going back to England and brought over to our settlers and not disturbed on this side of the Atlantic for when you put an innocent person to death? I think one might argue that there are no such settled uses and procedures for doing that. At least not within what we would call law.

JUDGE WOOD: Right. I want the audience to notice that I am not referring to the legislation in the Terri Schiavo situation, which perhaps comes closer in modern times to the sort of thing I am talking about: the persistent vegetative state person who is not flatlined in brain activity but who is, in fact, not, at least according to the medical judgments that were before the various courts, capable of further life.

Let me stand up now so that I can see and invite questions from the audience.

You may direct them either to the panel as a whole or if there is a particular member of the panel, that would be fine as well. Sir?

AUDIENCE MEMBER: I wonder if anybody would like to comment on Randy Barnett's new book *Restoring the Lost Constitution*?

PROFESSOR GRAGLIA: I have lots of comments on it.

JUDGE WOOD: This will come as a surprise.

PROFESSOR GRAGLIA: Randy Barnett is essentially arguing that courts should do the "right thing," and he knows what the "right thing" is. It is funny, these conservatives—with Roger Pilon at Cato you see the same thing—they berate Brennan for making it up, when their only objection really is they are making the wrong stuff up, and not making the stuff up they want.

What does Randy Barnett say? He is all for unenumerated rights. You do not need jurisprudential sophistication to understand that, as a practical matter, there is no alternative except for the judges therefore to make it up. What you are hearing is a distrust of the people that is inherent in the intellectual.

I mean, what if Oregon passed what some consider a questionable law? Must we thank the judges for keeping Oregon from doing that? I assume if Oregon passed such a law, it would have had reason to do so. Who am I to say that Oregon would be wrong? Do we need to improve on democracy? Is there a better way to make policy decisions, and the way is to leave it to the judges? That is a possible position. Plato thought that government by philosopher kings was an improvement on democracy. But lawyer kings?

JUDGE WOOD: Thank you. Professor Sherry?

PROFESSOR SHERRY: I long ago gave up trying to take on Professor Graglia, but I do have a comment on Randy Barnett. He has written a very persuasive article on the Ninth Amendment. It is called "The Ninth Amendment: It Means What It Says." If you want a copy of it, you can find it on the Boston University Law School Web site.

JUDGE MCCONNELL: Roger Pilon has pointed out that Ronald Dworkin's version of unenumerated rights, which holds that judges should simply act as philosophers and impose their moral views in the name of giving meaning to the Constitution, is not the only version of unenumerated rights. Roger asks: Is there not a theory of rights which the Framers and the people actually had and which can be enforced? I want to answer that, yes, but I am afraid that that theory of rights is too abstract to be usable as law. To find a way to articulate the theory of rights which is going to be sufficiently non-controversial to command a consensus either back then or for us today, it has to be at a very general level. All the interesting questions have to do with how the theory actually applies on the ground in the context of a particular case. And since we are talking about constitutional law and not, say, the development of common law and not the drafting of legislation, every case we are talking about is one in which the one moral position has been taken by the majority represented through the institutions of the legislature.

So we are, by definition, not talking about cases in which there is some sort of consensual standard or value that can be uncontroversially applied by the judges. Now, I would like to footnote that. There are a lot of different ways in which cases come up. *Moore v. City of East Cleveland* was mentioned a moment ago. It may be an example of the least problematic form of this kind of constitutionalism, because what *Moore* had to do with was a general and unobjectionable zoning ordinance which said that single family dwellings had to have a family in them. But then the question came up what happens when you have a grandmother living in a home with two of her grandchildren, but they are cousins. This is a case that no one had thought about. So there is an as-applied challenge. Not a challenge to the legislature's own deliberate acts, not a direct disagreement between the court and the representative institutions, but rather a claim that there exists a case that is rather unusual, that falls within the language of the zoning ordinance, but may well be beyond or in violation of a long standing and consensual norm having to do not with some fancy and newfangled desire to change the definition of families, but with the fact that grandparents and grandchildren are understood to be a traditional family unit.

Troxel v. Granville I think is one of the more interesting and theoretically difficult cases in recent years. The Court divided three different ways. As Roger knows, this is the case having to do with a breathtakingly broad power asserted by a state to require parents to send their children for overnight visits to essentially anyone that the state might consider to be in the best interest of the child.

Now, in practice, this statute was nowhere near as totalitarian as its broadest implications might suggest. Over the years, in Washington, as in most states, there was a certain understood limitation to what family courts would do in a situation like this one. But when the case became constitutionalized and went up to the United States Supreme Court, the Court held—and again it is a little bit hard to know exactly what their holding is, because they split three different ways—that at least in its unbridled, unlimited form, the state does not have the right to tell you that you must send your children off to spend time with others. If there is an example of a law challenged in the Supreme Court that violated long standing tradition and experience in this nation, this strikes me as being as close an example as I could find.

AUDIENCE MEMBER: If the Ninth Amendment was meant to be a ringing endorsement of the principle of individual liberty over corporate self-governance, then why is it that the same Congress that passed the Ninth Amendment did not overwhelmingly support Madison's desire and, in fact, his proposal to incorporate not even the entire Bill of Rights as it came to be written but only those rights that were believed by most people to be most fundamental so that those rights applied against the state governments? It would seem to me that if the Ninth Amendment was meant to have a broad meaning that Congress's failure to apply the rights in the First Amendment to the states would be intellectually inexplicable.

PROFESSOR SHERRY: It is an interesting point. I do not think that it is intellectually inconsistent, because I think there is a federalism overlay to this. That is, the states already had their own constitutions and their own bills of rights. Although Madison disagreed, the majority of Congress thought that that was sufficient protection and, therefore, that the federal Bill of Rights did not need to apply to the states. They also voted down, as you say, some of the very specific limitations that Madison proposed on the states. One last piece of evidence, though, is that the states themselves actually many of them, after the adoption of the Ninth Amendment, enacted constitutional provisions that were identical to or very similar to the Ninth Amendment, which undermines Professor Harrison's point a little bit.

I think the implication of what Professor Harrison was saying is that the Ninth Amendment was at least in part a federalism provision, designed to leave the federal government out of things and let the states take care of them. But the states also believed that the core of the Ninth Amendment was a good idea. After it was adopted, many states said, "Wait a minute, our bills of rights might be interpreted to be exhaustive, and we do not want them to be interpreted that way either." So, at least a dozen states, right up through the middle of the nineteenth century, enacted their own "baby Ninth Amendments."

PROFESSOR HARRISON: Can I?

JUDGE WOOD: Yes, please.

PROFESSOR HARRISON: I am going to about eighty percent agree with Suzanna Sherry. I want to stress here the extreme importance in understanding all of this of federalism. Because if the question is, did the Framers have a theory of rights that we can recover, the answer is, with respect to the national government, absolutely. It is in Article I, Section 8. It is in the list of federal powers. That they worked hard on. That they theorized.

The converse of that, the residuum, are everyone's primary rights against the national government. So, yes, they absolutely had that theory. It was built into a system of federalism. I do think that the Ninth Amendment itself, the federal Ninth Amendment, is fundamentally a principle about federalism, about the limited scope of the federal government. What that means is that the scope of power that is left to the states is very substantial and much harder questions arise with respect to state constitutions and the state Ninth Amendments which I suspect, if they protected anything else, of course they protected vested rights of property, because this was the nineteenth century and you could not take the property of A and give it to B.

Other than that, I am not sure. But those are very important questions of state constitutional law. The primary place to think about this ought to be the state constitutions. It is a big mistake to think that the federal Constitution is the primary guarantor of all of our fundamental freedoms. It is about mainly the federal government and it does a few things, important things like the Fourteenth Amendment, but only a few things about the state governments. Most of the powers and restrictions on the state governments are going to be found in state constitutions.

PROFESSOR SHERRY: May I make just one very small comment?

JUDGE WOOD: All right.

PROFESSOR SHERRY: John Harrison said that the Founders worked very hard on the list of federal powers in Article I, Section 8. In fact, they did not. They sent the Constitution to a committee to do the actual drafting, they instructed that committee simply to give Congress the powers that were needed. The delegates were not even sure that Congress should have specifically enumerated powers or whether Article I should just have something essentially equivalent to the Necessary and Proper Clause. It was the Committee on Detail that actually produced the list of enumerated powers in Article I, Section 8. Then, in fact, there was almost no discussion of any of those powers. There was a little bit of discussion about post roads, I believe—not something that comes up much today.

JUDGE WOOD: Walter?

MR. DELLINGER: I want to agree with John Harrison that the Bill of Rights clearly was intended to limit the national government and not the states. Indeed, it was the state legislatures that were insisting that there be limits on the national government. They had in their own constitutions their own bills of rights. They were perfectly comfortable that the state judiciaries would protect rights within the states.

It only was with the Fourteenth Amendment—and I probably think a lot of the disagreement over what the Court has done in the modern era is in some sense a disagreement with the Fourteenth Amendment, which really, for the first time, made the national government the guarantor of the rights of citizens against their own state governments. Whether that was wise or unwise, the Fourteenth Amendment did empower the national Congress, which could legislate under Section 5, and the courts with judicial enforcement, to protect rights against the states.

Now, it is important, I think, to separate out the question of unenumerated rights from the question of judicial restraint and judicial activism. Even if you believe that there are rights not specifically mentioned, like the right of parents to control the upbringing of their children, you can still be a restrained or an activist judge and exercise caution and restraint in other areas.

It is also important to note, I think, as the Institute for Justice and as Cato have in briefs they have filed in cases like *Lawrence*, that state "legislative power" does not encompass everything that passes with a majority vote. There are things that legislatures under our Constitution perhaps never had the authority to do—like enact *ex post facto* laws which are not laws, or take the property of A and give it to B. But there are other examples. There are limits. That, I think, is essentially the anti-totalitarian principle that is at the heart of American constitutionalism. Before the government can interfere with your liberty or your property it has to have a reason. "Just because we said so" is not a good enough reason.

PROFESSOR GRAGLIA: You can be sure it does have a reason or they would not do it. The question is: Does some judge get to say that reason is not good enough, in the judge's opinion? That simply is the policy issue.

What is clear here? We keep saying that one thing is clear. Can we not have a general principle that courts can enforce? For example, you cannot take the property of A and give it to B. That is the standard example given. It is hard to think of anything hardly more unclear. Of course we tax people. We tax the rich for welfare purposes. We have zoning laws that take the property rights of some property owners for the benefit of others. So the rule that you can not take the property of A and give it to B does not answer many questions.

Realistically, you have got specific difficult questions that are not answered by a general principle. Why do we not have some general rule, Roger Pilon says? Did they not have a theory? But as Mike McConnell said, if they had a theory, it was so abstract as to be useless to us today. What is accomplished by a theory that says "let good be done," or "let justice be done." We all agree on that. But it does not answer any of the hard questions in particular cases. One's answer comes down to one's policy views. The issue here is who makes those decisions? It is a terrible thing to trust the people. Democracy is terribly dangerous. Yes, government is dangerous. But being ruled by Justice Souter is more dangerous.

JUDGE MCCONNELL: I think Walter Dellinger is entirely right that the Fourteenth Amendment is at the heart of this matter and that goes to the federalism dimension. But there is also the separation of powers dimension of the Fourteenth Amendment, because some draw the conclusion that because there exists some fairly general language in the Fourteenth Amendment, the people, in adopting that Amendment must have wanted judges to have a much more open-ended role in enforcing the Amendment. But I think that is quite a misreading of the history of the Fourteenth Amendment, because in its penultimate draft the Fourteenth Amendment did not even contemplate a judicial role. The initial proposal was solely an addition to Congress's enumerated powers. Congress was given the power to make laws to protect persons from the deprivation of privileges and immunities of citizens and to enforce the equal protection of the law. It was only later that Section 1 was added to the Fourteenth Amendment, in order to protect against the horrible possibility that the Democrats might take over again and repeal the Civil Rights Act of 1866. But it is still quite clear that no historian that I know of even doubts that drafters of the Fourteenth Amendment thought that Congress and not the federal courts was to be the principle enforcement agent. This was the age of *Dred Scott*. When the framers of the Fourteenth Amendment thought of judges, they were thinking of Roger B. Taney and *Dred Scott v. Sandford*. It was *Dred Scott,* after all, that for the first time employs this doctrine of substantive due process in order to protect an unenumerated right to spread slavery to the territories. The Fourteenth Amendment reads almost sentence for sentence as a repudiation of the various doctrines of the *Dred Scott* case. To assume from the Fourteenth Amendment that it was some great act of faith in the judiciary to be able to second guess state legislation, I just think is historically inaccurate.

MR. DELLINGER: Ten seconds. I entirely one-hundred percent agree with that, Mike, that Congress was the central institution to enforce the Fourteenth Amendment and I agree with you that the Court has too narrowly read Congress's Section 5 powers.

Accepting, however, that the Court's role in enforcement was clearly secondary, we ought nonetheless to conclude in light of *Marbury v. Madison, McCulloch v. Maryland,* and *Fletcher v. Peck,* that surely it was not unanticipated that courts would enforce the Fourteenth Amendment. I agree with you that the central institution for enforcing the Amendment was Congress.

PROFESSOR SHERRY: And all the state courts that had also been enforcing rights.

JUDGE WOOD: Yes, you have been waiting.

AUDIENCE MEMBER: I would like to ask each side of the debate a question of self-criticism. For the proponents of the judicial protection of unenumerated rights, how do you dissociate yourself from the *Dred Scott* Court? And for the opponents of judicial protection of unenumerated rights, how do you protect against a legislature behaving like the Committee on Public Safety? Is Thomas Carlyle's criticism of Rousseau not right, that if there is any universal philosophical truth it is that all universal philosophical truths are flawed?

JUDGE WOOD: Suzanna?

PROFESSOR SHERRY: *Dred Scott* may be, or may not be, the first substantive due process case, but it is certainly the first originalist case. Since I am not an originalist, it is very easy for me to disavow *Dred Scott.* My purpose here this morning was to say that if you are an originalist you have to support unenumerated rights. But I am not an originalist.

PROFESSOR GRAGLIA: That really is a lawyerly dodge. The Ben Curtis dissent in *Dred Scott* points out that nowhere in the Constitution does it say that Congress cannot prevent the extension of slavery to the new territories. Where does the Constitution say, as Taney said in *Dred Scott,* that a state cannot make a black person a citizen? *Dred Scott* is not an example of originalism. It is rather an instance of the judges saying that you can not take the property of A (slaves) and give it to B (the slave). Everybody knows that is wrong! Although we all know today, most of us know, that it is perfectly legitimate to do that. Most historians agree that it was *Dred Scott* that gave us the Civil War. It made it inevitable. Now, I ask you, if we are going to do a cost-benefit anaylsis of judicial review—and I have to admit nothing is so bad that it does not occasionally do something good, and maybe that is even true of judicial review, although I have to stretch my brain to think of it— does the *Dred Scott* decision not settle this question?

MR. DELLINGER: No.

PROFESSOR GRAGLIA: The first significant exercise of the power of judicial review to hold an Act of Congress unconstitutional, its very first such major holding, gave us the Civil War, and six hundred and twenty thousand people dead? I would say that anything that failed so catastrophically was not a good idea.

JUDGE WOOD: Walter.

MR. DELLINGER: I think it is a very good question. Cases like *Dred Scott* are deeply sobering to any defense of judicial review. There is no question about that. It makes one very sober about trusting judges, no matter how clear the constitutional command or invitation might be. It is very sobering.

But it is not dispositive, because I think, for example, about how the Takings Clause has blunted what is a very strong redistributive instinct in this country. The Takings Clause has been essentially respected to a large degree because we all know that judicial review under it is available. At the end of the day, I am very agnostic about whether I think the level of judicial activism is on the whole good or ill. I am reminded of what Chou En-lai responded when he was asked—he was a great intellectual —he was asked, "What do you think is the significance of the French Revolution?" His response was, "It is too early to tell."

Eight

PANEL ON ORIGINALISM
AND PRAGMATISM

Dean Larry Kramer

In my ten to twelve minutes, I want to make two simple points. One is that the only way you can be an originalist is to not know history very well. The other is that there is no such thing as pragmatic originalism because originalism is by definition unpragmatic and at odds with legal pragmatism.

To understand why being an originalist works only if one ignores or misstates history, we actually need to do a quick history of originalism itself—to draw some distinctions that matter and recognize how originalism has been an evolving theory. Some notion that what the Framers or Founders thought is relevant to constitutional interpretation has been part of the legal landscape for a very long time, appearing as early as the 1790s. But constitutional interpretation as a discipline—as a distinct subject with a distinct methodology—actually came into being only in the late nineteenth century. If you read legal treatises and other works on the Constitution written before that, you will not find anything about theories of interpretation. The treatises discuss particular interpretations and offer descriptions of the proper or best understanding of particular clauses, but it takes the passage of some time before people begin to think about the problem of interpretation more broadly and systematically. For most of the nineteenth and early twentieth centuries, even as the problem of interpretation emerged into consciousness, the main controversy concerned how much deference courts should give to legislatures. It was about *who* should interpret, not *how* to interpret. When it came to the question of how to interpret the Constitution, there was general agreement on a kind of conventional approach that mixed different arguments without much systemization—something very much like the mix of arguments lawyers use when interpreting statutes or common law. The Framers' intent was one of these arguments, used alongside text and precedent and policy, but not superior to them.

The idea of originalism as an exclusive theory, as *the* criterion for measuring constitutional decisions, emerged only in the 1970s and 1980s. And it first appeared as, let us call it "original intent originalism." This is the idea that we care about what the fifty-five men who drafted the Constitution in Philadelphia thought they were doing when they framed the Constitution. That originalism first emerged in this guise is hardly surprising, given that the most readily available evidence about the origins of the Constitution's provisions consisted of notes from the Constitutional Convention collected in a neat four-volume set by Max Farrand. Consequently, a great deal of early originalist work asked what the Framers thought they were doing when they wrote this or that Clause of the Constitution.

Of course, relying on such evidence was immediately subjected to a strong critique that I think everybody is probably familiar with. The sparseness of the evidence was said to leave every question indeterminate. Some people found this sort of argument persuasive, others did not. But a more powerful critique of original intent soon emerged, this one arguing that relying on Framers' intent could not be justified as a normative matter. The intent of the drafters in Philadelphia does not matter, this critique argued, because the Constitutional Convention had no lawmaking authority. The underlying premise of originalism is one of positive law: the Constitution is a species of legislation, authoritative only because and insofar as it was enacted by an authoritative lawmaker. As such, the authoritative intent is that of the people who had the power to make it law, not of the people who drafted the Constitution in Philadelphia. Looking to their intent is like giving authority to a speech writer for the president. It is like giving authoritative weight to the intent of the lobbyists who drafted a bill for Congress, as opposed to the Congress that actually adopted it.

This was a pretty devastating critique, and it required a response. So originalism changed and reemerged in a second guise, which we can call "original-understanding originalism." Unsurprisingly, given the critique, originialism in its new guise evolved to focus mainly on the views of the ratifiers. It was, perhaps, more than serendipity that originalism in this second guise emerged just as extensive material on ratification became easily available to legal scholars through the publication at Wisconsin of the multi-volume Documentary History. Suddenly everybody could be an historian of ratification, because a vast reserve of primary sources were available in neatly bound volumes.

This development made sense as a response to the critique of original intent originalism. But originalism in this second guise soon ran into a similar set of critiques. The indeterminancy argument became stronger, as indeterminacy is obviously a greater concern when you expand the number of people whose views count from the small group of fifty-five in Philadelphia to include everybody who voted on the Constitution. Originalists found themselves trying to recover the understanding of an exceedingly large group of people, a task made more difficult by the fact that different issues were discussed from state to state. There were issues discussed in Pennsylvania that just did not come up in Virginia and vice versa.

Make of this what you will: again, some people found it persuasive, others did not. As with original intent originalism, however, there was a second critique that proved fatal to original understanding originalism—surprising partly because this critique came from the Right. It built on Justice Scalia's critique of statutory interpretation, which questioned the legitimacy of using legislative history to interpret a legal text. Many of the same arguments made in the statutory context applied equally to the Constitution, and so originalism evolved again—into the form that is prevalent today, which we can call "public-meaning originalism."

The easiest way to understand public-meaning originalism is to play out further the analogy to statutory interpretation. How do we understand the meaning of a statute if we are not using legislative history? We look to the language of the statute and ask about the public meaning of the words, which is to say, how those words are or ought to be understood by the relevant audience. We may, of course, disagree about what that public meaning is, and we may have to litigate the issue. There are arguments lawyers make about the proper way to interpret the public meaning of a statute: when to use ordinary parlance, when to use the dictionary, when to treat something as a term of art, and when to deploy a canon of construction. There are similar arguments that can be used to recover the public meaning of the Constitution, and the originalist argument became that the proper way to understand the Constitution is according to its original public meaning. This means interpreting the text using the kinds of arguments that would have been used in the late eighteenth century, at the time the Constitution was enacted and became law.

As I said, public-meaning originalism is the prevalent version of originalism today, which makes sense given the way it responds to the critiques of both original-understanding originalism and original intent originalism. Yet public-meaning originalism has some pretty serious defects of its own—the main one being that there was no agreed upon public meaning of the constitutional terms most often in dispute. This was something the Founding generation learned to its dismay early in the 1790s. There were huge disagreements about the meaning of many of the provisions we are still debating today. Interpretation, the Framers came to understand, was then, as it is today, a process of filling gaps, resolving ambiguities, and settling conflicts. And insofar as there were, at the time, two or more plausible positions on the correct original public meaning of a provision of the Constitution, all one does in embracing one of them today is to take sides in a historical dispute that was not resolved at the time of the Founding, and so is not resolvable on such terms today. As far as positive law is concerned, this has no more objective grounding or authority than what Ronald Dworkin does when he applies moral theory to interpret the same provisions.

It might be different if, at the time of the Founding, there had been an agreed-upon set of conventions for interpretation. Then you could claim to be applying the same principles of interpretation while disagreeing about their application. That happens all the time, and the test for whether there is a discernible public meaning does not and cannot require that there be unanimity as to its precise content. The problem is that there was *not* an agreed-upon set of conventions for interpreting the Constitution at the time of the Founding. On the contrary, the very concept of something we could call constitutional law was new. Such questions as whether constitutional law was like ordinary law and whether the same principles of interpretation used for statutes would or should apply to the Constitution were up for grabs, and it took two to three decades for the Founding generation to develop principles that applied to these matters. Even then, different and competing principles developed, and there was no more agreement about what the "correct" way to interpret the Constitution was or should be in the early years of the Republic than there is today.

That being so, it is impossible to talk about the notion of an original public meaning, because at that point you really are just making it up from the top down. You are deciding what principles should have been used in the eighteenth century to determine public meaning, because those principles were never settled. You then use those principles, from which you can generate a variety of plausible interpretations, to pick one that you think makes sense. Whatever that accomplishes, it is *not* ascertaining what would have been the original public meaning of the constitutional text at the time that text was adopted.

So, how have originalists handled this problem? They have ignored it. You see this in the originalist scholarship being done today, none of which looks remotely like the way those issues were or would have been debated at the time. As I said, there was no agreement on how to do constitutional interpretation. There were, rather, different modes of interpretation just beginning to emerge, with no general consensus or agreement on which was right. But whatever the debate was two hundred years ago, it did not look anything like the scholarship we get today from people who tell us they have deciphered the authentic eighteenth century public meaning of this or that clause of the Constitution.

What we have, in other words, when someone offers an original public meaning interpretation is a wholly fictitious construct: a construct made possible only by the fact that the person presenting it has managed not to learn too much about how the Founding generation actually thought matters should be handled. Because what one invariably discovers when one learns more about the Founding era is that there was no original understanding or settled means of fixing meaning. There was, rather, indeterminacy at the deepest level, at the level necessary in order even to begin the originalist project.

My second point is that originalism is by its very nature unpragmatic. To understand why, forget about the Constitution for a minute and think about ordinary legal interpretation. Suppose that yesterday a statute was enacted, and a case involving that statute arose today. The case comes to court. There will be questions under the statute that are easy: questions as to which everybody would agree about the proper interpretation and outcome. And then there will also be questions that are hard: questions as to which the proper interpretation is a matter of legitimate disagreement because the text is unclear. Assume one of the hard cases. Difficult or not, the court is going to resolve it somehow, employing some set of interpretive principles. For present purposes, I do not particularly care what those principles are. Whatever they are, we get a resolution.

Hard cases like this are inevitable, because language is unavoidably imprecise. There always are gaps, conflicts, and ambiguities. I am assuming a case involving one of these, and the court resolves it by whatever techniques it uses, and in so doing closes the gap, resolves the conflict, or eliminates the ambiguity. That solves the immediate problem, but it also inevitably creates new conflicts or new gaps or new ambiguities. So a day after that, or a week after, or a year after, at some later point in time, someone will confront the new problem and another case will arise. The court at that point will do the same thing it did in the first case. It will resolve the problem by whatever interpretive techniques it uses to decide cases. But it will do so not in light of the statute as it was originally enacted. It will do so in light of the statute as it has been modified by the first interpretation, which changed the law in some way by resolving the first problem and in so doing created the framework that gave rise to the new problem. And this will be an on-going process: cases are decided, reshaping the law, giving rise to new problems and so new cases, and so on. This is the way we interpret law, the way we understand it ordinarily to work. It is, moreover, a thoroughly pragmatic process. It is pragmatic because it recognizes the interdependency of legal rules and rulings, the "seamless webness" of the law. What you do in resolving one problem has effects on things around it. So when you get to the next problem, you need to resolve it in light of what the law has become through implementation and practice.

The same thing is true when it comes to interpreting the Constitution. Indeed, when it comes to the Constitution, we cannot think only in terms of judicial decisions and judicial interpretations, because every time the Court interprets the Constitution, all the other branches of government respond. They change how they think. They change what they do. And the constitutional system develops accordingly. When it comes to the Constitution, in other words, even more than with a statute, what you have over time is courts giving it meaning, the other branches adapting, courts responding to what the other branches have done, and so on. The interdependency argument is the same as with a statute, except it is more complex and elaborate because there are more moving pieces. To see the powerfully pragmatic premises here, consider the process by analogy to a classic philosophical metaphor. You are in a boat in the middle of the ocean. Whatever problems you may confront in the design or structure of your boat, the one thing you can not do—and this would be a core principle, I think—is to rebuild the boat from scratch, because then you are going to drown. You must deal with the boat as it is and take whatever problems present themselves, as they present themselves while doing your best to stay afloat. Think of the Constitution as, in effect, a blueprint for a boat. The Founding generation built and launched the boat, and we have now been out there sailing for a couple of centuries. The whole time we have been confronting and resolving problems, with each resolution changing the structure of the boat—sometimes in small ways, sometimes in large ways.

That being so, does it make sense, when you come upon a new problem, to fix it by going back to the original blueprint? To say "I am going to ignore everything that happened between then and now and resolve this in whatever way is most consistent with the original blueprint?" Well, maybe. Except if the engine started in the bow and now it has been moved to the stern, and some new thing appeared only because the engine room was moved, you may be making a huge mistake to say get rid of it, pluck it out, because it was not in the original design.

This is the sense in which originalism is deeply unpragmatic. Because if you take originalism seriously, it says that wherever we are at any given time, we are supposed to resolve problems according to the original design, ignoring what has happened since then and forcing the problem in front of us back into the original framework, whatever the consequences. Whether this is a good thing or a bad thing, it most certainly is *not* a pragmatic thing. Nor, speaking from my own perspective, is it a sensible thing.

It does not follow that originalism is irrelevant. To solve a given problem, I am still going to want to start with the original design. I need to understand the boat as it is now, but the only way I am going to do that is by understanding the original design and how and why it evolved to look as it does today. It seems to me, in other words, that the sensible way to think about constitutional interpretation is to begin with the original understanding. You will not find answers to a whole lot of questions, not complete answers at least. Instead, you will find partial answers that led to problems for the Founding generation, which resolved them, creating new problems, which were then resolved by the next generation, and so on. We have been, as a nation, engaged in the process of creating and giving shape to our Constitution from that original blueprint for more than two hundred years. Constitutional law is a form of customary law, albeit customary law refracted through a text. Every generation has faced its problems and resolved them according to its best understanding of the text, handing a refashioned constitutional law on to the next generation to do the same. And that being so, when called upon to interpret the Constitution, we may want to think about original intent as a place to start, but not a place to finish.

❦

Frank H. Easterbrook

Although the title of this panel is in the conjunctive—Originalism *and* Pragmatism—people usually assume that we must choose originalism *or* pragmatism. Pragmatists, such as Justice Breyer, think it both wise and appropriate to change constitutional norms to serve modern needs.[1] Pragmatists differ from Justice Douglas and other inventionists by giving the political branches what they view as healthy sway, through a Dworkin-like process that treats judges as authors of chain novels. The pragmatist is constrained by what earlier authors have done—but, like the inventionists, the modern pragmatists insist that in the end how much sway to allow is a question for judges, because judges write today's chapter. Originalists, such as Justice Thomas, deny that the Constitution has changed since its words were adopted; political society evolves informally and incrementally, but legal texts are fixed unless the rules for change (such as statutory or constitutional amendments) have been followed.

I want to defend the assumption of the panel's title—that both originalism *and* pragmatism play vital roles in constitutional practice.

The case for pragmatism is easy to state. Our Constitution is old, and modern society faces questions that did not occur to those who lived at the time of the Civil War, let alone those who survived the

Revolutionary War and wrote the Constitution of 1787. What is more, originalism requires us to understand how the linguistic community that approved the words understood their application. A phrase such as "due process of law" or "commerce among the several states" is so much noise unless linked to the original interpretive community. But language is a social and contextual enterprise; those who live in a different society and use language differently cannot reconstruct the original meaning except by feats of scholarship and cerebration. More often, alas, unsupported and hubristic assertion takes the place of hard work.

New problems pose unanswerable questions to someone who thinks originalism the sole method of interpretation. Denying the obvious gives textualism a bad name. And we have had "new" problems from the start: think for example of the Bank of the United States. When James Madison first considered the bank's constitutional status (while he was in the House) he thought it beyond the new national government's powers; on second take Madison (as president) signed the bill establishing the Second Bank; then Andrew Jackson vetoed the bill establishing the Third Bank with a constitutionally based explanation (to which Roger Taney contributed) that still repays reading. None of what Madison, Jackson, and their contemporaries did or said was encoded in 1787; most problems lack original solutions. So much is inevitable; the Constitution is a very short document.

But no one who had a hand in creating this nation was so foolish as to think that all interesting decisions are encoded in the original text. The decision was to create a federal republic and let the people work out, through their representatives, the problems of time still to come. We do so pragmatically. How else does democracy work?

When the Bank came to the Supreme Court in *McCulloch*, the Justices approved that process. The Bank's opponents pointed to two things: the Constitution creates limited federal powers, and nothing authorizes the national government to create financial intermediaries. To charter a bank, Congress needed to rely on the power to enact laws and 1816 it did (and would again between 1836 and 1913). By taking "necessary" strictly, the Court could have set itself up as a potent political force, reviewing the wisdom of laws.

The Court resisted. Chief Justice Marshall explained:[2]

> Among the enumerated powers, we do not end that of establishing a bank or creating a corporation. But there is no phrase in the instrument which, like the articles of confederation, excludes incidental or implied powers; and which requires that every thing granted shall be expressly and minutely described.....A constitution, to contain an accurate detail of all the subdivisions of which its great powers will admit, and of all the means by which they may be carried into execution, would partake of the prolixity of a legal code, and could scarcely be embraced by the human mind. It would probably never be understood by the public. Its nature, therefore, requires, that only its great outlines should be marked, its important objects designated, and the minor ingredients which compose those objects be deduced from the nature of the objects themselves. That this idea was entertained by the framers of the American constitution, is not only to be inferred from the nature of the instrument, but from the language....It is also, in some degree, warranted by their having omitted to use any restrictive term which might prevent its receiving a fair and just interpretation. In considering this question, then, we must never forget, that it is a constitution we are expounding.

There is that famous phrase: "We must never forget, that it is a constitution we are expounding." But now you see its context: as a description of legislative latitude. Marshall was explaining why the political branches have power to act pragmatically, while judges do not! He had *two* theories of constitutional authority—one for Congress, which wields explicit grants of power, and the other for judges. It should hardly be necessary to remind you that there is a real Necessary and Proper Clause, but no judicial review clause.

Congress and the president derive authority from election, and they act under open-ended language designed for an indefinite future. If a court is to do anything other than bless the product of the political branches, it must appeal to concrete decisions. Remember the rationale of *Marbury v. Madison*[3]: the Constitution is a set of laws, superior to statutes; having deciphered the meaning of both, judges need only apply standard choice-of-law principles. *Marbury* depicts the Constitution as a catalog of rules, usually having a meaning comprehensible to all who take the trouble to read carefully. When judges can reach such a firm conclusion, they may insist that the political outcome yield. That is the originalist constraint. Otherwise judges must respect politically pragmatic decisions.

Thus originalism is the tool of the judicial branch—not because it is the only right way to understand texts, not because it is easy, and certainly not because those who apply it will always be right, but because it is the *only* approach that explains why judges have the final word. When an issue lacks an original answer, the premise of judicial review is defeated. When originalism fails, so does judicial power to have the final say. And democracy remains.

Let us not lose sleep over a claim that this leaves a "wooden" Constitution or rule by a dead hand. Originalism is an approach to the allocation of power over time and among the living. Decisions of yesterday's legislatures (the 108th Congress is as "dead" for this purpose as the 50th or the 10th) are enforced not only because our political system does not treat texts as radioactive (there is no legal half-life) but also because affirming the force of old texts is essential if sitting legislatures are to enjoy the power to make new ones. Our rules for making law were encoded in 1787 and are no more or less dead than other aspects of the process.

To say that "the dead" govern through originalism is wordplay. We the living enforce laws (and the Constitution that provides the framework for their enactment and enforcement) that were adopted yesterday because it is wise for us to do so today. Old texts prevail not because their authors want, but because the living want. This is not a theory of *interpretation* but of political legitimacy. Originalists accept the Constitution's theory of political obligation, but it is important to separate the theory of political justification from the theory of interpretation appropriate to that theory of justification.[4]

The fundamental theory of political legitimacy in the United States is contractarian, which implies originalist interpretation by the judicial branch. Otherwise a pack of tenured lawyers is changing the deal, reneging on behalf of a society that did not appoint them for that purpose. This is not a controversial proposition. It is sound historically: the Constitution was designed and approved like a contract. It is sound dispositionally: it is the political theory the man in the street supplies when he appeals to the Constitution (or to the legitimacy of the electoral process, even though his candidate lost).

Contractual rights are inherited. If I buy a house with borrowed money, the *net* value of the house is what my heirs inherit; they can't get the house free from the debt. This is so whether my heirs consent to the deal or not; contract rights pass to the next generation as written.

Both private and social contracts are hard to change, but only someone distracted by babble about "contracts of adhesion" would think this an objection rather than a benefit. We the living accept the power of contract *because* deals are hard to change. Stability in a political system is exceptionally valuable. Someone who loses a legislative battle today accepts that loss in exchange for surety that next year's victory on some other subject will be accepted by other losers in their turn. People accept old contracts and old legal texts because they know that this is the only way to ensure that promises *to them* are kept; if all is up for grabs, they are apt to lose both coming and going.

The constitutional contract is no more hypothetical than the losers' willingness to accept the election results today, in the belief that they may win tomorrow. Today's majority accepts limits on its own power in exchange for greater surety that its own rights will be respected when, sometime in the future, power has shifted. An originalist system of interpretation facilitates and guarantees this allocation of power over time, and across groups.

Like other judges, I took an oath to support and enforce both the laws and the Constitution. That is to say, I made a promise—a contract.

In exchange for receiving power and long tenure I agreed to limit the extent of my discretion. Sneering at the oath is common in the academy, but it was an important part of Chief Justice Marshall's account of judicial review in *Marbury* and matters greatly to conscientious public officials. It should matter to everyone. Would *you* surrender power to someone who can be neither removed from office nor disciplined, unless that power was constrained? The constraint is the promise to abide by the rules in place—yesterday's rules, to be sure, but rules.

Originalism is the constraint for judges, as short tenure is the main constraint for political officials. These different constraints imply different modes of interpretation—just as judges under *Chevron* give politically accountable agencies more interpretive leeway than the judges allow themselves.

My point in the end is simple: meaning depends on the purpose to which we put it. Judges seek not enlightenment but right answers, the core meaning within which further debate is ruled out. That core will be smaller than the scope of all constitutional interests and proprieties. In the end, the power to countermand the decisions of other governmental actors and punish those who disagree depends on a theory of meaning that supposes the possibility of right answers.

So you can't view rules of interpretation as unitary. You must search for a norm simultaneously suited to the Constitution and to the actor's role—and judges fill roles different from political actors. We must demand not that the courts' interpretive norm conform to the reader's political theory, but that it be law.

A Pragmatic Defense of Originalism
John O. McGinnis and Michael B. Rappaport

Originalism and pragmatism are uneasy companions. This essay will attempt to make them friends. The usual view is that pragmatic interpretation has the essential virtue of making sure that the consequences of legal decisions will be good.[5] Originalism, by contrast, is thought to focus on fidelity to the past and therefore to permit the Court to reach undesirable, outdated results.[6] We argue that originalism, although it requires judges to focus on the past, actually produces desirable rules today. Thus, it is originalism that is the genuinely pragmatic way to interpret the Constitution.

Originalists, in our view, have largely failed to meet pragmatic objections. The argument that judges should be originalists, simply because that is what the Framers intended, not only is circular, but fails to offer any assurance that good consequences attend originalism. The argument that originalism advances democracy seems weak and undeveloped because originalism sometimes requires judges to strike down a result of the democratic process when statutes or executive action conflict with the original meaning of the constitution.[7] Finally, the argument that originalism offers clearer rules to constrain judges than other interpretive approaches contains some truth, but is not enough to sustain the case for originalism.[8] The benefits of judicial constraint are limited if judicial decisions, even though they are not discretionary, still impose substantial harms. Conversely, if constraint is the overriding objective, nonoriginalist doctrine may sometimes provide more constrained rules than the original meaning.[9]

However, pragmatic interpretation—which is usually thought to involve judges deciding particular cases based on their policy consequences—faces severe problems as an approach to resolving cases. People disagree about whether the consequences of particular decisions are good or bad. If the Constitution is to provide a framework for governance, it cannot simply replicate these disagreements.[10] Or, to put the objection to pragmatic constitutionalism in pragmatic terms, if a constitution is to have an independent settlement function in our polity—one that promotes the important ends of political stability, liberty, and prosperity—it cannot depend on judges' deciding the same issues that are endlessly politically disputed. Moreover, judges seem a curious group to interpret the Constitution if consequences are key. The Supreme Court is a small and insulated group of legal experts that lacks the institutional capacity or electoral accountability for evaluating policy consequences.[11]

We believe that originalism can be given a strong pragmatic justification by focusing on the process by which constitutional provisions are created. Provisions created through the strict procedures of constitutional lawmaking are likely to have good consequences. Sustaining these good consequences, however, depends on adhering to the Constitution's meaning when it was ratified. Justified in this manner, originalism allows judges to achieve good consequences through formal legal interpretation without having to make policy case by case.

In a paper of this brevity, we cannot provide exhaustive support for our views. Instead, we are content to sketch the main elements of a pragmatic defense of originalism. Because we believe that such defenses of originalism have been neglected, we hope that this essay will help encourage a broader debate about the consequences of originalism and other interpretative methodologies.

I. Supermajority Rules and Desirable Constitutional Provisions

Our pragmatic argument for originalism can be briefly summarized. First, entrenched laws that are desirable should take priority over ordinary legislation, because such entrenchments operate to establish a structure of government that preserves democratic decision-making, individual rights, and other beneficial goals. Second, appropriate supermajority rules tend to produce desirable entrenchments. Third, the Constitution and its amendments have been passed in the main under appropriate supermajority rules and thus the norms entrenched in the Constitution tend to be desirable. While there is one significant way in which those supermajority rules were not appropriate—the exclusion of African Americans and women from participating in the selection of constitutional drafters and ratifiers—this defect, which we address below, has rightly been removed.[12] Finally, this argument for the desirability of the Constitution requires that judges interpret the document based only on its original meaning because the drafters and ratifiers used only that meaning in deciding to adopt constitutional provisions. In short, it is the supermajoritarian genesis of the Constitution that explains both why the Constitution is desirable and why that desirability depends on its being given its original meaning.

Note the structure of this defense of originalism. It defends the quality of constitutional provisions by reference to the likely consequences flowing from the process that created them. It avoids the Scylla of completely formal defenses of originalism and the Charybdis of completely contestable assertions of what constitutes goodness. It is also consistent with perhaps the most common defense of originalism: that it generally ties judges to rules.[13] These rules consist of the interpretative rule of originalism itself as well as the substantive rules in the Constitution.[14] But to the virtue of rule following, it adds the even more important virtue of following beneficial rules.

The essence of our argument is that the strict supermajoritarian rules that govern the Constitution's enactment make it socially desirable. If the Constitution were simply enacted by majority rule, like statutes, there would be no strong reason to privilege provisions that happen to be in a document called "the Constitution."[15] The supermajority rules of the Constitution's enactment, however, make them good enough to enforce when they conflict with mere majoritarian enactments.

Entrenchment of norms offers great potential benefits.[16] It establishes a framework for government and sets out ground rules that protect against predictable dangers of ordinary democratic governance. Entrenchments, however, last long into the future and bad entrenchments are at least as harmful as good entrenchments are beneficial. While majority rule is thought to generally produce ordinary legislation that is desirable, permitting a majority to entrench norms would be problematic, because majorities will have a tendency to pass undesirable entrenchments for a variety of reasons.[17] By contrast, the passage of entrenchments under supermajority rules would compensate for these tendencies and produce on average good entrenchments. Given the brief nature of this essay, we here explain only a few of the reasons for the superiority and desirability of supermajoritarian entrenchment.

First, because entrenched norms cannot easily be eliminated, controversial entrenchments can be extremely divisive. Majorities, even narrow ones, will tend to pass such entrenchments if they believe that these norms will make for good entrenchments. Moreover, even if a majority recognizes that entrenchments should have consensus support, it might still be reluctant to refrain from entrenching controversial norms for fear that a future majority will entrench its preferred norms despite the lack of a consensus. If controversial entrenchments are enacted, minorities may strongly oppose them and be furious that the nation will be governed by bad notions that cannot be repealed by the ordinary democratic process.[18] Their alienation will lessen their allegiance to the Constitution and the regime.

Supermajority rules, however, address this problem by permitting only norms with substantial consensus to be entrenched. A broad consensus for the Constitution creates legitimacy, allegiance and even affection as citizens come to regard the entrenched norms as part of their common bond.[19] Such a Constitution helps individuals to transcend their differences, like ethnicity or geography, making them citizens of a single nation.[20]

Second, majorities in a party system tend to be partisan. Because of partisanship, majorities will tend to abuse their power for at least two reasons. First, partisanship may lead them to adopt a non-rational "us versus them" attitude that will focus their attention away from the merits of legislation. More rationally, majorities may decide to entrench legislation that they do not really believe should be entrenched if only to foreclose legislation that they fear the opposing party will entrench when it comes to power. For instance, legislators from one party might decide to entrench low taxes and low debt to prevent the other party from entrenching entitlements even if both parties believe the nation would be better off without entrenching either program.[21] Supermajority rules can also decrease the ill effects of partisanship by making it less likely that entrenchments can be passed only with the support of one party. If the two

Chicago and Yale Federalist Societies
Harvard Society for Law and Public Policy
Stanford Foundation for Law and Economic Policy
The Leadership Institute

present a symposium on

Federalism:
Legal and Political Ramifications

April 24 & 25 - Yale Law School

Participants

Prof. Paul Bator .... Harvard Law School
Walter Berns .... AEI Resident Scholar
Morton Blackwell .... Special Assistant to the President
Judge Robert Bork .... D. C. Circuit Court of Appeals
Prof. Thomas Brennan ..... President, Thomas M. Cooley Law School
Judge Stephen Breyer .... First Circuit Court of Appeals
Prof. Charles Fried .... Harvard Law School
Stephen Galebach .... Christian Legal Foundation
Prof. Lino Graglia .... Univ. of Texas Law School
Prof. Maurice Holland .... Indiana Univ. School of Law
Prof. John Jeffries, Jr. .... Yale Law School
Prof. Edmund W. Kitch .... Univ. of Chicago Law School
Prof. John Noonan, Jr. ..... Univ. of California at Berkley Law School
Hon. William Olsen .... President, Legal Services Corporation
Hon. Theodore Olson .... Assistant Attorney General
Judge Richard Posner .... Seventh Circuit Court of Appeals
Prof. Grover Rees III .... Univ. of Texas Law School
Prof. Antonin Scalia .... Univ. of Chicago Law School
Hon. Loren Smith .... Chairman, U.S. Administrative Conference
Judge Ralph Winter .... Second Circuit Court of Appeals

For further information,
contact Steve Calabresi,
432-2614 or
Box 401A, Yale Station

Funding provided by Institute
for Educational Affairs,
Olin Foundation, and
Intercollegiate Studies Institute

THE BILL FROM THE FEDERALIST SOCIETY'S first National Student Symposium, at Yale University in 1982.

A PROTESTOR at the 1982 Yale Symposium.

FEDERALIST SOCIETY CO-FOUNDER STEVEN G. CALABRESI, moderating a panel at the 1982 Yale Symposium with Judge Robert H. Bork.

ATTORNEY GENERAL EDWIN MEESE III, speaking to the Federalist Society Washington, D.C. chapter, shortly after delivering his famous November 1985 speech to the American Bar Association calling for a "jurisprudence of original intent."

SUPREME COURT JUSTICE WILLIAM J. BRENNAN, JR., whose response to the 1985 ABA speech Attorney General Meese credited with giving the originalist cause new life.

THE GREAT DEBATE:

INTERPRETING OUR

WRITTEN CONSTITUTION

J. MADISON

published by:

THE FEDERALIST SOCIETY

SPEECHES BY:
ATTORNEY GENERAL EDWIN MEESE III
JUSTICE WILLIAM J. BRENNAN, JR.
JUSTICE JOHN PAUL STEVENS
JUDGE ROBERT H. BORK
PRESIDENT RONALD REAGAN

PRESIDENT REAGAN delivering the September 1986 investiture speech, elevating William H. Rehnquist to Chief Justice of the Supreme Court, and University of Chicago professor Antonin Scalia to an Associate Justice.

SUPREME COURT JUSTICE RUTH BADER GINSBURG, fielding questions at the Federalist Society's 1985 National Student Symposium at Georgetown University.

SUPREME COURT CHIEF JUSTICE REHNQUIST, speaking at an early Federalist Society event. Rehnquist attacked the idea of "a living constitution" in a famous 1976 article in the *Texas Law Review*.

PRESIDENT RONALD REAGAN, delivering the keynote address to the Federalist Society's 1988 National Lawyers Convention: "[Y]ou are insisting that the Constitution is not some elaborate ink blot test in which liberals can find prescribed policies that the people have rejected. You are fighting for renewed respect for the integrity of our Constitution, for its fundamental principles and for its wisdom."

JUDGE ROBERT H. BORK'S *The Tempting of America* (1989), has become the best and most comprehensive defense of originalism to date.

VICE CHAIRMAN DAVID M. MCINTOSH and Counselor Kenneth T. Cribb, handing Judge Bork the Federalist Society's James Madison Award at the 1989 National Student Symposium at the University of Virginia.

SUPREME COURT JUSTICE CLARENCE THOMAS, delivering his famous 1999 speech on judicial independence to the Federalist Society, in which he stated, "Our judicial system is built upon a belief that those who judge will do so impartially, and in accordance with the law, without regard for race, creed, religious belief, or other affiliation. It is this ability to render judgment without concern for anything but the law, that should distinguish judges from members of the legislature or the executive branch."

JUSTICE ANTONIN SCALIA, addressing the Federalist Society at its 20th Anniversary National Lawyers Convention.

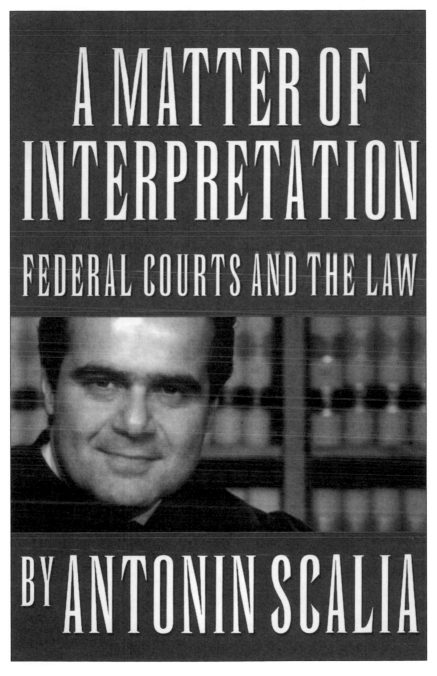

A MATTER OF INTERPRETATION
FEDERAL COURTS AND THE LAW

BY ANTONIN SCALIA

SUPREME COURT JUSTICE ANTONIN SCALIA followed up on Judge Bork's indictment of judicial activism with *A Matter of Interpretation* (1998), which defended "textualism" as the proper guide to legal interpretation.

STEPHEN BREYER

* * * * * * * * *

ACTIVE LIBERTY

INTERPRETING

OUR DEMOCRATIC

CONSTITUTION

* * * * * * * * *

"A brisk, lucid and energetic book, written with conviction and offering a central argument that is at once provocative and appealing. . . . Deserves a place of honor in national debates, now and in the future, about the role of the Supreme Court in American life." —*The New Republic*

JUSTICE STEPHEN BREYER responded to the arguments for originalism in constitutional interpretation with *Active Liberty* (2004). Justice Breyer said that the Constitution should be thought of as a guide for the application of basic American principles, rather than as a restricting document meant to keep a "static meaning."

JUSTICES BREYER AND SCALIA, discussing their opposing views of constitutional interpretation, in a televised 2007 Federalist Society event, co-spon-
sored by the American Constitutional Society.

WHO SPEAKS FOR THE CONSTITUTION?

THE DEBATE OVER INTERPRETIVE AUTHORITY

J. MADISON

published by:

THE FEDERALIST SOCIETY

including contributions to the debate by:

JAMES MADISON	THOMAS JEFFERSON
ANDREW JACKSON	DANIEL WEBSTER
STEPHEN DOUGLAS	ABRAHAM LINCOLN
JOHN BINGHAM	FELIX FRANKFURTER
RONALD REAGAN	GEORGE BUSH
EDWIN MEESE, III	PAUL BREST
JOHN HARRISON	BURT NEUBORNE
STEPHEN CARTER	FRANK EASTERBROOK

THROUGH MUCH OF ITS QUARTER-CENTURY EXISTENCE, the Federalist Society has sought to spark a debate about the interpretive authority of the three branches of the federal government respecting Constitutional issues. "Who Speaks for the Constitution" (left) was an important monograph addressing the history and philosphy surrounding this subject. Supreme Court Justice Samuel Alito most recently addressed the issue at the Society's 2006 Annual Dinner, where he stated: "All public servants, not simply judicial officers, play a role in shaping our law, interpreting our Constitution, and directing the actions of various legal institutions. It is wrong to think that the courts are the center of the universe when it comes to all legal questions. Legislators also have a duty to think about constitutionality when they draft and introduce legislation. Executive officials have a responsibility to consider the constitutionality of legislation presented to them.... It is wrong for any public official to ignore questions about the bounds of their authority under our constitutional system and simply say the courts will sort that out for them."

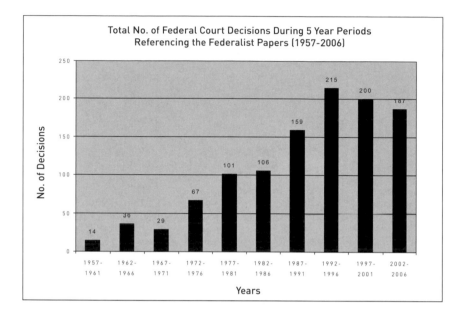

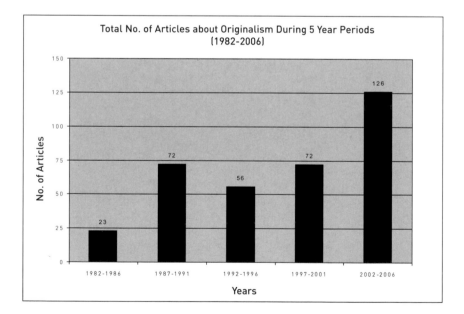

parties must cooperate to pass legislation, they are less likely to indulge in "us versus them" attitudes. Moreover, supermajority rules will prevent the destructive competition by which one party races to entrench its political program before the other party entrenches its own program.

Third, the long-term nature of entrenchments makes it less likely that legislative majorities will enact desirable entrenchments. Individuals have a heuristic problem in thinking about the future: they are too disposed to believe that current trends will continue.[22] They may, for example, be too prone to support constitutional provisions out of the mistaken belief that present circumstances will continue in the future. In addition, citizens cannot easily hold legislators accountable for their entrenchment votes, because most legislators will be long gone before the long-run effects of the entrenchments are felt.

While supermajority rules would not address these problems directly, it would improve legislative entrenchment decisions in other ways that would compensate for these deficiencies.

Supermajority rules restrict the agenda of proposals, because fewer proposals have a realistic chance of passing. A restricted agenda encourages a richer stream of information about the proposals, improving legislative determinations. More significantly, a strict supermajority rule (coupled with the requirement that the constitutional entrenchment can be repealed only by a similarly strict supermajority) also improves the quality of entrenchments by helping to create a limited veil of ignorance. Because proposals so entrenched under supermajority rules cannot be easily repealed in the future, citizens and legislators cannot be certain how the provisions will affect them and their children.[23] Hence they are more likely to consult the interests of all future citizens—the public interest—to determine whether they will support a provision.

For these reasons, strong supermajority rules are likely to overcome the problems that afflict majoritarian entrenchment and produce beneficial entrenchments.

II. The Benefits of Supermajoritarian Enactment of the Original Constitution

It is clear that the Constitution and its amendments were in the main a product of the kind of stringent supermajority rules that generate beneficial entrenchments.[24] Constitutional amendments must be approved by two thirds of each house of Congress and ratified by three quarters of state legislatures.[25] The original constitution was also a product of a double supermajoritarian process. Article VII expressly required nine of the thirteen states to ratify the Constitution before it took effect.[26] But what may be less clear is that a supermajority of states also had to support the convention in the first place. [27]

This kind of consensus-forcing process is not merely good in some abstract sense; it creates very substantial real world benefits. Take the effect of the veil of ignorance: in considering the extent of the president's power, citizens had to recognize that sometimes they would like the president and sometimes they would not, and therefore they parceled out his authority based on public interest rather than partisan considerations.[28]

It is the supermajoritarian constitution-making process that helps to account for the beneficence of the Constitution. While most Americans believe that the amended Constitution is an exemplary document, there are few explanations for its excellence. Rather than view the document as the product of a few great men, we see it as largely the result of the supermajoritarian process that enacted it. That process generated some of the most distinctive and praised features of our Constitution. Because of the need to compromise to obtain consensus at the convention, the most nationalist forces conceded an indestructible role for the states and gave us constitutional federalism.[29] To obtain ratification in the necessary nine states, the nationalists had to promise that a bill of rights would be enacted once the new government was established.[30] Thus, the supermajoritarian ratification process was the big bang of our Constitutional universe— bringing into effect the key elements of a document admired around the world.

III. Originalism as the Necessary Means for Preserving the Supermajoritarian
Basis of the Constitution

A last step to our argument is that beneficial judicial review requires originalism, because it was the original meaning that was crucial to obtaining the consensus that makes constitutional provisions desirable. The ratifiers in the supermajority of states approved the provisions based on commonly accepted meanings and the interpretative rules of the time. Some of the provisions approved had clear meanings. Others may have seemed ambiguous, but the ratifiers would have believed their future application would be based on the interpretative rules with which they were familiar. Following the original meaning of their provisions as construed through the Framers' own interpretative rules thus remains faithful to their expectations of the likely effects of the provisions.[31] In contrast, following a meaning whose substance or derivation was not endorsed at the Framing severs the Constitution's connection with the process responsible for its beneficence.

Parenthetically, if interpretative rules at the time of the Framing are as important as we believe they are, this suggests that originalist constitutional scholarship should be reoriented. The first model of originalism focused on original intent. When originalists recognized that focusing on original intent wrongly emphasized the subjective purposes of the Framers, most originalists embraced the original meaning of the text as a better, second model of originalist interpretation.[32] A debate then arose over how to define the original meaning and the best means of ascertaining it. While some originalists eschew using interpretative rules from the Framers' time, our view suggests that these rules are necessary both for the definition of originalism and for originalism to have beneficial consequences.[33] Thus, the third model for originalism will help resolve ambiguities in meaning by deploying the Framers' interpretative rules.[34]

A comparison of constitutional lawmaking with case-by-case Supreme Court norm creation reveals what is wrong with the theories that usually fly the flag of pragmatism. First, only a very small number of Justices generate norms through their decisions, but constitutional lawmaking requires the broader participation of many. Second, the Supreme Court is drawn from a very narrow class of society: elite lawyers who then work in Washington.[35] In contrast, constitutional lawmaking includes diverse citizens with a wide variety of attachments and interests. Finally, constitutional lawmaking is supermajoritarian, while the Supreme Court rules by majority vote. In short, these several reasons suggest that the doctrines fabricated by Supreme Court justices are likely to lead to worse consequences than doctrines that flow from the original meaning of the Constitution.[36]

Sometimes it is claimed that the Supreme Court will provide better results by embracing the incremental and case-by-case manner of the common law rather than following the original meaning.[37] But traditional common law crafted by judges crucially differs from constitutional common law. The legislature could overrule common law decisions, while judges through constitutional review can invalidate the decisions of the legislature. Thus, to justify common law constitutionalism, one would have to show not merely that it is good enough to exist in the absence of statutes, like the ordinary common law, but that it is good enough to override statutes. To our knowledge, no one has made a persuasive case that constitutional common law possesses such extraordinary quality and the very characteristics of Supreme Court judging we note above—its insularity and lack of consensus—militate against claims of quality.

Thus, not only is our Constitution's original meaning of high enough quality to displace ordinary democratic lawmaking, more free-form methods of judicial interpretation do not provide similar assurance of their superiority to democratic lawmaking.[38] While we here defend originalism as a pragmatic interpretive approach, originalism cannot be evaluated in isolation. The salient question—and the question any good pragmatist should recognize as salient—is what other approach is more likely to reach as sound consequences as is originalism? We do not believe originalism is ideal, but we do believe it is likely to have better consequences than competing approaches.[39]

IV. Counterarguments: Ancient Origins and the Exclusion of Blacks and Women

The cornerstone of our pragmatic defense of originalism faces two significant challenges. The first is that the Constitution was made by bewigged ancestors long dead rather than by the living; the second is that these ancestors excluded crucial parts of the polity, such as African Americans and women.[40] These lines of attack have not been limited to academics but have been pressed more generally in the public sphere for many years. Thus, these critiques themselves enjoy a sufficient consensus, as it were, to be taken seriously, and their public resonance confirms that the key question for originalism is whether the process of framing was good enough to be respected now.

A. Ancient Origins

The first complaint has been around at least since the Progressive era.[41] Today is for the living and Americans should no longer be ruled by those long buried.[42] An extreme version of this "dead hand" complaint—that a current majority must be able to change the past constitutional rules at will, either directly or through free form interpretation of their own—is simply inconsistent with constitutionalism. A constitution is designed to restrain current majorities—either to prevent temporary passions from doing damage to the social order or to prevent majorities from trampling on minority rights.[43] Moreover, if the dead hand objection is really right, why should we ever pay attention to the constitutional text, formulated long ago, regardless of whether it is to be given its original meaning? That text is as much a product of the past as the meaning a past generation understood it to convey.

Finally, even if this critique were sound, it would justify judges only in upholding current democratic decisions when they conflicted with the original meaning. A focus on the dead hand hardly suggests that the Supreme Court—itself the product of the original constitutional settlement—enjoys the power to displace the decisions of living legislators.

A more plausible concern about relying on a historical document would ask whether a past generation had more power to influence the document than the current generation. If the Framers could insert provisions into the Constitution more easily than we can, the Framers would have an unjustified advantage in establishing our fundamental law. There is no purpose served by granting an earlier generation more influence on the content of the Constitution than any other generation. Originalist constitutionalism, however, does not suffer from this malady. The original Constitution came into being through stringent supermajority rules and each generation can amend the Constitution through similar, even if not exactly the same, rules. Thus, each generation has essentially equal formal authority to place its political principles into the Constitution.

It may be harder practically to amend the Constitution today than it was to frame the original Constitution or to amend it earlier in the republic, but that is largely the result of the Constitution's success: people are loathe to amend a document under which the United States has become the most prosperous large nation on earth. The difficulty of amending the Constitution is also sadly the result of the Supreme Court's now frequent disregard of the original meaning. There would be more constitutional amendments if the Court itself did not frequently revise the Constitution every time a principle becomes popular enough that the public might be willing to place it in the Constitution.

This judicial anticipation of the amendment process, moreover, is not harmless. First, the Court is unlikely to establish the same norm that the amendment process would have produced, because it is difficult to know what consensus would have emerged from the supermajoritarian process. Second, the Court is unlikely to seek to limit its decisions to the probable political consensus. For instance, the consensus likely favors a right of contraception without encompassing the right of abortion, but justices who strongly favor abortion rights are motivated to include them within a nebulous right of privacy. Third, the prospect of non-originalist judging makes it harder to obtain a consensus on an amendment, because ratifiers of the amendment are understandably concerned that a subsequent activist court will unwind the deal they encode in the constitutional text. The Equal Rights Amendment foundered in part on fears that activist courts would seize on it to enforce unisex bathrooms and other ideological extravagances.[44]

A variation on this progressive attack might be thought to have more bite than the dead hand objection per se. According to this view, it is all very well to say that the consensus nature of constitutional provisions made them desirable when they were enacted but they are now very old and no longer produce the benefits they once did in a changed world. This kind of attack may be implicit in translation theories of the Constitution that purport to take account of social change by applying the Framers' values in the context of the present day.[45]

This objection might have force if the Constitution purported primarily to frame a code of rules of primary conduct, but of course the Constitution does not.[46] Those who framed the original Constitution and the amendments *never forgot that is was a Constitution they were enacting*.[47] They thus already took account of the fact that the Constitution should contain only a framework for government that would respond to the enduring realities of human nature and problems of social governance.[48] Thus, the fact of change was already taken into account in the making of the Constitution.

The best proof of the Framers' perspective lies in the Constitution itself. The Constitution permits substantial avenues to address social change. The states themselves have few restrictions on their powers absent congressional action.[49] Their experiments to address changes can be readily adopted by other states in a continental republic with a free press.[50] Congress can legislate, under the Commerce Clause and the Necessary and Proper Clause, both of which grant Congress substantial power, albeit not the unlimited power modern case law has bestowed.

Finally, the Constitution creates an amendment process by which to replace provisions that have become outmoded. It is, of course, no accident that a legal document produced by a high quality process would offer many ways to address social change: its many avenues for democratic change reflect its quality.

In the face of this structure, why should one be at all confident that a clamor for judges to substitute a new meaning for the original meaning is a response to changing social conditions and not an attempt by special interests, numerical minorities, or transient majorities to change the Constitution to reflect their peculiar values? Even if the Supreme Court is sincerely attempting to update the Constitution, the Court as an elite and centralized institution lacks the ability to elicit the consensus that can reliably differentiate responses to social changes from constitutional putsches.

B. The Exclusion of Blacks and Women

For the second attack on constitutional lawmaking we move from the progressive era to the 1960s. The complaint here is that until recently African Americans and women did not vote on the Constitution and key amendments.[51] Thus, this defect in constitutional lawmaking deprives it of legitimacy or at least should lower our estimation of the Constitution's quality. We certainly agree that the exclusion of these groups from constitutional lawmaking is a defect. In fact, we believe that these exclusions go to the theoretical heart of the supermajoritarian argument: the desirability of supermajority rules requires that all interests be reflected in the electorate. Thus, the absence of African Americans from the Framing and the blatant disregard of their interests may well have meant that the Constitution was not even binding on them.

But from today's perspective, these defects in the Constitution have been corrected. The Thirteenth Amendment prohibits slavery, the Fourteenth Amendment forestalls government racial discrimination, and the Fifteenth Amendment prevents denial of the franchise on account of race.[52] Moreover, the Voting Rights Act has implemented these constitutional provisions to guarantee that African Americans can fully participate in elections.

That the Constitution now grants all people the freedoms of white, male property owners suggests that the defects of the Founding have been eliminated. It is true that the Constitution does not contain items like a mandate for racial preferences, but given the disagreement about such policies even today, it is implausible to believe that the Constitution would have included them if all groups were represented. Thus, these defects of the original process do not provide reasons for ignoring the original meaning as amended.

A related criticism of the original Constitution is that its tragic countenancing of slavery was the fatal defect that rendered the document illegitimate.[53] While slavery was certainly tragic, the responsibility cannot be laid at the feet of the Constitution or its supermajoritarian basis. A serious attempt to eliminate slavery would have defeated any constitution and probably caused a fracturing of the nation. Despite its acquiescence to slavery, the original Constitution contributed to a social order based on markets and freedoms that helped persuade Americans that slavery is wrong.[54] It seems unlikely that African Americans would have been better off with a failure of the Constitution in 1789 and a retreat to sectional governments.

A similar complaint can be made about the absence of women. But this complaint is less powerful, both because there is stronger argument that women were virtually represented at the time by their male relatives and because many women apparently believed that they should not have the right to participate. In any event, the Nineteenth Amendment now grants women the right to vote.[55] Moreover, the Constitution would have likely been amended to prevent government sex discrimination had not the Supreme Court itself guaranteed such a right through its construction of the Fourteenth Amendment.[56] In short, the Constitution has now been corrected to provide equal rights to all Americans.[57]

One final kind of objection to this pragmatic defense of originalism is simply to find a constitutional provision that is widely believed to be defective, and suggest that the provision demonstrates that the Constitution is not of high quality. An example might be the provision that prevents a foreign-born citizen, like Arnold Schwarzenegger, from becoming president.[58] But our argument is only that the Constitution taken as a whole is of high enough quality that its original meaning should be enforced. It is to be expected that some provisions may become undesirable and yet remain law because they are not so bad that a supermajority will repeal them. But following any legal rule has costs. Retaining a bad constitutional provision is simply a cost of following a supermajoritarian enactment rule when that rule generates a constitution with benefits that exceed its costs.

Conclusion

Debates about originalism have often resembled skirmishes between two armies that never really confront one another. Originalists talk about the rule of law and democracy, while non originalists talk about indeterminancy, social change, and the consequences of individual cases. By providing a consequentalist defense of originalism itself, we have mapped out a new field of engagement. Our theory recasts the old arguments for originalism sounding in democracy and the rule of law into a defense of originalism's consequences. We argue that originalism provides a theory of constitutional interpretation that has good consequences even though it does not force judges to assess consequences on a case-by-case base.

Thus, we present a new, frontal challenge to non orginalists. To meet this challenge, non originalists must show that their theories both generate better consequences and provide some metric for assessing those consequences that does not merely reflect a narrow theory of substantive good. Until this challenge is met, originalists can defend their respect for the meaning attached to the Constitution by those long dead as the best protection for the living.

❦

Professor Jeffrey Rosen

P rofessor McGinnis suggested that pragmatism and originalism should be thought of as friends. I want to suggest this afternoon that the friendship they provide is pallid and unsatisfying, because both promise more than they can deliver. In a cheerful bipartisan spirit, I want to suggest that the idea that either pragmatism or originalism can restrain judges meaningfully in hard cases is illusory.

Both pragmatism and originalism are defended by their most prominent champions as ways of promoting democracy and judicial restraint. Judge Easterbrook, one of our most distinguished originalists, gave that defense when he said, "When originalism fails, democracy remains," and Justice Breyer's new book makes a similarly passionate consequentialist defense of pragmatism as a way of promoting both values of democracy and restraint.

I am not convinced, when I study the hard cases and watch the results of originalists and pragmatists, that indeed either theory follows through on this promise. Therefore, it seems to me better for those of us who care about promoting democracy to abandon these abstract and ultimately unproductive methodological debates and embrace openly a tradition of bipartisan judicial restraint.

This is the tradition of Thayer, of Holmes, of Frankfurter, most recently of the lamented Justice White. It is a tradition that has no consistent defenders on the current Supreme Court. It would require deference to democratic processes in most situations, simply striking down very few federal or state laws, something neither originalists nor pragmatists are willing to embrace. So when Professor McGinnis asks what is a better theory? I say, the theory is clear: defer, defer, defer.

I should confess that I come before this distinguished crowd speaking as something of a recovering originalist. Like many of you in this room, I was a student of the admired Professor Akhil Amar at Yale, and imbued his infectious enthusiasm for the promise that originalism, when applied in a principled way, might lead to genuinely bipartisan results. Learn the history better than the judges, said Akhil Amar, and you can be more principled than the originalists themselves. I was caught on fire with the promise of that wonderful teacher. I took it seriously and devoted years of my early career trying to learn enough about the history of the Fourteenth Amendment in particular to try to be able to interpret it in a principled way. Imagine then my earnest sense of disappointment and shock when I read the U.S. reports and found in case after case no trace of the complicated history that Akhil Amar had taught me to learn about. Instead, a deafening silence on all of the issues where one would have most expected it to be found.

In particular, I want to talk about three of these issues today: affirmative action, federalism, and religion. There is no justice on the current Supreme Court who has studied the history of Fourteenth Amendment with the rigor that one should expect of a principled originalist. Few appellate judges have put in that dark and lonely work either.

Now there is one judge in particular who has done that work. He is here today, and is right now illuminated by a very dramatic spotlight as I gaze on him. This is the esteemed Judge McConnell, who is in our audience. I am delighted to see him here. If I had to pick an Originalist-in-Chief, if I could just turn over the whole enterprise to a single person in the United States, it would be Judge McConnell. He deserves a bipartisan hand of applause for the scrupulousness and care with which he has studied the history and with which has tried to apply it.

Should not we then be angry, indignant, appalled that Judge McConnell's history, his insights, and the complicated lessons that he reminds us that history teaches are absent in all of the most important cases in the areas I have described?

Very briefly—you know this debate, and I will only rehearse it quickly here. First, consider affirmative action. The simple question, one would think, is affirmative action in public contracting? This is the question in the *Adarand* case. Is affirmative action in public contracting a violation of the original understanding of the Fourteenth Amendment? Well, Judge McConnell has taught us in his important scholarship not to ask whether there is a rule of colorblindness across the board for all state action. Instead, he says the question is whether or not a particular public benefit should be considered a privilege or immunity of citizenship. If it is, the government must be colorblind. If not, it is free to discriminate against or in favor of whomever it chooses.

But the question of figuring out whether the rights of the subcontractor on a highway project are or are not a privilege or immunity of citizenship is a complicated question. One could argue either way. First take the case against, because it is easier. Privileges or immunities, says McConnell, are uniform from state to state. They do not vary. They are demandable as a matter of entitlement, rather than being a discretionary privilege.

So, at the time of the Fourteenth Amendment, building highways was mostly a concern of private businesses. It was work that was contracted out. Let us imagine it is not a kind of civil right, like the right to make or enforce contracts, which the Framers would have thought would have been a privilege or immunity. Well, the consequences of that conclusion are jarring. That means that the government is free to distinguish on the basis of race. It is free to discriminate against or in favor of people when it chooses contracting, something that no current justice would be willing to embrace.

But the issue can be argued the other way. Imagine that the right to be a subcontractor is a privilege or immunity of citizenship. That has vastly disruptive consequences. It means not only that the right to work on federal highway projects, but indeed many of the benefits that the government doles out would be subject not only to a color-blindness rule but to a general prohibition on discriminatory classifications. If the right to be a subcontractor has to be given to everyone on equal terms, presumably any discrimination among subcontractors would have to be evaluated under strict scrutiny rather than under rational basis review.

So, much of the post-New Deal jurisprudence would go out the window. Think of *Williamson v. Lee Optical*, the case that upheld as rational a distinction between opticians and ophthalmologists. The Williamson case would go out the window. The *Beazer* case, involving whether methadone users can be excluded from working on railway cars, would go out the window. Essentially, we would be ripping up root and branch the bulk of the post-New Deal jurisprudence.

Now I know that this possibility might gladden the hearts of that small and shadowy movement that a few liberal conspiracy-mongers have called the effort to resurrect "the Constitution in exile." I know that that movement for many of you in this room is really just a conspiracy cooked up by me, Cass Sunstein and the *New York Times Magazine* photo department—for which I offer an unqualified apology. But it would be impossible to claim that this prospect of striking down the New Deal—I see Randy Barnett grinning with joy at the prospect; he can barely contain himself as he thinks about it, salivating happily—although it would gladden Professor Barnett and a few of his colleagues, to claim that it is consistent with judicial restraint would be preposterous. Adopting Professor Barnett's approach would require a radical uprooting of much precedent and practice, as well as being dramatically activist in striking down a great many federal and state laws.

That is my first example, affirmative action. I will not belabor the rest. The second example—federalism—is known well to you. Judge McConnell has reminded us that the framers of the Fourteenth Amendment expected Congress, not the courts, to be the primary enforcer of Section 5 rights. Imagine what they would have made of cases like *Kimmel* and *Garrett*. Surely they would have thought that *Hibbs* was the correct case, the one that deferred to Congress, not the other way around.

The objections to the atextual, ahistorical Eleventh Amendment jurisprudence are now a commonplace. They need an answer. All of you in this room, if you are going to be principled originalists, think of the earnest skeptic, that Akhil Amar student. He sends them out every year happily into the world, like innocent sheep. They go out into the world like little lambs, eagerly looking for principled debate about originalism. But they find no answer to legitimate questions. So answer these charges.

The third and final example of ahistorical originalism I want to talk about involves religion. Judge McConnell has made a very powerful case for the importance of neutrality as the preeminent vision contemplated by the First Amendment. He has said that, according to this neutrality vision, graduation prayers would be difficult to defend on grounds of neutrality. What, then, are we to make of the religious supremacists, like Justices Thomas and Scalia, who know far less of this history than Judge McConnell, but insist that these prayers are constitutional? Taken together, these three examples amount to more than the thirteenth chime of the clock. We have the most contested cases facing the country, the ones most closely watched—affirmative action, federalism, and religion—and it turns out that the history not only is contested but fails to constrain justices in any meaningful way. When the history is ignored by the justices in question in a way that instead leads to the enactment of what one has to assume are their political preferences, we have to conclude that the claim that originalism is a meaningful way of constraining judges, and promoting democracy is illusory. As I say, I once took that claim seriously, but have now reluctantly abandoned it.

And, indeed, originalists are not constrained when you take the most neutral definition of judicial restraint. I do not want to have a dreary debate about what counts as judicial restraint, because I know that each person in this room will have a different definition. But I do like the neutral definition which Cass Sunstein has offered. I think it is a useful definition. Judicial activism is the decision to strike down a federal or state law. Judicial restraint is the decision to uphold it.

This definition does not say whether judicial restraint or activism is good or bad. It just describes it. Judged by this neutral standard, who are the most activist justices on the current Court? Any guesses who are the most activist justices? It is not Thomas. It is Kennedy and O'Connor, followed by Scalia and Thomas. Rehnquist, Breyer, and Ginsburg are the most restrained. So the pragmatists, Rehnquist and Breyer, are on the restrained side. But you also find a pragmatist, O'Connor, among the most activist.

This leads to my second thought, which is that if pragmatism includes both the most activist justice, O'Connor, and one of the most restrained justices, Breyer, then it must be a very big tent. And it is hard to see pragmatism as a reliable constraint on judicial discretion.

Let me just say this about pragmatism. In his new book, Justice Breyer claims that pragmatism is defensible on two grounds. First, that it promotes democracy, and second, that it promotes restraint. Although there is much to be said for his provocative book, I find ultimately unconvincing his claim that those two goals—promoting democracy and promoting restraint—are not in tension.

First, consider promoting democracy. For a purported empiricist, Justice Breyer offers us surprisingly little empirical evidence about the effects of Supreme Court decisions in his book. He claims, for example, that upholding the campaign finance laws would promote democracy because more citizens would participate. But he does not stop to examine empirical evidence suggesting that the same amounts of money have flowed instead through five hundred and twenty-seven committees, and that the basic proportion of donations has not fundamentally changed.

Similarly, in saying that affirmative action would help people learn how to live together as democratic citizens, Justice Breyer provides us with no empirical evidence to support his view. So like Justice Brandeis, who claimed to be interested in empirical evidence in theory, but who was not that interested in it in practice, I think Justice Breyer is vulnerable to a similar charge. When Justice Breyer is upholding laws, as he does most of the time, there is really nothing to object to, because he is being restrained. But Justice Breyer is not always restrained. And just as I was harsh with the originalists who failed to talk about their Achilles heel in affirmative action, federalism, and religion clause cases, so was I disappointed in Justice Breyer's vote to strike down vouchers in the *Zelman* case because of the empirically contested claim that vouchers would promote social divisiveness. Justice Breyer did not examine the empirical evidence that suggests that, on the contrary, by allowing the education of a small percentage of kids of minority parents, vouchers might decrease divisiveness rather than promoting it. Similarly, in the partial-birth abortion case— another activist decision by Justice Breyer—there was no actual empirical discussion of whether the law might be construed in a more modest way, in the way that Judge Easterbrook admirably construed it on the lower court, to avoid constitutional difficulties and to affect very few abortions. So, Justice Breyer then has to be held accountable for the cases in which he is not restrained and when push comes to shove, he too does not always come through. I am more skeptical than he is that restraint and promoting democracy can always be achieved at the same time.

So, I will close on a simple note, which is merely to say that we can continue to have these wonderful panels. I am delighted to be invited by the Federalist Society every time you are kind enough to invite me. It is an honor to be here. But I find myself losing interest ultimately in the question of which methodology is best in abstract terms. Judges should be evaluated by what they do, not what they say; by their willingness to embody the restrained virtues of modesty and deference, not in theory but in practice. There is a tradition of this. It began with Holmes and Frankfurter. Justice White embodied it admirably. I have come to regret a juvenile article I wrote years ago questioning Justice White and have come to revere his principled devotion to bipartisan judicial restraint.

And I hope on the current Court that Chief Justice Roberts, who strikes me as more of a pragmatist in the restrained tradition of his boss, Chief Justice Rehnquist, than a doctrinal originalist, will keep up this tradition. But, whether he does or not, remember, members of the Federalist Society, that there is a small group that is trying to keep alive the flame of bipartisan judicial restraint. Please join us.

Thank you so much.

Discussion
Moderated by Douglas H. Ginsburg

JUDGE GINSBURG: We will begin the discussion by giving each panelist a moment to respond to what the other panelists have said. Dean Kramer, two or three minutes.

DEAN KRAMER: The use that has been made here of pragmatism is not one that is comprehensible or meaningful to me. That is to say, I do not understand pragmatism to mean doing what you think produces the best consequences in some seat-of-the-pants judgment sort of way. To me pragmatism means understanding that the world we confront is a complex web of practices and beliefs. We do things. We have justifications for why we think we do them. Most of the time, hopefully, what we do and why we do it match and then things are okay. But, inevitably, because the world is a complicated place, dissonances arise:

inconsistencies in our practices and our beliefs about why what we do is justifiable or right. We might go a long time without noticing these inconsistencies before something forces them to our attention. But, once that happens, we have to adjust to resolve the tension.

We can do that either by changing the practice or by changing the belief, either by changing the legal rule or by changing the rationale that has been offered for that rule. Pragmatism does not have anything to say about what should change or how it should change. It says only that you need to do something to resolve or eliminate the inconsistency. And the only other principle I take from pragmatism is that we should make the most economical change possible because, as I explained before, all our practices and beliefs are interdependent and you cannot predict what the unintended consequences of a change are going to be.

For me, the problem with originalism with respect to pragmatism is that originalism does not adequately confront the fact that our practices are changing all the time and that the relationship among them is complex. So, originalism creates problems that do not need to exist and ought not to exist. I know there are people here who really think we should dump the entire post-New Deal jurisprudence. To me that would be—I do not know how to put this strongly enough while remaining polite—a completely insane thing to do. It is one thing to say that post-New Deal jurisprudence has produced horrible pernicious consequences and we need slowly to undo it and find small steps to push the world in a different direction. But originalism says to just dump the whole thing now, completely, because it is not what the Constitution originally authorized. And that strikes me as utterly, disastrously foolish. The problem with originalism, in other words, is the fundamentalism that underlies it. That is the only point I wanted to make about pragmatism. I am not embracing a thorough-going form of consequentialism.

JUDGE GINSBURG: Frank?

JUDGE EASTERBROOK: No, I'll save time for questions.

PROFESSOR MCGINNIS: Can I respond to two points here. One, I thought Jeff's remarks were interesting, but I am not sure they constitute a theory of interpretation.

PROFESSOR ROSEN: That is exactly the point.

PROFESSOR MCGINNIS: The question is do you need, though, a theory of interpretation to do anything, even to defer? Because the question of judicial deference, it seems to me, focuses on the distance between what the Constitution requires and what Congress has done. Unless we endorse wholesale judicial abdication, there has to be some measure of that distance. If an interpreter, even a deferential inter- preter is to invalidate a statute with reference to the Constitution, you have to have a theory by which you can understand what the Consti- tution means. But I agree that it is certainly open to originalists to be deferential originalists. You might adopt a rule of clear mistake, as far as Congress is concerned. And doing that seems to me the rule Chief Justice Marshall adopts, and thus it may well be one of the orginal interpretative rules about which I spoke that are to guide the resolu- tion of constitutional questions.

With respect to the issue of precedent, I think the Framers did have a theory of precedent which we must recover. It is quite clear that Hamilton believes in the authority of precedent. There is defi- nitely an idea in the early Republic that the meaning of the constitu- tional text may be liquidated by a series of decisions. Following such liquidated meanings may be another of the originalist rules of inter- pretation. So, it just does not follow, I think, that if one is an origi- nalist one is going to have to overturn a lot of New Deal precedent. *Roe v. Wade*, however, is another matter.

So, all I would say is I think originalism is somewhat more nuanced than sometimes it is being given credit for. I think it may well have a theory of deference built into it, and yet it still provides what we need: a theory of how to interpret the constitutional text.

PROFESSOR ROSEN: Well, I am happy to call myself an origi- nalist still, if originalism means deference, even though very few orig- inalists are consistently deferential. I agree with the basic defense in *Federalist* 78 about the relationship between originalism and popular sovereignty. So, sure, let us look at the historical evidence; look at the text; look at the history. And unless the answer is clear, unless all of the methods of interpretation—text, history, original understanding, precedent, perhaps even pragmatic considerations—argue in favor of invalidation, then defer. Then defer. It is a version of the clear statement rule.

I am just struck and, I have to say, distressed that I cannot think of a single prominent originalist on the bench or in the academy who applies originalism in that restrained sort of way. The idea that for all the virtues of the effort to strike down the New Deal—and, for what it is worth, Randy and others, I do have some libertarian leanings as a policy matter. But the idea that the Constitution clearly compels these results is so patently unconvincing to those of us who are not inclined to accept that methodological claim that I struggle like Larry Kramer to come up with adequate adjectives to describe it.

So, fine, if we want to begin our discussion by positing that we are all originalists now—as even Ronald Dworkin, of all people, said a few years ago—that is fine with me. So long as we are not going to strike down a lot of laws unless the arguments for doing so are very, very, very clear, then I am still happy to be called an originalist.

JUDGE GINSBURG: Thank you all. Jeff, your remarks put me in mind of those made forty-some years ago that could be paraphrased along the lines of saying that judicial activism in the face of unconstitutional action is no vice, and judicial restraint no virtue.

We have two mikes. We will alternate sides. Sir?

AUDIENCE MEMBER: Do you think it is fair to label as an activist an originalist judge who is striking down what he considers to be activist decisions of liberal judges or justices in the past? In other words, if Justice Clarence Thomas were to rule against affirmative action, could you say that he is an activist simply because he is trying to undo an activist liberal court from several decades ago?

DEAN KRAMER: Very quickly. I think the opposition of activism and judicial restraint is generally unhelpful because it depends on one's baseline. If the proper baseline is the original understanding of the Constitution, then it is not activist to overturn decisions that departed from that understanding. All the Court is doing is restoring the original meaning. But not everyone agrees that this is the proper baseline, and there are others one could use: the text, Supreme Court precedent, the results of political decision-making, custom, and so on. All of those provide defensible baselines, and any decision that departs from the baseline you pick—whatever it is—can be attacked as activist. In my view, the proper baseline is definitely *not* the original understanding of the Constitution. I think it is more complicated than that.

JUDGE GINSBURG: Dean Kramer, let me ask you to extend that a bit. Judge Bork, in his confirmation hearings, when he spoke in favor of the original understanding, he also said that it would be impractical to undo everything that was done in departing from the original understanding. Taking the example of the New Deal, which I think you raised, he said that it would be impractical to reconsider that. He said that there have been reliance interests formed, institutions that have grown up around this; and it is just not the role of the Court to undo those reliance interests and institutions. But Judge Bork also said that to allow further transgressions would be a misfortune. So does that make him a pragmatist?

DEAN KRAMER: In the way I think of it, yes.

JUDGE GINSBURG: So it seems to me what is wanting here, to fill in the gap, is a principled theory of when one adheres and when one does not adhere to precedent that is aberrant relative to the original understanding.

DEAN KRAMER: Again, not necessarily. To arbitrarily pick any one of these baselines is too simple. And this is why I think the use of the terms activist or restrained does not help. We need a theory that includes some room for evolution. There are different ways in which such evolution can occur, whether it be through political practice, or judicial practice and precedent, and so forth. Activist or restrained is just a conclusion that in my personal opinion the interpreter did not have an adequate justification for the departure he or she made from what I think is the proper baseline.

JUDGE GINSBURG: Judge Easterbrook?

JUDGE EASTERBROOK: Yes, the short version of this is: Is there some way we could agree to stop using the word activist? What it means is, depending on context, either judges behaving badly or judges behaving really badly. Neither one of those definitions helps unless you know what it means for judges to behave badly. So, it seems to me, one should really talk about whether judges are deciding correctly.

Obviously, theories of precedent and reliance interests and so on play a large role in how judges decide correctly. But the term 'activism' does not help, because it usually shelters behind it some assumption about the right roles of precedent, or the right interpretative theory, and so on, rather than stating them openly and then critiquing judges for not following the correct ones.

JUDGE GINSBURG: Professor Rosen?

PROFESSOR ROSEN: Thank you. Actually, "judges behaving badly" sounds like a good reality TV show. Judge Luttig just offered a very interesting theory of precedent. In an effort to respond to your challenge, sir, he said that there should be a theory of super precedents which suggests that when a particular decision has been accepted by different courts, made up of different justices, appointed by different presidents, confirmed by different Senates, they are entitled to special weight.

JUDGE EASTERBROOK: Like *Plessy*.

PROFESSOR ROSEN: The reason that his theory deserves to be taken seriously is because it introduces something which has not yet come up in our discussion, which is the important relationship between the Court and public opinion. We are assuming—originalism assumes that you should just enforce the original understanding and damn the consequences. But this is preposterous as a description of how the Court has behaved over time. The political scientists remind us that the Court over time has almost always mirrored national opinion. On the rare occasions it has not, it has provoked backlashes that have gotten it into trouble. Robert McCloskey's wonderful book, if you have not read it, is just the best historical account of this.

So that is a serious failure of originalism—the failure to have a theory of precedent which recognizes that it matters what a majority of the country thinks at a particular moment in time. A theory of precedent along these lines certainly does not mean a Court has to follow a decision like *Plessy*, when segregation is no longer accepted by the political branches. Overruling *Plessy* in *Brown* was appropriate once the president, as well as Congress, although more weakly so, came to reject segregation. It is even arguable that when *Plessy* was decided, a majority of the country was not intensely committed to Jim Crow—only nine southern states had embraced it in 1896. But sensitivity to popular views about the Constitution is what the Court has always done and always will do and that is also what makes possible the stability of the rule of law. So I think Judge Luttig's suggestion deserves a conference of its own. We really should think about it.

JUDGE GINSBURG: I thought we learned in *Casey* that sometimes the Court would educate us rather than the other way around. Sir?

AUDIENCE MEMBER: Ed Whelan of the Ethics and Public Policy Center and National Review Online Bench Memos. I have two quick interrelated questions: one for Dean Kramer, and one for Judge Easterbrook.

Dean Kramer, do you accept that on questions where originalism is indeterminate it follows that judges should yield to the decisions made in the democratic process? Or do you think that somehow judges are then liberated to make things up?

Judge Easterbrook, I want to make sure I understand. I understood you to say that originalism is tied to judicial review and constraining judges. I thought you seemed to suggest that other government actors are not constrained by originalism. Is that simply because originalism is indeterminate in certain areas, and where it is indeterminate, they are obligated to act? Or is there some other way in which there is some alternative method that you view as equally legitimate for non-judicial actors?

DEAN KRAMER: I will go first, I guess. I cannot answer quickly for the following reason. One of the things we have not yet discussed is the doctrine of judicial supremacy, which distorts everything. The reason we have to agonize about this as much as we do is because we build in a second premise, which is that once the Court has spoken everybody else is supposed to yield.

PROFESSOR MCGINNIS: Who wants that?

DEAN KRAMER: Well, if you take judicial supremacy off the table, then a lot of these questions about interpretation become less important, because there are responses to get around or override a judicial decision short of having to produce a constitutional amendment.

That said, I would not accept originalism as a sensible theory of interpretation, even if we were to stipulate that there is an original intent that is clear as applied to today's circumstances. My view would still be to think of the Constitution as a form of evolving and unfolding law.

The choice would be between that original intent, if we assume there is one and its application to present circumstances is clear, and my view that people before us have already struggled with most questions of constitutional law and we need to understand what those people said and did to make sense of the doctrine.

There are very few issues as to which no supervening events have occurred to affect the question of construction. Most questions in constitutional law have come up before, and they have been resolved one way or another. Those post-Framing resolutions, in turn, provide a new starting position for further development with respect to the issue in question. I think in order to understand what the question is and how to think about resolving it you have to go through that process.

JUDGE GINSBURG: It strikes me, Dean Kramer, that all the talk about the difficulty of discerning the original meaning of the Constitution may be somewhat circular, in the sense that there has been a lot of originalist scholarship in the last two decades. There is Judge McConnell's originalist scholarship and the work of many others on original meaning of various clauses in the Constitution. This work places those clauses in an historical context and describes their original meanings with a specificity that is almost impossible to refute. But, as Jeff Rosen has pointed out, there has been very little demand for this kind of originalist scholarship on the Supreme Court. If there were demand for it, maybe finding the original meaning would not be so difficult. If the Supreme Court actually wanted and consumed such originalist work, inevitably a lot more of it would be produced.

DEAN KRAMER: There are a lot of scholars who do originalist work that I respect, but having spent basically twelve years of my life doing nothing but reading, and not just the original legal sources but also the social history and political history that informs those legal sources. I must say that most originalist work reads to me like essays people write about America in French or German papers. They may not misstate facts, but they are very far off in nuance and feel. That is how most originalist scholarship reads to me. There is not a hard question that I have come across yet where I could not, if you gave me a little time, shred the originalist scholarship that has been done.

JUDGE GINSBURG: Maybe the reason you feel that way is because you have been looking too much at the social context instead of looking at the relevant legal documents? A lot of these terms were legal terms that were in use?

DEAN KRAMER: If the question is how did the Framers understand the legal terms they used, you cannot make do without both. To illustrate, Saul Cornell has a wonderful book on the meaning of the term "to bear arms." He looked much more broadly at arms and weaponry and hunting, and it turns out that the phrase had a meaning that is obscured if you look only at the legal doctrine—a meaning that would have been apparent to people at the time but that we have since lost. That is what I mean by needing to look at the social history.

JUDGE EASTERBROOK: The other question, which you may have forgotten by now, was whether the political branches are bound by originally taken decisions that apply to them. The answer is plainly yes. In the argument I was giving—really Chief Justice Marshall's argument which I was parroting—is that the Constitution is full of lacunae and they are to be filled up through decisions made by the representatives, rather than invented by the courts.

But there are a number of things, a number of very important things that are in the Constitution as an original matter. Suppose for example, to take a wild and exceedingly implausible example, suppose Congress were to pass a statute saying that the decision of a single house of Congress would be sufficient to knock out a decision by an administrative agency or a president. That would just blatantly violate the provision of the Constitution, which says Congress acts bicamerally and submits it to the president. If Congress were so absurd as to enact such a law, it would be unconstitutional on originalist grounds. Some people tell me that they once did that kind of thing, but I have kind of lost....

JUDGE GINSBURG: Actually two hundred times.

DEAN KRAMER: They still do it.

JUDGE EASTERBROOK: And by the way, it would not be useful to talk about whether *INS v. Chadha* was an activist decision, because it took out two hundred statutes. Similarly, if Congress enacts a law tomorrow, the Legislative History Act of 2005, saying, "We are tired of all of these filibusters and votes and needing to run back to the Senate to vote. What we are going to do is hire the Gallup organization to take a poll of members of Congress, and anything having majority support shall be deemed to be the law." That would be unconstitutional, even though it would make legislation really easy. The fact that what judges often do in the name of looking at legislative history is exactly that is, by the way, a very good reason why they should stop consulting legislative history.

JUDGE GINSBURG: I take it your argument would extend to a statute that says that all legislative power is hereby delegated to agencies, and we will see you in two years?

JUDGE EASTERBROOK: Unless, of course, those powers are delegated to the Supreme Court. Then the justices would be very happy. We call that the antitrust laws.

JUDGE GINSBURG: Next question?

AUDIENCE MEMBER: I want to pick up on a couple of the themes that John McGinnis has raised and direct my question to Dean Kramer. One of the things that John spoke about was that one needs to have a theory of interpretation before one can defer. He made the same point with respect to Jeff Rosen's remarks. Dean Kramer's critique of originalism seems to me to be deeply rooted in a claim about indeterminancy, which to my mind, is very much overstated. Dean Kramer, what is your theory of interpretation? What say you?

JUDGE GINSBURG: Before you say it, the queue is closed. I'm going to ask each answerer and each question to be limited to a minute.

DEAN KRAMER: Wow, one minute. In a nutshell, my understanding is that constitutional law is best conceived as a form of customary law refracted through a text. I do not think this is empty, unless you believe that all forms of common law and customary law are empty. Under this approach, we begin by recognizing that the various institutions of government are, at all times, addressing themselves to the text, coming up with their best understanding of it, and adapting the text to their world. Our responsibility is to pick up where they left off and continue the process of interpretation from that point.

Now you can agree or disagree with me about whether this is a good approach, but certainly it is a coherent theory. It is, in some sense, a thoroughly conventional theory of legal interpretation akin to common law adjudication—the only additions being 1) that interpretations are always refracted through the text, and 2) that interpretations of all of the institutions of government need to be considered, not just the courts, because they are responding to each other. So when you face a question of constitutional interpretation twenty or thirty years after the Court decided something, it is not just the Court's last decision that counts, but also what Congress and the President and the states have made of that decision in the intervening decades. You need to take all of that into account.

AUDIENCE MEMBER: Thank you for clarifying that.

DEAN KRAMER: Was that a minute?

JUDGE GINSBURG: Yes, I think we can call it even a constitutional moment.

JUDGE GINSBURG: The next question will be from Lino Graglia.

LINO GRAGLIA: I would like, if I may, to make two preliminary points, and then my main point. My first preliminary point is that I disagree with Judge Easterbrook that the term judicial activism does not mean anything. I defined it in my talk earlier today quite clearly.

Activism is holding things unconstitutional that are not unconstitutional. Overruling *Roe v. Wade* therefore is not activism. My point is that I think there is a large element of unreality in most of these discussions about how to interpret because, in fact, it all comes down to the meaning of four words: "due process," and "equal protection." The problem is that the judges have quite wrongly said that "due process" and "equal protection" mean that all laws must be "reasonable" or "just" or serve "a public purpose," and we the judges are the ones who get to say what that is. That is the essence of the problem. The rule should be that the Court should only hold something invalid if it *clearly* is. Now, often we do not know what the original intent is and, if so, fine the policy choice by the political branches stands. Why is that not the whole answer?

JUDGE EASTERBROOK: What Lino Graglia just said is in many ways similar to my proposition that there are a lot of lacunae in the Constitution. It is very hard for judges to claim the authority to act in the name of words like equal protection. It does not mean that there is nothing there. The argument I was making is actually very similar to part of the argument that Judge McConnell made this morning. The Fourteenth Amendment certainly is ambulatory, but it has a clause in it saying who it is that is to interpret it and how. That is, it is a grant of power to Congress. That is what Section 5 is. If Congress were to say, using its Section 5 power, that certain things have to be done in order to protect the privileges and immunities of citizens or to provide equal protection, I think it would not be appropriate for a judge to say, "Well, that is not how I would have understood those terms, so I refuse to enforce the legislation if the grants of power should be construed as granting a discretion in proportion to the difficulty of reconstructing a single original meaning."

JUDGE GINSBURG: Don't feel obligated.

PROFESSOR ROSEN: No, just to say that I had not realized that long journey from Akhil Amar's embrace would culminate in the arms of Lino Graglia. We may be closer than I thought. I admire much of your work. I am not as familiar with your views on the federalism questions, but, if you are as deferential to Congress as you just said the Court should be to the states, we are on the same team.

AUDIENCE MEMBER: If I may say so, the answer is yes. I wrote a long article saying *Lopez* was wrongly decided. The problem Dean Kramer is worried about is will they repeal the New Deal? I would not do so.

JUDGE GINSBURG: Randy Barnett?

AUDIENCE MEMBER: Jeff, the bad news for you is that you really are in Lino Graglia's embrace.

PROFESSOR ROSEN: I am delighted to be there. That is why I came today, actually.

AUDIENCE MEMBER: You had better learn to enjoy it. Actually, I....

PROFESSOR ROSEN: I already am.

AUDIENCE MEMBER: I only got up because I saw Lino get up and I figured if I got in line after Lino, I would have a lot to disagree with. But then I realized that if Lino talks long enough, he ends up revealing that his position is that nothing is unconstitutional. I rest my case.

JUDGE GINSBURG: I am sorry to say that we have run out of time.

Nine

PANEL ON ORIGINALISM
AND PRECEDENT

Steven G. Calabresi
Text vs. Precedent in Constitutional Law

Conservative constitutional law scholarship is divided into two camps. First, there are the originalists and textualists like myself, Randy Barnett, John Harrison, Gary Lawson, Michael McConnell, Michael Stokes Paulsen, Saikrishna Prakash, and, at times, Akhil Amar. We believe that the text of the Constitution, as it was originally understood, is controlling in most constitutional cases. Second, there are the followers of Supreme Court precedent, who sometimes claim incorrectly that they are Burkeans. This group includes Thomas Merrill, Charles Fried, Ernie Young, and, in some respects, Richard Fallon. These scholars all follow the doctrine over the document and believe in a fairly robust theory of *stare decisis* in constitutional law. The key case in recent times where the textualists and the doctrinalists have clashed is *Planned Parenthood of Southeastern Pennsylvania v. Casey*.

My argument in this brief chapter is that the doctrinalists are wrong in arguing for a strong theory of *stare decisis* for three reasons.

First, there is nothing in the text, history, or original meaning of the Constitution that supports the doctrinalists' strong theory of *stare decisis*. Second, the actual practice of the U.S. Supreme Court is to never follow precedent, especially in big cases. In other words, precedent itself counsels against following precedent. And, third, the doctrinalists strong theory of *stare decisis* is a bad idea for policy reasons. I will take up each of these three arguments against *stare decisis* in turn below.

I. Textualist and Originalist Arguments

First, the textualist and originalist arguments as to why following precedent is wrong. Beginning with the text: it is striking that there is not a word in the Constitution that says in any way that precedent trumps the text. In fact, Article V specifically sets forth a procedure by which the constitutional text can be changed through the amendment process. This is the *only* process the constitutional text provides for making changes in the document. Five to four or even nine to zero Supreme Court decisions do not trump the text, at least according to the text. Moreover, in the Supremacy Clause, the document says that the Constitution, Laws and Treaties shall be the supreme law of the land, but it makes no mention of Supreme Court decisions. It is absolutely crystal clear that under the text of the Constitution the Supreme Court has no power to follow its own decisions when they conflict with the text.

Moreover, the Supremacy Clause of the Constitution makes *this* Constitution the supreme law of the land, and this Constitution is the one that we know was submitted for ratification under Article VII. It says nothing about Supreme Court case law being the supreme law of the land. The text, then, simply does not support a strong theory of *stare decisis*.

The original history of the Constitution leads to the same conclusion. The records we have from the Philadelphia Convention and of the ratification debates do not mention anywhere a power of the Supreme Court to follow precedent over constitutional text. If such a power had been contemplated surely it would have been discussed and debated during the heated and close fight over ratification of the Constitution. Alexander Hamilton to at least some extent does mention in *Federalist* 78 that the courts might sometimes be bound by precedents but he does not claim a power to follow precedent where it plainly conflicts with the text. At most Hamilton's comment, and a few other early comments like it, suggest a power to follow past interpretations of the constitutional text which are plausible and not in contradiction to the text. Absolutely no one in the Framing generation, not even the most die hard anti-federalists, imagined a doctrine of stare decisis trumping the constitutional text of the kind the Justices found in *Casey*.

Moreover, early practice under the Constitution, I think, shows that the Framers themselves did not follow a strict theory of *stare decisis* on the biggest constitutional issue of their day—the constitutionality of the Bank of the United States. It is worth rehearsing quickly the history of the debate over the constitutionality of the Bank during the first forty years of the Republic.

The Bank of the United States was created in 1791 on the recommendation of Alexander Hamilton and almost two-thirds of the members of the first House of Representatives and all of the first Senate thought the Bank was constitutional. This is significant because the First Congress was full of delegates to the Philadelphia Constitutional Convention and so its decisions have always been thought to be especially probative of constitutional meaning. The bill establishing the bank was signed into law by President George Washington, who had presided over the Philadelphia Convention and without whose support the Constitution would never have been ratified. Washington signed the Bank bill even though his secretary of state and attorney general advised him the bill was unconstitutional. He thus must have been especially sure that he was right that the Bank was constitutionally okay, and the public must have realized as well that Washington felt that way.

The question of the constitutionality of the Bank would continue to be debated from when it was first enacted in 1791, up until the 1830s. And throughout that period of time, most of the people who commented on the matter did not think that the question of the constitutionality of the Bank was settled as a result of the first Congress and President Washington having participated in creating the Bank. The Bank was allowed to lapse in 1811 after its twenty-year charter expired, and members of Congress continued to debate its constitutionality. A bill renewing the Bank was ultimately passed by Congress during the War of 1812, and President James Madison ultimately signed it into law. This was significant for several reasons. First, Madison is often called the Father of the Constitution because of the important role he played at the Philadelphia Convention and as an author of the *Federalist Papers*. Second, Madison had said in Congress when the First Bank was approved that he thought the Bank was unconstitutional as a matter of original meaning. Third, Madison ultimately let the Second Bank become law because he felt that practice and precedent had settled matters in favor of the Bank's constitutionality. Strikingly, as we shall see in a moment, Madison's conclusion on this point was to be decisively overruled.

The question of the constitutionality of the Bank finally reached the Supreme Court in 1819 in *McCulloch v. Maryland*. Chief Justice Marshall could easily have said in *McCulloch* that the question of the constitutionality of the Bank had been settled by twenty-eight years of practice and precedent. The Supreme Court had said something like that in a case called *Stuart v. Laird*, where the Court relied on practice or precedent. Chief Justice Marshall did not say this. Marshall did not rely exclusively on practice or precedent in *McCulloch*. Instead, he reviewed the question *de novo* making a number of famous textualist, structural, and originalist arguments. Chief Justice Marshall treated the question of the constitutionality of the Bank as still being open even after twenty-eight years.

In 1832, a full forty years after President Washington and the First Congress had created the Bank, the question of the constitutionality of the Bank came up again when the Bank came up for renewal a third time. President Andrew Jackson vetoed the renewal bill, saying the Bank was unconstitutional, and he used some key language in his veto message that bears on whether the Founding generation believed in precedent or not. President Jackson said:

It is maintained by the advocates of the Bank that its constitutionality in all of its features ought to be considered as settled by precedent and by the decision of the Supreme Court. To this conclusion I cannot assent. Mere precedent is a dangerous source of authority, and should not be regarded as deciding questions of constitutional power except where the acquiesence of the people and the States can be considered as well settled.

For Jackson, forty years after the First Congress and President Washington had approved the Bank, the question of its constitutionality was not well settled. Jackson's veto killed the Bank, and it was not to reemerge until eighty-two years later during the administration of Woodrow Wilson when the Federal Reserve Board was created.

So, original practice, then confirms that on the most contested constitutional issue of their day—the constitutionality of the Bank— the first generation of Americans did not follow a precedent set forty years before by the First Congress and President Washington. Early practice then confirms what the constitutional text and original history show. The Framers of the Constitution did not believe in a strong theory of precedent in constitutional cases.

II. Arguments from Practice

Second, what is the actual practice of the Supreme Court with respect to following precedent? I believe that the actual practice of the Supreme Court is to never follow precedent, especially in big cases. In fact, the Court appears to have overruled itself 174 times, mostly in constitutional rather than statutory cases, according to a question Senator Sam Brownback asked John Roberts during his hearings to be Chief Justice of the United States. The September 2005 issue of the *Atlantic Monthly* quotes leading D.C. Circuit Judge Laurence Silberman as saying in an opinion that the "Supreme Court is a non-court court" that "rarely considers itself bound by the reasoning of their prior opinions." The same article goes on to quote Richard Posner, one of our leading Circuit Court Judges and a leading scholar of the federal court system, as saying: "The Supreme Court has never paid much heed to its own precedents—that's nothing new." Posner is clearly right. Consider ten big occasions from the last seventy years where the Court explicitly or implicitly overruled itself relying on textual first principles or originalist arguments.

First is the Constitutional Revolution of 1937. The Supreme Court abandoned the *Lochner* era doctrine of economic substantive due process in the face of a withering textualist and originalist critique thus displacing a body of caselaw that stretched back for almost forty years. In *West Coast Parish Hotel*, the Court explicitly overruled its decision in *Atkins v. Children's Hospital*—a major and landmark case. The Court also adopted, as part of the Constitutional Revolution of 1937, a much broader reading of the Commerce and Necessary and Proper Clauses. It reached this reading after resorting to first principles and a Marshallian originalist understanding of the scope of national power. The New Deal Court's federalism caselaw explicitly overruled *Hammer v. Daggenhart* and was also inconsistent with a forty-year-old line of precedent. There can be little question but that the Revolution of 1937 constitutes a big break with precedent.

Second, is *Erie Railroad v. Tompkins*, which overruled the one hundred year old doctrine of *Swift v. Tyson* on originalist grounds. *Erie* is an unabashed triumph for originalism since the Court's opinion begins by claiming that *Swift* has been fatally undermined by the new historical research of Charles Warren. This is the doctrinalist's worst nightmare of what originalism might lead to. A scholar emerges from the library with new evidence about the original meaning of a text and decades of practice gets up-ended. Yet, that is what the Court did in *Erie*.

Third, is the Flag Salute Cases where *West Virginia State Board of Education v. Barnette* overruled *Gobitas* on textual first principles. This is a clear and sharp overruling of a recent and major constitutional precedent. *Barnette* may not be an originalist victory, but it is a victory for those who want to use the first principles implicit in the text of the Constitution to change sharply the doctrine.

Fourth is *Brown v. Board of Education*, which implicitly over-ruled *Plessy v. Ferguson* on textualist first principles. The opinion in *Brown* is openly non-originalist, but *Brown* is again clearly a victory for those who want to use the first principles implicit in the text of the Constitution to change sharply the doctrine.

Fifth, is the school prayer decision in *Engel v. Vitale*, which upended a 172-year Burkean tradition of legal school prayer on the grounds that such prayer violated a hitherto unappreciated original meaning of the Establishment Clause. *Engel* may well be wrong as a matter of originalism, but it is certainly another example of the Supreme Court not caring a whit for precedent or practice.

Sixth, is *Jones v. Alfred H. Mayer Co.* which implicitly overrules the *Civil Rights Cases'* discussion of Section Two of the Thirteenth Amendment for originalist reasons. Again, this is a triumph of text and in this case original meaning over decades and decades of con-trary precedent.

Seventh, is *Gregg v. Georgia*, where the Supreme Court brought back the death penalty for originalist reasons after the Supreme Court's decision in *Furman* had seemed to call it into question. The Court in *Gregg* quoted at length from the constitutional text and from originalist sources to prove that the death penalty was not always and everywhere unconstitutional.

Eighth, is the Supreme Court's Tenth Amendment line of cases. Here the 1969 decision in *Maryland v. Wirtz* was overruled by the five to four 1976 decision in *National League of Cities v. Usery*, which in turn was overruled by the five to four decision in the *Garcia* case—which has itself been rendered a dead letter by *Seminole Tribe* and *Alden v. Maine*. The number of overrulings in this one area of doctrine alone are staggering and suggest no willingness whatsoever by the Justices to adhere to stare decisis in constitutional law.

Ninth, is the Rehnquist Court's federalism cases, which displaced forty-eight years of contrary post-1937 case law. These cases include: *United States v. Lopez*, which is inconsistent with almost five decades of Commerce Clause case law; *City of Boerne v. Flores*, which explicitly limits and alters the meaning of *Katzenbach v. Morgan*; *New York v. United States*, which is inconsistent with *Garcia*; and *Seminole Tribe* which overruled a decision from the 1980s called *Union Gas*. This is clearly another big area of constitutional law where the Court has acted in ways sharply inconsistent with precedent.

Tenth, and final is the Court's recent overruling of *Bowers v. Hardwick* in *Lawrence v. Texas*, where the Justices held that a Texas sodomy statute was unconstitutional as a matter of substantive due process. The Court's decision in *Lawrence* not only flew in the face of *Bowers*, but was also inconsistent in its substantive due process methodology with the Court's 1997 decision in the assisted suicide case of *Washington v. Glucksberg*. This is then a clear triumph again of textualist first principles over contrary precedent. *Lawrence* is blatantly wrong as a matter of originalism, as I have explained in another article, but it is certainly an example of the Court not following—and indeed upending—long-established precedent.

Taken together, these ten explicit and implicit overrulings show that it is simply *not* the U.S. Supreme Court's practice to follow precedent. In fact, the Court almost never follows precedent on big issues having done so only in *Casey* and in *Dickerson*, to my knowledge, in recent times. All good Burkeans in this country must admit that we have a tradition here of following the written Constitution and not Supreme Court case law. Thus, in the United States, Burkeanism leads back to the text.

III. Policy Arguments against Following Precedent

Third, and finally, is it a good idea as a matter of policy for the U.S. Supreme Court to follow strictly its own precedents? The answer is "no" for two big reasons.

First, it is almost impossible to amend the U.S. Constitution. We have the most difficult constitutional amendment process of any big democracy that I am aware of. Constitutional amendments must receive a two-thirds vote in both houses of Congress and be ratified by thirty-eight States (three-fourths of the current fifty) in order to become law. That means that if only one house of thirteen state legislatures rejects a constitutional amendment, the amendment is dead. If one groups together the thirteen least populous states, they have a combined total of only 4.48 percent of the U.S. population. That means that, in theory, constitutional amendments in the U.S. could be supported by 95.52 percent of the American people, and they could still fail for ratification.

A strict rule of *stare decisis* in constitutional cases, therefore, would make it impossible ever to correct the Supreme Court's errors, even by appointing new members and hoping for overruling. This would eliminate the only formal check and balance on the Supreme Court that actually works. The other two checks are the amendment process, which as I have already explained does not work, and in theory impeachment which could have become a check on the Supreme Court but does not work because it has not been tried in two hundred years and has never been used successfully. So, if we think the Supreme Court is going to make mistakes, and I certainly do think they do from time to time, it is necessary to be able to correct those mistakes by getting them overruled.

I cannot imagine why it would be good public policy to allow 4.48 percent of the population to have an absolute veto on changes in Supreme Court doctrine, but this is, in practice, what a strict rule of stare decisis would lead to. Given the casual way in which the Court decides cases and given the Court's refusal often to be bound by text, original meaning, or precedent, I cannot conceive of how anyone could believe it would be good public policy to eliminate the only check and balance on the Supreme Court that actually works in practice.

Second, a strict rule of *stare decisis*, I think, is also a mistake for policy reasons because it fails to take account of the long time horizon one should have in constitutional law. Thus, I disagree with leading doctrinalists like Professor Thomas Merrill who argue that the Supreme Court ought to follow precedent because it: 1) promotes the rule of law, 2) preserves continuity with the past, 3) reflects an appropriate skepticism about powers of human reason, 4) enhances democratically accountable lawmaking, and 5) promotes judicial restraint. Let us examine each of Professor Merrill's five arguments in turn asking whether they would countenance overruling the precedent of *Roe v. Wade*, a case that Professor Merrill thinks *stare decisis* protects.

First, would the rule of law be promoted by retaining or overruling the thirty-four-year-old precedent of *Roe v. Wade*? The answer, I think, depends on how long your time horizon is. Is it more important to the rule of law to be consistent with the constitutional law on abortion of the last thirty-four years or is it more important to be consistent with the tradition of banning abortions outright from the mid-nineteenth century to 1973? Is it more important to the rule of law to maintain abortion rights or more important to get rid of the doctrine of substantive due process which has led to *Dred Scott* and to *Lochner v. New York*? I think in constitutional law that it is the long view which one ought to take and that being consistent with centuries of law regulating abortion and getting rid of the destabilizing constitutional monstrosity of substantive due process does more to promote the rule of law values of stability and consistency than following a thirty-four-year-old precedent that was controversial from the day it was handed down.

Second, is continuity with the past best promoted by retaining or overruling the thirty-four-year old precedent of *Roe v. Wade*? Again, this depends on whether one adopts a long or a short term time horizon in constitutional law. Do we want to be consistent with the past thirty-four years or with centuries of laws regulating and forbidding abortions? It seems obvious to me that in constitutional law one's time horizon must be multi-generational and not confined to the past thirty-two years. The whole point of constitutional law is to allow one generation to bind its descendants by enshrining fundamental rights in the Constitution. This enterprise of multi-generational lawmaking would become impossible if one preserved continuity with only the recent past and not with the last few centuries. Again, continuity with the past is best preserved by overruling *Roe v. Wade*.

Third, is skepticism about the powers of human reason most enhanced by retaining or overruling *Roe v. Wade*? Once again, the answer is clear. For hundreds of years, it has been our tradition to forbid abortion from the moment we first knew that fetal life had come into being. It was for this reason, that the common law banned abortion from the time of quickening onward and it was for this reason that abortion was outlawed altogether in the nineteenth century once we learned that fetal life starts before quickening. Obviously, skepticism about the powers of human reason should lead us to defer to longstanding practice and not to a thirty-four-year-old dictate that was controversial from the very moment it was handed down. Conservatives like to believe with Friedrich Hayek that tradition embodies the wisdom of the ages and is a spontaneous source of order that ought to be followed. But, calling a Harry Blackmun opinion from 1973 the "wisdom of the ages" strains credulity. Skepticism about the powers of human reason suggest *Roe* ought to be overruled.

Fourth, is democratically accountable lawmaking enhanced or diminished by overruling *Roe*? Again, the answer is obvious: *Roe* took the highly controversial question of abortion and removed it from the legislatures of the fifty states while creating a sweeping and congressionally unalterable rule. Overruling *Roe* would not make abortion illegal. It would simply return the question to the fifty state legislatures, most of which would probably keep abortion legal. Supporters of *Roe* claim there are powerful reliance interests on the part of women that have grown up around *Roe* and counsel in favor of keeping abortion legal. If that claim is true, then there is every reason to expect that state legislatures will respond to the wishes of women who are after all a majority of the population. There is no question but that democratically accountable lawmaking is enhanced by overruling *Roe* and not by retaining it.

Fifth and finally, does judicial restraint counsel in favor of overruling or retaining *Roe*? Here again the answer is obvious. Overruling *Roe* means no more invalidations of state and federal laws regulating abortion, and it is the striking down of democratically initiated laws that are constitutionally permissible that constitutes judicial activism. The defenders of *Roe* like to play on words by implying that it is "activist" for the Supreme Court to overrule *Roe* because the Court would be taking action. This is nonsense! Failing to continue a practice of striking down abortion laws is not activist: it is restrained. Judicial restraint counsels in favor of overruling *Roe*.

Constitutions are about inter-generational lawmaking where one generation binds the next. Accordingly, it is a mistake to think it is restrained for the Court to follow a thirty-two-four-old precedent rather than the tradition of the last millennium where we never aborted a life in the womb once we knew it had begun. We need a long time horizon in constitutional law. Judicial restraint and the rule of law are promoted when we follow the fundamental constitutional principles of our great-grandfathers, secure in the knowledge that if we pass an Equal Rights Amendment or a Balanced Budget Amendment, it will be followed by our great-grandchildren. This, to me, is what constitutional government is all about.

Conclusion

In summary, the text of the Constitution, its original meaning, the early practice of the Framers, the modern practice from 1937 to 2005, and policy arguments all counsel in favor of textualism and against a strong theory of *stare decisis* in constitutional cases. Conservatives in the United States ought to embrace textualism and originalism in place of rule by a biased, cultural lawyerly elite on the Supreme Court. True Burkeans in the United States will realize that America's tradition is one of following the written Constitution, and not the decisions of five superannuated life tenured lawyers. It is not our practice slavishly to follow precedent and there is no good reason why we should suddenly make that our practice today.

Professor Akhil Amar

It is a great honor and pleasure and privilege to be here before such a distinguished group, and to be on such an extraordinary panel with such extraordinary colleagues, whose work I have so long admired.

I think, until recently, the conversation on this issue has been dominated by two main camps, which I will call unoriginal originalism and unprecedented precedentialists. By unoriginal originalists, I mean to refer to people who purport to pay close attention to text, history, and structure, and then you say, well, what happens when that conflicts with precedent? And they basically do not quite have a theory at all, or the theory is sort of muddling through; or sometimes we follow precedent and sometimes we do not. But if you are just going to muddle through, or be pragmatic about when you follow precedent, does that not undercut the very grounds on which you claim to be an originalist in the first place? Why not then muddle through across the board or be pragmatic across the board?

So, if it is tolerably clear, for example—to pick just one issue—that the exclusionary rule is completely made up from a constitutional perspective, and that no Framer ever believed that illegally seized evidence should be excluded from court; that England never had an exclusionary rule; that the Fourth Amendment definitely does not provide for an exclusionary rule; that no state excluded evidence for the first hundred years after the Declaration of Independence, even though most of the states have Fourth Amendment counterparts. So, if anything is pretty clear, it is that the exclusionary rule is inconsistent with the original meaning of the Fourth Amendment. And yet none of the supposedly originalist justices on the Supreme Court reject the exclusionary rule. Even Justices Scalia and Thomas exclude evidence pretty regularly, and do not ever quite tell us why they do so when it means abandoning the original meaning of the Fourth Amendment.

Now, I am actually going to instead argue that what originalists ought to do is to actually try to deduce a theory of precedent from the text, history, and structure of the Constitution itself, and to see what are the proper metes and bounds of precedent, reasoning from the document. We have not seen a real sustained effort to do that yet. This is why we have unoriginal originalists.

The other side of the text versus precedent debate fares no better. On the other side of the debate, we have the unprecedented precedentialists—scholars and justices who cannot explain why sometimes the Court ought to overrule and sometimes it ought not to overrule. Consider here the following important statement from the decision in *Planned Parenthood v. Casey:* "A decision to overrule should rest on some special reason over and above the belief a prior case was wrongly decided." This is the point of view that has recently carried the day on the modern Supreme Court, at least since the *Casey* decision. But the problem with this thesis is that it is inconsistent with precedent, both pre-*Casey* precedent and, even, post-*Casey* precedent. The *Casey* Court claims its view of precedent has been "repeated in our cases," the view that a decision to overrule should rest on some special reason over and above the belief that the prior case was wrongly decided. Again, the *Casey* Court says that is a view that has been "repeated in our cases." But to support that proposition the Court cites only dissents! Neither of the dissents cited are squarely on point, which leaves the careful reader with a sneaking suspicion that perhaps the *Casey* Court's view of precedent was not well-established, after all, in the pre-*Casey* case law on when to overrule precedent.

I did a strict count of the number of cases where the Supreme Court overruled itself on the basis of text, history, and structure. I excluded from my count cases where there were overrulings because the doctrine was unworkable or because of some other pragmatic or doctrinal argument. I just looked at pure, naked overrulings, where the Court said that the case it was overruling was wrong as an originalist matter. And, after doing this, I came up with five important cases in the twentieth century pre-*Casey*, and there may well be more, where the Court overruled itself simply because of an originalist argument that a precedent was wrong. In doing this, I was as strict as possible in confining myself to only overrulings that were based on a changed view of the original meaning of the constitutional provision in question. It is this analysis that led me to the conclusion that *Casey* was putting forward a view of the sanctity of precedent that was itself unprecedented.

So, let me now, in the few minutes I have left, tell you a little bit about how I would analyze the question of when to overrule a precedent based on the original meaning of the document itself. And here I am summarizing views that I have written about in the *Harvard Law Review,* in a Supreme Court Foreword published in 2000, called "The Document and the Doctrine." In my foreword, I talk about a great principled divide that cuts across liberalism and conservatism in constitutional law scholarship. This great principled divide among lawyers separates out documentarians—people who believe in the primacy of text, history, and structure, like Steve Calabresi on the Right, who is mentioned in the opening paragraph of the piece, or Justice Hugo Black on the Left who reaches the same conclusion—and the great doctrinalists in constitutional law, like David Strauss on the Left, who I also mention on the first page, or the second Justice Harlan, who was a great doctrinalist on the Right. I argue that there is a great distinction in principal between those who pay more attention to the document and those who tend to privilege the doctrine.

I am with the document people, and let me try, from the perspective of the document, to give you its account of doctrine. And it is an account in which doctrine has an important but ultimately subordinate place. I say in my *Harvard* foreword that a thorough-going commitment to the document would leave vast space for judicial doctrine, but doctrine would ultimately remain subordinate to the document itself. Now, Article III of the Constitution proclaims that the text of the Constitution is to be enforced as justiciable law in ordinary lawsuits. So, the document itself envisions that in deciding cases under it, judges are going to offer interpretations, give reasons, develop mediating principles, craft implementing frameworks to enable the document to be construed in court as law. So, these interpretations, reasons, principles, and frameworks, are, in a word, doctrine, and the Constitution contemplates that doctrine will exist.

In *McCulloch v. Maryland*, the great Chief Justice Marshall properly reminded us that our Constitution does not and cannot properly partake of the complexity of a legal code. Why? Because if it were that detailed it would not have been understood by the public, the people who would have to have been able to read it to decide whether to vote it up or down in the ratification process. So, the text of the Constitution could not read like a tax code because it would not have been understood by the people, its authors and amenders if it had so read during the ratification process. What that means is that the broad dictates of the Constitution, in order for the document to work in court, will have to be concretized in all sorts of ways.

Think of the Fourth Amendment. It establishes general parameters. The parameters are not, as I understand them, that every search and seizure requires probable cause. That is not what the text says, no matter what Ron Allen may or may not claim. It does not say, actually, that a warrant has to issue before each and every search can take place. It does not say that, and actually that has never been the case. It does not say that the exclusion of evidence is the proper response to an illegal search.

So, we have some parameters, but the text does not quite specify what they are. What the text does say is that, "Every search and seizure has to be reasonable." Now, what does an open-ended word like "reasonable" mean in this context? How do we cash that out? Well, that is going to require a vast number of strategic, pragmatic, empiric, institutional, second-best judgments by courts today about how to create a framework of what searches are reasonable in today's world. And I think thorough-going documentarians do not mean to displace an inquiry of this sort. We think that as long as the doctrine really does properly exist as an implementation of the proper principles that people did authorize, we can make our peace with that.

So, we documentarians do not begin and end with the document. We begin with the document, and we insist on its priority and fundamentality, and we try to ponder how to translate that wisdom into rules that can be made to be enforceable in court. Now, let us distinguish how to think about those rules in court. Well, here is one important distinction. The doctrine talks about a supreme court and inferior courts. And inferior courts, in general, are not judicially authorized to disregard the doctrine of the Supreme Court, even if those inferior courts think that doctrine is wrong, because the Constitution itself creates a structure of vertical authority. There may be rare cases in which a judge might act as a civil disobedient—Mike Paulsen has written very acutely about that problem—but there is no general judicial authority of an inferior to overrule or, if you will, under-rule or undermine the views of the Supreme Court. This is the case even if the inferior court judge thinks that the Supreme Court's rules are incorrect, because the

Constitution itself creates lines of authority that make the Supreme Court superior in authority to the lower federal courts.

Now, what should the Supreme Court think about its own precedent? Should the Supreme Court itself be bound by its own prior precedents? Well, here again, I think the document itself gives us some broad outlines to the answer, even though it does not answer all the questions that are raised by this issue. The Constitution itself creates the Supreme Court as a continuous body, and as a continuous body it is one that is ideally structured to think about what it has done in the past, and to anticipate what it is going to do in the future. All of that seems to me to argue for an idea that precedent may properly be taken as the default rule. There ought to be a presumption that the Court will do again what it has done before, unless and until the justices are persuaded that their prior decision was wrong. Accordingly, it makes sense to say that the burden of proof is on someone who wants to prove that a precedent is mistaken, just as the burden of proof ought also to be on someone who wants to prove that a law is unconstitutional. We have a presumption of the constitutionality of statutes, and someone who wants to overcome that presumption must give reasons if they are going to succeed in doing so. In other words, the Court ought not to treat its precedents as if they were more important than statutes, which are the people's own pronouncements. Rather, the Court should treat precedents as if they were comparable in force to statutes; that is to say, as if they were on a coordinate par with statutes.

We might even not only treat a past precedent as a sort of default or the starting point but even give it a certain epistemic weight. The mere fact that our predecessors, thoughtful men and women, came to a certain result might be a reason for thinking that that result is actually the right one. It is not an irrebuttable reason, but if the precedent came from the pen of John Marshall, for example, it might be a very strong reason.

But, it seems to me, having said all of that—that, when a court comes to a settled conviction that the previous decision really was a mistake and that the burden of proof has been overcome, I do not agree with *Casey*, for example, when it says we are not going to try to even tell you whether what we really did was to make a mistake in the previous case. For the Court to do that is for the Court to privilege its own case law even more than statutes. After all, when Congress makes a constitutional mistake by passing an unconstitutional statute, the Court is quite happy to say that Congress has made a mistake, and to correct it.

I am running out of time, so I will just make one more point and then I will quit. Certain mistakes may have been ratified by the people in some way, or ratified by the passage of time. Another structural feature of the judiciary is that it acts late in the process and only after the legislative and executive branches have already acted. Thus, a case involving the constitutionality of the Bank of the United States only reached the Supreme Court many years after the political branches had passed on the question. And John Marshall actually says in the *McCulloch* case that there have been important reliance interests created by the Bank that the Court could not lightly disrupt. That is why we have a presumption of constitutionality when it comes to statutes, and it seems to me, similarly, that certain precedents may have been, in important respects, relied-upon by institutional actors. And because courts act later in time, and act on things that have already happened, courts must have a certain respect for the reliance interests that may have grown up around a law. But the existence of such reliance-interests goes only to the question of what is a proper judicial remedy for a mistake. It does not go to the question of whether a mistake was made in the first instance.

It might very well mean that the Supreme Court cannot undo its mistakes on a dime, but the Court's first obligation, when it has made a mistake, is to tell us it that it has; and at least issue a declaratory judgment to that effect. Perhaps Congress or the legislature may respond to the news that the Supreme Court made a mistake by phasing in a new regime over a course of years because legislatures can act differently in some ways than can the Supreme Court. Perhaps the Supreme Court will respond to the conclusion it made a mistake by gradually trying to get back to a more proper constitutional approach.

But it does not seem to me that when the Supreme Court has made a mistake it ought to respond by not telling the citizenry that because they fear the American people cannot handle the news, because telling the truth would undermine the people's confidence in us, the Supreme Court. I am not making this language up by the way. This is what the Court actually said in *Casey*, and I find it problematic. I find it unprecedented, and I find it in tension, also, with the document itself.

Thank you.

Professor David Strauss

Good morning. I am also honored to be on such a distinguished panel. At some point when we were having our preliminary conference call to put together the logistics for this panel, someone—I do not remember who it was—commented that Steve Calabresi had put together a perfectly balanced panel. There was one liberal originalist, one conservative originalist, one liberal precedent guy, and one conservative precedent guy, and then one judge who actually knew what was going on. I do not want to vouch for any of the others except for the judge, but to the extent that allocation of roles is correct, I guess I am the liberal precedent guy. So, thank you for putting up with me.

What I really want to talk about, the pitch I would like to make, though, is why conservatives should not be originalists, and why conservatives should be receptive to a precedent-based approach to the Constitution rather than to originalism. A good way to think about this question is to ask yourself what theory you would want your opponents to operate on. If someone else were appointing people, someone you did not like were appointing people to the Supreme Court, what theory would you want them to use? If it is people whose basic orientations and inclinations you agree with, then it is kind of easy to assign them a theory. But when it is people whom you think are likely to go in the wrong direction, what approach would you then want them to use? It seems to me that a precedent-based approach is much more satisfactory from that point of view than originalism, and here is why: I think originalism leaves too many things too wide open and suppresses too many important considerations—suppresses in the sense that it gives people an incentive not to talk about them.

There are three reasons why I think originalism leaves things too wide open. The first you could call the problem of ascertainability, which is simply the difficulty of doing the historical research needed to figure out what the original understandings were; not so much the mechanical difficulty but the difficulty of knowing what inferences to draw from the historical materials. It is a hard intellectual process to reconstruct original understandings—not in every case, but in plenty of instances where there are going to be live controversies before the Supreme Court.

The second reason that originalism leaves things too wide open is what I would call the problem of indeterminacy. Even if you have accomplished the first task and you have figured out what the understandings were, the original understanding might not resolve the issue you are trying to resolve. This is a familiar problem from the ordinary legislative process: people might agree on a form of words but not agree on what the form of words is going to entail. A statute gets enacted or a constitutional provision is adopted because everybody can live with the words, but they have different understandings about what the words have committed the document to. Even if you do the work of figuring out what the understandings are, do that work successfully, you might find yourself in that position.

The third problem is what I will call the problem of translation. Even if you have figured out what the understandings were, even if the understandings are clear, it is often not going to be clear—I think routinely it is not going to be clear—what those understandings say about today's issues. Unless the original understanding was "here is how we are going to answer this question now and forever," you are not going to have a clear response to the objection that goes like this: "Well, okay, that was their understanding about how to deal with the problems of their time in the society they lived in, with the technology they had, with the population they had, with the problems they were confronting, but what was their understanding about how those problems should be confronted in a wholly different world, like the one we live in today?"

Now, it is theoretically possible that the original understanding will be that a particular constitutional provision settled some specific issue for all time. For example, it is theoretically possible that the original understanding was that the federal government should never regulate some particular kind of activity, no matter what. That is theoretically possible but practically unlikely. The Founders' understanding is overwhelmingly likely to be focused on their times, not on other circumstances that might have been literally unimaginable to them. And if that is so, then there is the difficult, interesting question of, well, okay, how do we translate that original understanding and for our time?

I think all three of these problems—ascertainability, indeterminacy, and translation—are sources of great uncertainty, and the temptation will be, even for the most rigorous interpreters, to put their own judgments in place when confronted by these sources of uncertainty. Let me just give you one example of this, really speaking to the point of ascertainability. It has to do with the extraordinary and brilliant article written by my former colleague, Judge McConnell. You know how people say, "Chief Justice (formerly Justice)," in parentheses? Well, I have got here in my notes "Judge (should be Justice) McConnell." Judge McConnell has an article arguing that, contrary to the conventional wisdom that was entrenched for a generation, *Brown v. Board of Education* was consistent with the original understandings. I am not sure I am completely persuaded by the article, but let us assume it is correct.

Now think about this. In 1953, the Supreme Court asked the lawyers in *Brown v. Board of Education* to brief that precise question, what do the Framers of the Fourteenth Amendment's own original understandings say about school segregation? All the best lawyers in the country, all the best historians in the country, virtually, were engaged in the project of trying to find an originalist justification for the outcome they wanted to produce, the unconstitutionality of segregation. They spectacularly failed. The opinion in *Brown* begins with what can only be read as a concession; there is some language about how we cannot turn the clock back. We know what is going on when they say they cannot turn the clock back. They are saying, "We looked at the original understandings and they're against us." That is how the opinion of *Brown* begins.

Now, if Judge McConnell is right and the original understanding actually does condemn school segregation, that means that the best lawyers in the country, the best historians in the country, the Supreme Court justices and their clerks, with all the resources available to them and with every incentive to discover the original understanding, did not succeed in recovering that original understanding. And what does that tell you? I think it tells you that originalism, as a practical matter, is not a good approach to constitutional interpretation, at least in any difficult case. It tells you it is very, very hard to do originalism right, even when you have every incentive to do it right, and that the chances of getting it wrong—even in something like ideal circumstances, the chances of getting it wrong are very great.

At the root of these difficulties with originalism is the lack of any real explanation, except one, for why we should follow the original understandings. There is no real answer to Thomas Jefferson's famous question, why should we allow the dead to rule the living, except one. The only plausible answer is, if we do not follow the original understandings, then the judges can do what they want. I think that, in the end, this is where originalism gets its appeal.

What I would like to suggest is that, if that is your concern, then you should not be an originalist. You should emphasize precedent instead as the source of constitutional law. That is, because precedent does is much better at limiting judges, at confining them, at keeping at them from reading their view into the law. It is common to say, as Professor Calabresi and Professor Amar have said with great force and great persuasiveness, "Look, judges pick and choose among precedents; judges often overrule precedents. Judges follow precedent uncertainly; sometimes they do, and sometimes they do not."

There is really no theory, people say, of precedent. Well, there is a theory. The theory is not the plurality opinion in *Casey*. The theory is one that was developed over centuries by common lawyers, culminating in Burke's great work. The theory is one of humility, of respecting the limits of human reason, of making judgments about morality and fairness and justice but making them only within the narrow confines left open to you by tradition. That is the theory of precedent. It is not an algorithm. It does not dictate results. It does not preclude you from making judgments about what is right and wrong, and allowing those judgments to influence your view of what the law is, but it limits the scope within which judgments like that can influence legal conclusions. And it seems to me that that is a much more satisfactory way to approach constitutional interpretation.

The evil of school segregation ought to have been part of the reason for the outcome of *Brown v. Board of Education*, emphasis equally on the words *ought* and *part*. If you think abortion is evil, that ought to be part of the reason for calling for the overruling of *Roe v. Wade*; and again, emphasis on the word *part*. What precedent does, I think, is to insist that judges be confined, but to allow them to say that part of the reason I am reaching this result is the moral rightness of the result; precedent leaves it open, or the precedents are in conflict, and one outcome, authorized although not dictated by precedent, seems to me to be much more sensible, or morally imperative, so I will rule that way.

The great virtue of this kind of common law approach, I think, is that it enforces a kind of candor that originalism tends to suppress. The temptation for an originalist is always to say, "Wow, what do you know? The Framers thought the same thing about this issue that I do. Isn't that great?" That is the temptation. And then, the argument comes across as: "This is not me; I do not have to put up my own views for argument; I am just channeling the Framers." I think a precedent-following account is better because it acknowledges that the precedent takes me only this far, leaves me this much flexibility, and the rest really is my judgment. Those are the terms in which I am putting it, and we can argue about the correctness of my judgment; I may be vulnerable on that point. But a precedent-based approach does not suppress the basis of the disagreement, by insisting that it is only about what the original understanding was and that the decision-maker's own views play no role at all.

Just one more thought about part of the appeal of originalism. I am not sure this is right, but I think there is something to it. I think part of the appeal originalism has, paradoxically, is precisely its indeterminacy, precisely its availability as a set of arguments that can be used by people who are unhappy with the *status quo*. This is the protestant use of the text. If you think what has been built up over time is corrupt and you want to sweep it away, one way you can sweep it away is to say: "Let's go back to first principles and get rid of everything that has happened since then."

This is what Justice Black did. He was attacking a different tradition from what today's originalists are attacking, but it was in his view a corrupt tradition. For Justice Black, it was the tradition of the pre-New Deal Court, and I think present-day originalists are often attacking what they see as a different, corrupt judicial tradition. If that is what you are doing, then the text is available as a weapon. But it is available pretty much to anyone, just because it is so flexible and open-ended.

That is my final pitch to conservatives about why originalism should not be their methodology of choice. Increasingly, the constitutional order is going to become something that conservatives like. And when the next generation of liberals comes along and wants to attack what the current generation of conservatives has done, those liberals, I guarantee you, will invoke the Framers. They will say, "No, no, the Framers did not want all this conservative stuff. They wanted our liberal stuff." I think the debate should not be conducted on those terms. I think the debate should be conducted in fully candid terms, in which the judges acknowledge that they are bound by precedent but not entirely, and where, to the extent they are not bound, they say where they stand, and they do not attribute their views to the Framers.

Thank you very much.

Professor Thomas W. Merrill

It is also a pleasure to be here. As David described, the way the panel was set up, I am supposed to be the guy who talks about the conservative case for precedent. I guess since David has already given the conservative case for precedent, the trap has been set for me, as I am now supposed to give the liberal case for precedent. But I am going to forgo stepping into the trap, and will instead give you some more conservative reasons why I think precedent ought to be given greater weight than originalism in constitutional adjudication.

Let me first just say a few preliminary things about the debate. First, I think the debate over originalism versus precedent has been dominated to far too great an extent by particular controversial cases. And of course, I have *Roe v. Wade* here in mind, above all else. It is very distressing for me, as I am sure it is for many of you, that it seems the only issue in the recent confirmation hearings that matters is what a nominee thinks about *Roe v. Wade*. And I think similarly in the precedent versus originalism debate, much of the discussion, even in the law reviews, is animated by what we think about *Roe v. Wade*. And so, if you think *Roe v. Wade* was an illegitimate usurpation of power by the judiciary, then you want to overrule that precedent, and then it somehow follows that you think that all of constitutional law should be based on something besides precedent. If you like *Roe v. Wade*, on the other hand, then you think we have got to stand fast and support our candidate, our guy here, *Roe v. Wade*, and so precedent must be a good thing. I think this is an extraordinarily myopic way to think about this problem.

The people who regard themselves as conservatives, people who embrace some of the values that Professor Strauss was talking about—respect for the rule of law, respect for stability and predictability in the law, respect for judicial restraint, and the desire that social policy decisions be made by the elected representatives of the people rather than by the judges—the people that embrace those values ought not to have their views on precedent versus originalism driven by one case.

A second point I would make is that I do not think we can resolve the debate by adopting the conceptual apparatus of one school or the other, and then point out that the rival approach has no place within the school of thought we adopt. To a large extent, originalism and precedent are parallel universes that do not intersect. The case for originalism starts from legal positivism, with the idea that only enacted law is the law of the land. When there is an ambiguity in the law, we have to seek out what the meaning of the lawgiver was. And so, naturally that leads to looking at originalism as the source for interpreting the law. And then we ask, "Does originalism say that precedent can trump the enacted law?" As Steve Calabresi frames the question, the answer, of course, is, "No, it does not." So, if we start from originalist premises, we do not have much room for precedent or *stare decisis*.

Conversely, however, if you start from the universe of precedent, that universe starts from the Holmesian observation that what the law is, ultimately, is the judgment of the courts. And if you start from that perspective, you say, "Well, what predicts the judgments of courts is the precedents of the courts, and therefore precedent is law." And therefore if want to know whether or not precedent following is permissible, we find the answer by looking to precedent. And guess what we find? Yes, judges say we ought to follow precedent. And so, precedent it is. That universe does not leave much space for the Constitution and enacted law. And so, we have these two universes, and I do not think you can reason from the premises of the one to oust the other.

The reality is that every justice, at least since the days of the Marshall Court, has relied to some extent on both originalist reasoning and precedent. Steve Calabresi is absolutely correct that when moments of high drama and crisis occur, the justices tend to revert to the constitutional text and to the statements of the Framers. On the other hand, I would point out that more careful studies of the justices have indicated that approximately eighty percent or more of the authorities that they cite in their constitutional law opinions are precedents of the Supreme Court. The most careful study was done looking at the opinions of Rehnquist and Brennan, who were the prototypical ideological outliers at the time the study was done. Presumably, centrist judges rely on precedent to an even greater extent. Even Scalia and Thomas, of course, routinely rely on precedent. So, to some extent, precedent also has to be considered in the equation.

The last preliminary point I would make is that the ultimate question for conservatives or people who value rule of law is not so much the technique or the theory that a judge applies, but the judicial attitude that goes along with it. I think we want our judges to try to apply the law in good faith, seeking the best answer that the law provides, rather than judges who try to advance their personal policy preferences by manipulating legal authorities to reach those ends. It is very hard to legislate this attitude. We are all familiar with it as lawyers because, as lawyers, sometimes we are asked by clients to tell them what the law most likely is on some point, so they can correct their behavior or guide their behavior accordingly. And when you get this kind of request for fair and impartial advice, you adopt one approach to analyzing legal authorities. And then another time, we are asked to write a brief defending a client in court. In this situation, we are in the position of being an advocate, and we adopt a very different mode of looking at legal authorities. I think what we really want is for judges to adopt the first mode in deciding cases, not the second mode. It is very hard to screen that out or prescribe that attitude by using any particular technique of decision-making.

Having said that, I think that technique does matter at the margins, and that the key issue here in terms of precedent versus originalism is whether the courts adopt a strong theory of precedent in constitutional law cases—they already have one in cases of statutory interpretation— or whether they should adopt a weak theory. I agree completely with Steve Calabresi and Akhil Amar that the Supreme Court is speaking with a forked tongue here, that they say they have a strong theory of precedent in constitutional law—at least since *Casey*—when, in fact, they have a weak theory of precedent. I think, for a number of reasons, a strong theory of precedent would be better. David Strauss has given a number of reasons, which I think are excellent. Let me just briefly mention four others, and then I will sit down.

First, I think the norms, the legal norms that we apply in resolving disputed questions of law are much thicker if we look at the universe of precedent than if we look at originalist materials. Take a question like whether or not Congress could ban advertisements for pharmaceutical drugs in newspapers and magazines. If you had to answer that using originalist materials, who knows what the answer would be? It would be extremely indeterminate. There is virtually nothing in the originalist materials that speaks to that. If you had to answer it by looking at Supreme Court case law, there is still some room for argument, but the norms are much thicker and the likelihood of the answer being one that people could reach consensus on, much greater.

Another point is accessibility. The precedents of the Supreme Court are published in the U.S. Reports and similar volumes. They are online; they have been indexed; they are easily searchable; every judge in the country can readily get her or his hands on them. The materials that bear on original understanding are vast, are frequently inaccessible, and in some cases are only now being discovered. People find new documents all the time that might bear on original understanding. So, it is much harder for us to get our hands on that material.

Lastly, I think—and I think David Strauss alluded to this to some extent—the style of reasoning from precedent is much more congenial with the skill set of the typical American judge or justice, than is reasoning from originalist materials. Now, this is a contingent fact. It could change, if we had different judges or if we taught them differently in law schools. But the reality is that people are much more comfortable dealing with precedent, and I think that produces greater restraint and predictability than there would be using originalist materials.

The last point I would make is really, again, a kind of contingent, pragmatic, political point, which is that I think many of us would like very much to see a very different process by which our judges and justices are picked in this country. I think we like to see a process by which people are chosen to be judges because of their legal knowledge and their legal skills and their judicial temperament, not because of the ideology and the particular political beliefs that they hold. And ask yourself, which style of constitutional reasoning over time, at least in our time, is more likely to push us to a system in which we pick people based on their competence and their legal abilities, and which is more likely to produce tempestuous proceedings in which we pick people based on ideology?

I think if the Court were to commit itself to a strong theory of precedent in constitutional law, that would lock in some decisions the conservatives do not like. It would also lock in some decisions that they do like. But I think its greatest impact would be that it would make the Court a less attractive forum for achieving social policy through litigation, and that the interest groups that are trying to get their various positions advanced through the courts would get bored and decide that this is not really the best hole in which to go fishing. They would decide that maybe they should just try to get some laws passed by the legislatures of this country or to get their policy preferences adopted by amending the Constitution.

And so, a judiciary that stood firm with a strong theory of precedent I think would re-channel our nation back toward democratic institutions, away from using the judiciary to make social policy. I, for one, would rather live in that world than the one we apparently live in today, and so I would endorse a strong theory of precedent on that basis alone.

Thank you.

Justice Stephen J. Markman

Descending for a moment from the rarefied atmosphere of the United States Supreme Court, I would like to offer several perspectives on the topic at hand from my vantage point as a Justice of the Michigan Supreme Court. What I hope may make these perspectives of some interest at this conference is that a majority of the Michigan Supreme Court, four of its seven justices, are self-described

Federalists and indeed are quite passionately committed to the judicial values that are often identified with this Society, in particular a commitment to giving faithful meaning to the words of the law. It is a court on which fine jurisprudential matters, such as, for example, the existence of an 'absurd results' rule, the significance of legislative acquiescence as an interpretative tool, and uses and abuses of legislative history are routinely, and I hope thoughtfully, addressed in our conferences and in our opinions.

What in my experience most differentiates the Michigan Supreme Court during the past six years from other state courts, including those routinely described as "conservative" or "judicially restrained" or "strict constructionist," has been the Michigan Supreme Court's treatment of precedent. Although respectful of precedent, as any judicial body must be, in the interests of stability and continuity of the law, the court has also been straightforward in its view that regard for precedent must be balanced with a commitment to interpreting the words of the law in accordance with their meaning. That is, what most distinguishes the Michigan Supreme Court from other such courts has been its unwillingness to serve as a mere foil for those who have previously served on the court who, like Justice Douglas, preferred to "make precedent, rather than to follow precedent." We have been unwilling to allow this ratchet process to operate in Michigan by which periods of punctuated equilibrium periodically occur where the law lurches in the direction favored by Justice Douglas and his philosophical allies, in which new precedents are adopted that bear little relationship to the language of the law, then to be followed by interregnum periods of conservative judicial rule in which these new precedents are affirmed and institutionalized. Rather, the Michigan Supreme Court has been committed to resisting the ratification of recent precedents that are clearly incompatible with the language of the law and the constitution of Michigan. The court's dominant premise has been on 'getting the law right,' moving toward the most accurate interpretations of the law, rather than acquiescing in decisions that essentially reflected little more than the personal preferences of predecessor justices.

The default position of the court in addressing questions of constitutional and statutory interpretation has been that, in exercising the "judicial power" of our state, it is our responsibility to say what the law "is," not what it "ought" to be. This responsibility derives from *Marbury v. Madison*, from the Preambles to the United States and Michigan constitutions that direct us that it is "this" constitution to which "we the people" have assented, from our "oath of office" in support of "this" constitution, and from the inferences drawn from Article V, the amending provision of the Constitution. This responsibility also derives, of course, from our sense of constitutionalism—that to exceed this authority is necessarily to trespass upon the authority of the executive and legislative branches of government. Moreover, there is, in our judgment, no alternative rule of interpretation that both precedes a decision and that better communicates that such a decision is more than a function of a judge's own personal preferences.

Also underlying this position is the sense that a truer long-term stability and continuity in the law—the very rationales for respecting precedent—are achieved when the law means what it says rather than merely what Justice Doe imagined it to say fifteen years ago. When "up" means up, not "down." When "public use" means "public use," not "public purpose." When the words of the law increasingly achieve equilibrium through convergence between the interpretations of the law and the actual language of that law.

Moreover, as the meaning of the law increasingly tracks what the lawmaker has actually written, as the "judicial power" is increasingly exercised to elevate the product of the lawmaker rather than that of predecessor judges, it seems to me that the law increasingly becomes more accessible to "we the people," and less exclusively the domain of lawyers and judges. When, to use a mundane illustration from Michigan law, the law requires that a person must file a certain type of lien within "thirty days" and "thirty days" means thirty days, that law remains relatively accessible to ordinary citizens. They can read the law and more or less understand their rights and responsibilities under this law. When, on the other hand, "thirty days" means "thirty-one days" if there has been an intervening holiday, "thirty-two days" if your car broke down on your way to the registration office, "thirty-three days" if you have been in the hospital, and "thirty-four days" if you are a particularly sympathetic character, then the only way to understand that law and its various unwritten exceptions is to consult an attorney. To read the law consistent with its language rather than with its judicial gloss is not to be harsh or crabbed or Dickensian, but is to give the people at least a fighting chance to comprehend the public rules by which they are governed.

Other benefits have arisen in Michigan from a jurisprudence that elevates faithfulness to the law over reflexive adherence to precedent. I have heard from legislators in my state, for example, that the approach of this court has caused them to be more precise in their draftsmanship, recognizing that this court is not going to bail them out from poor decisions and that they are responsible for their work product. I have heard from litigators that, although they do not necessarily agree with the court's philosophy, they understand that they must articulate arguments drawn from text, not only in arguments before my court, but also necessarily in arguments before the lower courts of our state. I have heard from academics that the court's decisions, and the extensive debate within these decisions, have produced energetic discussion in their classes and have afforded students a perspective on the judicial role to which, to say the least, they have not routinely been exposed. And I and my colleagues have delivered thousands of speeches around Michigan, describing the ongoing judicial debate in our country and exposing the people of Michigan to judicial campaigns for the first time based on something other than a pleasant family portrait or an attractive ballot surname.

While restoring discipline to the law of a state that had become a patchwork of decisions with no discernible consistency has had some dislocations—dislocations more properly attributable to the court that said twenty years ago that "up" means "down" than to the court today that says no, "up" means "up"—the benefits for the rule of law have been substantial and both the people of our State, as well as many in the media, have given support to the majority Justices in the face of a remarkably explicit public debate and a sometimes very hostile and well-funded opposition.

But getting the law "right" is only our "default" position. For, just as it seems to me the liberal judicial temptation is to do justice, rather than justice under law, the conservative judicial temptation, one that occasionally needs to be resisted, is to perfectly define that law. I say this not to denigrate this objective, since indeed it is one to which I myself subscribe. But my court, properly I believe, has recognized that there are considerations that sometimes argue in favor of adherence to precedent, even when that precedent is wrong. For example, the longstanding nature of some precedents and their effective institutionalization within the law; and the existence of *bona fide* reliance interests such as where one group of individuals has been encouraged by a precedent to purchase insurance against some hazard and another group of individuals has not.

I would note incidentally that respect for precedent is more indispensable in the realm of the common law where there is no definitive external standard, *i.e.* the text of the law, available to guide the interpretation of the law, but I will leave that discussion for another day.

Professor Calabresi raises legitimate concerns that the mere calculation by which these and other factors are taken into consideration itself constitutes an essentially discretionary exercise of the judicial power, appearing in some ways to resemble the kind of balancing more properly a part of the legislative process. I take this concern seriously and do not have a fully satisfying answer. I can only state uncertainly that in attempting to responsibly restore the law and the courts to their proper realm, these cannot be a force for turbulence or turmoil. While the law should never move further from the design of the lawmaker, and the court should never stray further from its assigned role, prudence and judgment must also be exercised. I must acknowledge that I am often torn by the sense that the more generations of judges that have concurred in an interpretation, the more modest I should be in correcting those interpretations, and the more cognizance that I should give to an assumption of legislative acquiescence. As Justice Frankfurter once said, respect for precedents sometimes "reveal

the wisdom of a court as an institution transcending the moment."
Perhaps it is my conservative impulses sometimes coming to the fore.
I very much look forward to further discussion on these matters.

Perhaps, to some members of the Michigan bar, the Michigan
Supreme Court has only received its just deserts. But it has been this
court's understanding of precedent that, more than anything else
probably, has been at the heart of several multi-million dollar campaigns directed at the four justices in the majority, including one campaign in which three of us were joined together on the ballot and over
ten million dollars was spent to defeat us. We have been the subject
of academic and popular studies focused upon our alleged lack of
regard for the rule of law. We have been characterized as "judicial
activists" and "renegades." We have been subject to invective from
our dissenting colleagues. And, of course, we have been accused of
being corrupt, partisan and beholden to the special interests. Most
dastardly, we have even been accused of being members of a conspir-
atorial legal cabal known to be meeting this weekend in Washington.

Yet, I believe if any one of you were to carefully read our decisions, you would, I hope, find an intellectually vigorous court, an
honest and conscientious tribunal, an even-handed and impartial
court, struggling on an everyday basis to accord reasonable meaning
to the law—whether that law be the Constitution of Michigan or of
the United States, the enactments of the people's representatives in our
legislature, the ordinances of Kalamazoo or Flint, or the contracts and
deeds of our citizens. We are attempting responsibly to bring to bear
in our decision-making in two hundred and fifty cases every month
the constitutional values that this Society has done so much to rein-
vigorate by conferences and panels such as this one—the constitutional values that have given our nation the freest, the most
prosperous, and the most stable democracy in the history of the
world.

While there are many difficult issues that must be confronted by
a court committed to a federalist jurisprudence, any judicial body that
hopes to contribute seriously toward the restoration of a legal culture
that is in accord with traditional constitutional values must first con-

front the issue that is the focus of this panel—how to properly balance respect for text and precedent. I do not suspect that the Michigan Supreme Court has achieved a perfect equilibrium in this regard, but I think that it has usefully engaged itself in this critical debate.

Thank you very much.

Discussion
Moderated by Steven G. Calabresi

PROFESSOR CALABRESI: I think I would like to now take questions, if possible, because that will give everyone a chance to bring out some of the ideas that you all have been thinking about. And I am sure some of the panelists, in the process of answering questions, will want to respond to things that other panelists have said. So, let me start over at that microphone.

AUDIENCE PARTICIPANT: Does a strong theory of precedent lead to a very complicated and difficult to understand body of case law with lots of multi-factored tests and is not this a reason to prefer textualism?

PROFESSOR CALABRESI: David Strauss or Tom Merrill?

PROFESSOR MERRILL: That is a very interesting and excellent point, I think. The common law has a certain tendency in this direction, I suppose, but not so much as constitutional law. I agree with your perception that the sort of common law-based constitutional law that we have in the First Amendment area, for example, or in, say, the Eleventh Amendment area, increasingly becomes more and more arcane and complicated. There are multi-factored tests, exceptions to the tests, balancing here, and so forth. And only the experts can really figure out what is going on. My only response to that is that, you know, this goes back to Steve Calabresi's point about the difficulty of amending the Constitution. This is the system within which we have to live. I am not sure that admixing precedent with frequent overrulings, based on presumed originalist understandings, would produce a less complicated system. I think it might even be more chaotic and hard to parse than a precedent-based system would be.

PROFESSOR CALABRESI: Randy Barnett.

RANDY BARNETT: Thanks, Steve. I used to think that the only good constitution was a dead constitution until I heard Ed Meese say that a living Constitution is one that still binds the Court, one the Court still has to adhere to. I say that in opening because I want to align myself with Steve Calabresi and Akhil Amar before I put my question to Tom Merrill and David Strauss.

If it turns out that the best theory or the best approach to original meaning acknowledges that original meaning, in fact as David Strauss has pointed out, is oftentimes underdeterminate—and underdeterminate is not the same thing as wholly indeterminate; underdeterminate means that it defines a range of possible meanings within which choice has to be made when you are dealing with new circumstances; but it also defines a range of possible interpretations that are outside the frame and are to be excluded . . . .

Once you understand that original meaning in many, many controversial cases is underdeterminate, which means a good deal of choice has to be made, why is there not, then, a very strong role for the kind of precedent that Tom Merrill and David Strauss are talking about? The only disagreement, then, between those who favor precedent—and I see Akhil nodding because this really does reflect a lot of what he thinks—then at that point, what is really separating people who are the precedentialists from the originalists is what to do when a particular case clearly falls outside that range of underdeterminate meaning. What should we do if a precedent is clearly contrary to the original meaning of the text? And in that case, it is really the text that should be binding, and not precedent. Why would that not capture ninety percent of the benefit that Professor Merrill and Professor Strauss see as coming from adherence to precedent, while still preserving a valuable living Constitution that is binding on judges?

PROFESSOR STRAUSS: I guess the question is to me. Of course, you know, a more complete statement of the way I would envision constitutional interpretation would have originalism playing a major role, because when the issues are first presented to the court there are no precedents to look to. You look to the text and you have to look to the original understanding.

The same thing is true when one is interpreting a statute. The first time a statute comes before the court, the court has to look at the text of the statute and what it understands the meaning of the statute to be, and decide how to interpret it. And then it is only later in time when judicial interpretations, and subtle expectations of a society and government, coalesce that a kind of strong theory of precedent begins to kick in, and you do not go back and revisit things that are settled by reference to discoveries of new things in the original understanding.

So, I really do not agree with your characterization. I guess my perception would be that most of the disputes that deeply divide society in the constitutional realm have to do with issues that are under-determined, as you would say, by the Constitution. We have to decide how to resolve those issues—whether to resolve them by looking to prior precedent or to some other theory of subtle expectations, or whether to resolve them by having each generation of judges go back and look at the text, stare hard at it, and look at the skimpy materials that we know about original meaning, and make up its mind anew. With respect to those sorts of issues, I am just making a pragmatic, Burkean case that, for all the reasons I discussed in my talk, the approach of following precedent would be better.

AUDIENCE PARTICIPANT: Does your answer depend on whether the original decision was itself originalist textualist, or whether the original decision, that is the precedent, disregarded originalism and textualism? Would your answer depend on that?

PROFESSOR STRAUSS: It might.

PROFESSOR CALABRESI: I just want to comment on a few things that Tom Merrill said. Tom has argued that precedent might be more constraining than the constitutional text because it is, he says, thicker than originalism. I have two responses to him on that point. First, if there were more originalist judges on the Supreme Court, there would be more originalist scholarship, and much more originalism in briefs, and that would in turn work its way into Supreme Court opinions, and would have an impact. So, I think that to some extent, the reason originalism seems not to be as thick as arguments from case law and precedents is because the Supreme Court has not paid as much attention to originalist arguments until very recently. Now that there are two justices, Scalia and Thomas, who are originalists, the Court is paying a lot more attention to original sources than it was in the 1970s or the early 1980s. And so, now there is actually a lot more material out there that is readily available to practitioners, and originalism is actually becoming thicker, as it were.

Second, I guess it could be argued that precedent is bulkier than originalism simply because there is more of it. There are more than five hundred volumes of the U.S. reports, whereas the text of the Constitution is obviously relatively spare. One problem with that is the fact that there are so many precedents means that one can find precedents on either side of most issues. So that, I think, suggests that precedent, like legislative history, may be very bulky but it may not be very constraining on the discretion of a judge, because you can find precedent on both sides of whatever proposition you're arguing for.

PROFESSOR AMAR: And Steve, just a couple of riffs on what you just said. Not only would a more sustained commitment to originalism impact lawyering and maybe scholarship, but it might feed back into the appointments process itself. And there would be a particular premium placed on those candidates who actually may have studied the Constitution, rather than just those who, for example, have followed precedent, as lower court judges who, of course, are mainly obliged to follow precedent. At the risk of embarrassing again, our friend Michael O'Connell—you see, he is not just a judge but, he is also an originalist scholar, and that is one of the reasons I agree with David Strauss about hoping a Supreme Court appointment is in his future—my hopes for the future would be for a court where we had someone like Justice Black alongside someone like Justice Scalia: both a liberal and conservative originalist to really thicken the conversation about originalism on the Court, in the academy, in the briefs, and in the nomination and confirmation process.

PROFESSOR CALABRESI: That would be a great thing. Over here.

AUDIENCE PARTICIPANT: Professor Strauss mentioned Jefferson's question, why should the dead rule over the living, and to me, the answer to that has always been pretty obvious. It is because the dead said so. They are the ones who have promulgated a Constitution that does not have a sunset clause, that purports to be the supreme law of the land, and that requires a supermajority for amendment. And it is sort of up to the living to say otherwise, if they disagree, either by amending the Constitution, or by trashing it and establishing a new regime.

But focusing specifically on the role of judges, does the judge's fidelity not have to be to the dead? If the judge is required to cast his lot between the living and the dead, does the judge not have to choose the dead? Is the judge empowered not because he is a creature of the dead? Does he not derive his authority from the dead? Does he not owe his position to the dead? Does he not at least cloak what he does in supposed interpretations of what the dead have done? Is the judge who casts his lot with the living not betraying his role?

PROFESSOR STRAUSS: Well, on the first question, is the answer to Jefferson's question not obvious? I think your answer is circular, right? You say we have to comply with the will of the dead because the dead said so, which simply raises again the question of why we should comply with the will of the dead.

JUSTICE MARKMAN: The preamble to our Constitution specifies that it is designed to "secure the blessings of liberty to ourselves and our posterity." In that sense, it is explicitly intended to govern generations that are yet unborn, and to govern them by the rules of those who are already dead. By not exercising their rights under Article V to amend the Constitution, I believe that each generation effectively reaffirms that they continue to be a part of "we the people" in whose name our Constitution has been proposed and ratified.

As a conservative, I have regard for the common law, for prescriptive law, for tradition, for the continuity of the law, for precedent. Virtually all of the precedents that have been reversed by the Michigan

Supreme Court over the past seven years, during which it has had a conservative majority, are of relatively recent vintage, and reflect an understanding of the judicial role that is also of relatively recent vintage. More often than not, our reversals have restored longstanding precedents that were abruptly overturned by recent generations of judges, sometimes without acknowledgment that this was even being done.

To the extent that, on rare occasions, I have questioned older precedents, I have given great weight to the fact that these decisions have been sustained by multiple generations of judges, that they may have been institutionalized within our legal system, and that reliance interests may have grown around such decisions. I have tended in these cases—and Professor Calabresi raises thoughtful objections to doing this—to give greater weight to the accumulated wisdom reflected in these decisions—to the combined judgments of dead jurists—than to my own perspectives that some of these cases may have been decided imperfectly.

PROFESSOR AMAR: And when we think about which past to look at, let us imagine actually—let me move the question away from what we are bound to do because I as a scholar, you see, have not taken an oath of office to do one thing or the other, to follow the opinions of the justices or the meaning of the Constitution. I can choose. I can learn a lot from the past. I think I have actually learned more from the text of the Constitution than I have from the cases. I read them both, and a lot of times I do not get that much wisdom, frankly, from some of the case law. I think about recent cases, and I think, you know, those are not even my "A" students, the clerks, who were writing these things in June, in a very hurried way. And I actually do not quite have that same unsettled feeling when I read the Constitution.

So, even if judges were not bound by the text of the Constitution, I actually do not think there is a good excuse for their not looking at the original meaning just because they do not have the skill set required to be good originalists. But, again, this builds on Steve Calabresi's point about how originalism could feed back into the larger legal culture. I want law students to learn how to study the original meaning of the constitutional text. I want law professors, especially people who teach constitutional law, to actually study the Constitution, alongside the cases, even if they are completely free to disregard the Constitution, because they could learn a lot from it. There are a lot more people that were involved in defining moments, not just in the history of this country but the history of this world—the Founding, the Reconstruction, the Progressive Era—hundreds of thousands of ordinary people, and they have to actually agree on the text for it to become our supreme law. Having the text as a common point for all Americans tends to emphasize the text and structure more than history, actually, as a common basis for coming together in accessibility.

And there are all sorts of things to which case law does not speak, even though sometimes it might be thicker than the text. Sometimes the case law is a lot thinner on issues that are not justiciable but that are hugely important constitutional issues that Presidents have to think about, that Senators have been thinking about during the appointment process, or during an impeachment process.

So, even if we were not bound by the text of the Constitution, even if we were just looking to the past for wisdom, there is a lot of wisdom to be drawn and deduced from the text of the Constitution itself, above and beyond the case law.

PROFESSOR CALABRESI: I just wanted to say something quickly about being bound by the dead hand of the past, and that is to point out that with the passing of Chief Justice Rehnquist, all nine justices who sat on the Supreme Court that decided *Roe v. Wade* have now passed away. So, if one is worried about being bound by the dead hand of the past, one could as validly ask that about being bound by *Roe* as to ask it about being bound by the Framers.

Now, it does seem to me that in situations where there is a deep societal acquiescence in precedent that such precedents should not be cast aside. I do not believe, as does Gary Lawson or Michael Paulsen, that it is actually unconstitutional for the Supreme Court to follow precedent. I think it is constitutionally permissible for the Court to follow precedents that the whole of American society has long since accepted, and I do think there are areas of constitutional law like the First Amendment where you can not make sense out of the law without allowing for the courts to follow precedent.

It seems to me you have to distinguish between situations where, as Andrew Jackson said, acquiescence in practice and meaning is well-settled among all of the people of the United States. There has to be a three-branch consensus on a constitutional issue, and it cannot be the case that the issue in question has been hotly debated in recent times. For those following that principle, I would certainly say that Supreme Court decisions upholding the constitutionality of paper money and many of the New Deal-era statutes should be respected as a matter of precedent. I would not say that about *Roe v. Wade*, which was a decision that was controversial from the day it was handed down to the present.

JUSTICE MARKMAN: I would like to make one additional comment concerning the difficulties of textualism. I recognize that there are often difficulties in interpreting, and giving meaning to, the written law, especially to the Constitution. The interpretative process is not a mechanical process, and reasonable people can disagree on what is the most reasonable meaning of the law. However, in my experience, there are too many judges who, when the law is difficult, are too quickly inclined to declare it "ambiguous," and thereby short-circuit the traditional interpretative process. When a law has alternative possible meanings, these judges feel that they have *carte blanche* to do what they will with a statute. The better approach, I believe, is to use every available interpretative tool—including looking to dictionary definitions, looking to the context of words and provisions, parsing punctuation and grammar and syntax, assessing the structure and organization of a law, understanding a statute's purpose as defined by its language, considering default rules as set forth in various maxims of law, and ascertaining the most reasonable, although imperfect, interpretation of the law. It is the obligation of the responsible judge to struggle through the interpretative process as conscientiously as he can, in order to adduce the best meaning of the law, and not to summarily rely upon the easy conclusion that a law is "ambiguous." There are also default positions that assist in the decision-making process when a law cannot be definitively given meaning. The side carrying the burden of proof, the party seeking to alter the *status quo*, for example, probably loses.

PROFESSOR CALABRESI: Over here.

AUDIENCE PARTICIPANT: Did Judge Randolph's remarks last night suggest perhaps a way of limiting certain types of precedent? He indicated, in discussing Judge Friendly's unpublished abortion case, that Friendly basically argued that *Roe,* or what became *Roe,* was totally illogical in the extension of *Griswold*, and indeed inconsistent with the reasoning of *Griswold*. So, could one say that, if there is a precedent which is purportedly based on earlier precedent, but in truth, upon objective analysis, is entirely wrong, if it incorrectly cites or applies an earlier precedent?

And, second, and more generally, is there a theory of weaker precedent? Weaker precedent is what you have when there is a precedent that has overruled a prior precedent, which in turn has overruled an earlier precedent. In some sense, is there a theory of the stability of certain precedents? Do precedents acquire a greater weight of authority precisely because they have, over a longer period of time, enjoyed a certain degree of approval?

PROFESSOR MERRILL: Your question raises the issue of whether there are so-called super-duper precedents which we have heard so much about recently. I am skeptical about this, myself. I am skeptical about whether because a certain controversial precedent has been challenged and reaffirmed on multiple occasions, that somehow it takes on greater and greater force and weight in our legal system. I think that kind of conception of things falls into the fallacy of thinking of the Supreme Court as a sort of House of Lords, of nine legislators who render these decisions that are entitled to respect based on the authority of the Court itself, rather than the fact that the Court is interpreting the Constitution.

I do think there is such a thing as precedent which is entitled to extraordinary weight, but they would be precedents that have been incorporated into the settled expectations of the polity, and that are therefore sort of woven into the fabric of society in a way that would make it unthinkable to undo them.

The development of the administrative state in this country, which started in the late nineteenth century and accelerated during the New Deal, I think is an excellent example of this. To read the original Constitution as not permitting administrative agencies, say, to engage in legislative rulemaking, which I think would be a plausible original meaning of the document, would be so massively disruptive in our society that I do not think any justice, however gung ho on originalism, is likely to embrace that opinion. So, that would be what I would regard as a sort of highly entrenched precedent that ought not to be revisited. Something like the sequence that Steve Calabresi described, where *Maryland v. Wirtz* has been overruled by a *National League of Cities*, which has been overruled by *Garcia*, which is then subvertly overruled by *Ashcroft v. Gregory*, or whatever—that, I think, is probably entitled to less weight as precedent because the line of cases reflects an inherent instability in the law, which is one of the factors cited as justifying overruling, even under a strong theory of precedent.

PROFESSOR STRAUSS: I agree with Tom Merrill, really, on all points. I think that follows directly from the premises of a system of precedent, that what you do not want to put yourself in the position of is questioning judgments that many thoughtful people have made over a long period of time. And, if those judgments are at variance, you should be more comfortable questioning it.

You know, when Tom Merrill originally said that he thought argument about *Roe v. Wade* had distorted this debate, I was not sure that that was true. But now, listening to these questions I am beginning to think that Tom is right. If you envision the case for precedent as being the case for not overruling *Roe v. Wade*, then I think you misunderstand what the case for precedent is all about. As far as I am concerned, the debate about originalism versus precedent is not a hidden debate about whether to overrule *Roe v. Wade*. I think, as precedents go, *Roe v. Wade* is pretty fragile. It has not settled into the culture.

People have not accepted it. A lot of people have strong objections to it. It continues to be challenged.

Compare *Roe* to, for example, the best known Warren court precedents. Many of those Warren Court decisions were intensely controversial at the time. But today they have settled deeply into the culture. No one seriously challenges the "one person, one vote" decisions, which were extremely questionable, to say the least, on originalist premises. I think the school prayer decisions have more or less settled into the culture. *Miranda* has also apparently settled into the culture. *Brown*, of course, quintessentially has settled into the culture. Those are the instances of possible contrary-to-original-intent decisions, where an account of precedent says we should not go around upsetting the apple cart. Or the claim, the position that states cannot establish churches is also, as Justice Thomas has said, extremely vulnerable on originalist grounds. Akhil Amar has written brilliantly on this subject as well. But that, too, I think, is a line of precedent which is now deeply settled. Those are the kinds of decisions that we should be focusing on in this debate, because they are questionable, or often just clearly wrong, on originalist grounds, but well-settled as precedents. Those cases present the question of whether originalism or precedent is the better approach to constitutional interpretation.

You know, we can have a debate about *Roe v. Wade*. You can invite me back to talk about *Roe v. Wade* some other time. That is not what this debate ought to be about.

PROFESSOR CALABRESI: Let me just try to follow up on that. Tom Merrill said earlier in his remarks that the premise of the pro-precedent camp is that the law is the judgment of courts, and so one should look at the judgment of courts in order to figure out what the law is. And I think for me, in thinking about constitutional law, I am very influenced by departmentalism, by the idea that constitutional interpretation takes place in Congress and in the executive branch, as well is in the courts. And all three branches of the federal government are to some extent constitutional interpreters. And so, it seems to me that, as to constitutional law, the law is not simply the judgment of the courts or of the Supreme Court, even a couple of supreme courts.

It rather is reflected by situations where there is a longstanding three-branch consensus about what constitutional law is. And, as to many questions, there is such a three-branch consensus. Thus, I certainly agree with David Strauss that there is a broad consensus that many of the Warren Court decisions, which were originally controversial, are completely accepted now, and are essentially not challengeable. The incorporation decisions certainly fall in that category. Likewise, the constitutionality of paper money has been in that category for more than a century. Many New Deal statutes and programs do, as well, although I continue to question *Wickard v. Filburn*.

I do think we should recognize that the Court does not have the sole authority to speak for the Constitution and enforce it, but that the Court shares that power with the other two branches of the national government. We should recognize that there has to be a really broad-based consensus with the other branches that a decision is right to help separate out the situations where precedent can be overruled and where it cannot be.

PROFESSOR AMAR: And I just cannot resist saying one sentence or two about incorporation, because I think it is more of a problem for David Strauss than he realizes. David can explain now why incorporation is settled law today. Everyone on the current Supreme Court accepts it. But can David account for why incorporation was done in the first place, given that it disregarded a lot of pre-existing precedents? Not merely one or two pre-existing precedents, but a whole lot of them. And incorporation was accomplished by Justice Hugo Black on largely originalist grounds. Justice Black laid the foundation for this even before Justices Brennan and Marshall and Warren were on the Supreme Court. Incorporation ultimately happens on Brennan's watch, but, basically, it happens because Hugo Black was arguing for it on originalist grounds. David Strauss is living in the house that Justice Black built, but if he were around in the 1940s, would he say to Black, "Gee, you should not be doing this because it's actually disrupting and disregarding existing precedents and practices?" This point is connected to the ratchet issue that Justice Markman raised.

PROFESSOR CALABRESI: Over here.

AUDIENCE PARTICIPANT: Professor Amar used the word "reasonable" in the Fourth Amendment as an example of a situation where the Constitution contains terms that require more precise definition and rules to be able to effectively implement it. I would be interested in the panel's views on the respective roles of the judiciary, both federal and state, versus the legislative branch, in coming up with those rules. And where the legislative branch may have stepped in first and attempted to come up with those definitions and rules, should that be subject to the same deference, for those of you who believe that the Court should follow precedent, as the instances where the Court itself may have attempted to first formulate those definitions and rules?

PROFESSOR AMAR: If I could just jump in, I am with Steve Calabresi in thinking that the Constitution is addressed to all three branches of the government. And toward the end of an article that I wrote called "Fourth Amendment, First Principles," I tried to map out regimes of legislative reasonableness, of judicial reasonableness, of administrative and executive reasonableness, and even jury-based reasonableness, and tried to identify which branches of government I thought would be particularly good at dealing with which aspects of constitutional reasonableness, of which there are many. And I do not think it is only about judges, at all. I think there is space for many other constitutional actors to help give meaning to a richly textured term like constitutional reasonableness.

PROFESSOR STRAUSS: Let me just say quickly, I think the correct theory of precedent from a Burkean perspective is a departmentalist one, in the sense that, in deciding whether something has been determined as a matter of precedent, we should look at the opinion of all three branches of the government. A precedent can become settled because of the non-judicial branches of the federal government, and indeed of state governments, and even the people acting in a nongovernmental capacity. For example, in deciding cases about the constitutionality of discrimination on the basis of sex, the courts are entitled to, and should, look at how the status of women has changed in society. I think a genuine Burkean would not necessarily rule out any of those sources, and would not say that the Supreme Court is the only body that counts.

PROFESSOR CALABRESI: That raises a question, maybe, which I can ask Tom Merrill. I should mention by way of background that Tom and I were colleagues for twelve years and we have been arguing about this topic and discussing it for the entirety of that time. I guess the question would be, in a situation like *Casey*, where the Solicitor General's office, where both Tom and David once worked, shows up in the Supreme Court representing the president and arguing for overruling—in that type of situation, should the Court be particularly bound to decide a case according to the original meaning, rather than giving weight to reliance interests? After all, the judgment about reliance interests, as Michael Paulsen has pointed out, is very much a policy judgment. It is a judgment that the harm being done by a precedent, and the wrongness of it, are outweighed by the fact that it has been around for a long time. If the political branches as represented by the president and the S.G. say that reliance interests should not get weight here, should not the Court presumptively in those situations almost be forced to decide according to the original meaning, rather than falling back on precedent?

PROFESSOR MERRILL: I would not go quite that far, but I do agree with you that when the executive branch repeatedly challenges the Court to overrule a decision interpreting the Constitution, this is not an occasion for the Court to say this is a super-duper precedent and you know, shame on you, Mr. Solicitor General, for even questioning the wisdom of one of our decisions—which is sort of the reaction the Court had initially to this. I think it is an occasion to say that this is a precedent which is not settled into the fabric of the law, which is one which is—continues to be deeply controversial, and that is one criterion under a strong theory of precedent that would warrant consideration.

PROFESSOR CALABRESI: I agree with that. Over there.

AUDIENCE PARTICIPANT: Yes. I guess I am the exception that proves David Strauss's rule that the one-person, one-vote principle is settled. But my question is for Justice Markman. Would a Supreme

Court that seems to factor in reliance interests, say the recent idea of evolving standards of decency, especially—would such a Court have read the decision of your court overruling *Poletown* before they decided a case like *Kelo*? Could it be said that the reliance interests of other branches of government are best handled through the political process, when in a sense you do not have private actors alleging the reliance interests?

JUSTICE MARKMAN: What constitutes "evolving standards of decency" may sometimes be a legitimate consideration within the legal process. But I agree with Justice Scalia in his opinion in *Stanford v. Kentucky,* that this is largely a consideration to be evaluated by the legislative branch of government.

You are right that it was the *Hathcock* decision in which my court overruled an earlier decision in *Poletown,* concerning the meaning of the eminent domain provision in the Michigan constitution. And there were reliance interests in that case, because there was a governmental jurisdiction involved that was seeking to condemn property at least partly on the basis of our earlier decision. However, in the end, we interpreted our eminent domain provision to require that the "taking" involve an actual "public use," rather than merely a "public purpose," because the former is what is actually provided for in our Constitution. Words matter, and the subtle change in words effected by *Poletown* authorized takings that were never contemplated by the framers of our Constitution.

In the *Hathcock* decision, as in other decisions reversing precedent, we did consider options such as applying our decision prospectively only or in a more limited manner. But we chose not to do so, not only because the reliance interests did not rise to a sufficiently high level but because the prospective-only application seemed to partake too much of the legislative process.

Again, however, I believe that Professor Calabresi, and Professor Paulsen in the article which he cites, have raised some very legitimate concerns about how consideration of which precedents ought to be reversed, and which ought not to be, bears resemblance to the legislative process. To what extent can we consider factors, such as the reliance factors, in assessing whether a wrongly decided precedent ought to be reversed?

PROFESSOR CALABRESI: Thank you. Over here.

AUDIENCE PARTICIPANT: I am going to address my questions primarily to Professors Merrill and Strauss.

When I hear a defense lawyer argue *stare decisis*, or precedent, I am reminded of what Ghandi said when a reporter asked him, "Mr. Ghandi, what do you think of Western civilization?" He said, "I think it would be a good thing."

As a practitioner primarily in the state courts and the lower federal courts, I find that there is an extraordinarily cynical use of what purports to be precedent, and that, in fact, outcomes of cases are not by any means predictable simply because the parties have tried to make a good faith argument about the application of precedent to the facts of their own case. What you see in judicial opinions may have string cites in it, but it sure does not bear any relationship to the principled application of precedent, to the actual facts of the particular cases.

As members of the Federalist Society, one of our goals is restoring the legal culture. Do you or any of the other panelists feel that our legal culture is one in which precedent is really that entitled to respect, as opposed to originalism?

PROFESSOR MERRILL: I think what you are raising is what I alluded to as the problem of good faith versus manipulation. I could not agree with you more. I think our legal culture is in a rather sorry state in this regard, that increasingly you read decisions at all levels of the judiciary that appear to be driven by an attempt to manipulate precedents to achieve outcomes. But I do not think the situation is beyond hope. I think that people can lead by example, and that the culture can be changed.

For example, the lower federal courts adopt a super-strong theory of precedent with respect to the Supreme Court's precedents in constitutional matters, and statutory matters as well, and I think by and large the lower federal courts do try in good faith to follow the Supreme Court's decisions. So that suggests to me that it is at least conceivable that judges can orient themselves in a properly restrained and respectful manner toward precedent.

I admit it is a bit utopian, because the current system that we have is not one where people follow precedent in good faith. But, I think it is possible to create such a system, and I think the only way to start doing that is to urge the appointment and confirmation of people to the U.S. Supreme Court, in particular, who share that attitude. I think the Bush administration has made an excellent start in that direction.

PROFESSOR STRAUSS: I would just add one thing, along the same lines as Tom Merrill—that although the situation is bad in many respects, it may not be nearly as bad as one thinks. The cases that are litigated in appellate courts make up a very unique sample. If you are looking to see whether precedent is really a constraining force, you have to keep in mind that many, many potential cases are resolved before they get to appellate courts, and often they are resolved because, under the precedents, only one outcome is possible. When a case is litigated up to the appellate courts, it is because there is uncertainty in the law. And then there are opportunities for judges to play fast and loose with the precedents, if they are so inclined. But an awful lot of issues, constitutional and common law and otherwise, simply do not get litigated. People just know what the law is and they live with it. Or, if they litigate, the case is settled very quickly. In those cases—the vast majority—precedent is often the principle constraining force. Precedent puts many arguments and positions off limits— so clearly off limits that we often do not realize how much work the precedents are doing.

JUSTICE MARKMAN: Campaigning throughout Michigan, I believe that the debate on this panel largely mirrors the differences of opinion among lay people, concerning the proper role of the courts. There are many of these people who understand a responsible court as being one which follows precedent; maintaining the law as it is, not changing it. However, there are also many people who understand a responsible court as being one which interprets the law and does not "make it up." Both of the perspectives on this panel find some support within the overall population. However, I am inclined to believe that in the case of a precedent that itself gave little respect to the laws enacted by the people's representatives, the overwhelming number of the people, if the alternatives were fairly presented, would be inclined to have the judges "get the law right."

PROFESSOR CALABRESI: We have time for one final question over here.

AUDIENCE PARTICIPANT: You guys told us this panel was going to be about precedent and originalism, but it has been to a great extent about precedent versus originalism. My question is what the Framers thought about precedent, and particularly when they established courts and gave them the judicial power, to what extent was that with the thought that that power would include a respect for precedent?

PROFESSOR CALABRESI: I tried to address that, to some extent, in my opening comments. I think the first evidence of what the Framers thought is to be found in the text of the Constitution, and the text of the Constitution does not seem to command that courts ought to follow precedent. It is possible that the judicial power includes an ability of the Court to bind itself in the future. But the fact that Article V sets forth a process for changing the Constitution does make me think that, in fact, the text of the Constitution does not envision constitutional change and updating happening through Supreme Court case law.

There is very little evidence from the debates at the time of the Philadelphia Convention and ratification. Alexander Hamilton does refer, in *Federalist* 78, in an indirect way, to the notion that judges will be bound down by many precedents, and that it will take time to study them. But he does not say a great deal about how those precedents are derived, or in what sense they have to be well settled.

The reason I wanted to talk about the Framers' controversy over the Bank of the United States is because that was the *Roe v. Wade* fight of their day. It was the big constitutional issue that raged for forty years, where people fought about it back and forth. And my sense of that is that, with the exception of James Madison, everybody else who participated in the debate about the Bank thought that it was not settled as a matter of precedent. It was, relatively speaking, an open question.

The one other thing from the Founding era that points a little bit in the other direction is that, in the case of *Stuart v. Laird*, where the Supreme Court was asked whether the re-creation of circuit-riding by the Jeffersonians was unconstitutional. The Court, in a brief opinion, said we have had circuit-riding for twelve years; that question is settled as a matter of practice. So, my impression of the Founding generation is that they did contemplate precedent, that they contemplated some room for precedent, but they certainly did not think that big issues like the question of the constitutionality of the Bank of the United States that were very hotly contested were things that might be settled by precedent.

It might also be a question about legislative precedent; precedent from Congress and precedents in the Court.

Akhil, did you have anything else?

PROFESSOR AMAR: Just to reiterate a few basic structural points, rather than searching for little micro-bits of history, which Steve did not do, but which some originalists might be tempted to do. The Constitution comes from the people. It is a short document, so ordinary people can read it. It is about all three branches of the federal government. The judiciary, in case you were looking carefully and counting, was listed third out of three. Less attention is devoted to it textually. So, that argues for the Supremacy Clause. It says the Constitution is the supreme law of the land. That is what everyone takes an oath to, not to precedent. And there are other branches of government, again, that are not within the judiciary. This seems to me an argument about the fundamental priority of the Constitution, the role of the other branches, the role of the people and of popular understandings, and the importance of the text.

Now, when you look at Article III itself, there is a distinction between the Supreme Court and the inferior courts, the importance of vertical precedent, and a recognition that courts are acting by— they are a continuous body, so there is going to be some attention to what they have done before, and what they are likely to do after.

There is not a presumption that a continuous body would reinvent the wheel every day, and not begin at least with the premise that what we decided yesterday is our starting point, at least, for what we decide today. It is justiciable law, says Article III. The Supremacy Clause says that the Constitution is the supreme law. In almost the same language, Article III says there is judicial power over all cases arising under the Constitution, laws, and treaties of the United States, so we are supposed to work so there is room for doctrine.

And structurally, judges are acting not just as the third branch, in a democratic sense, but also as the third branch chronologically. So, when they are acting, often other things will have already happened. A law might have been in place for a large number of years and that argues for a certain restraint *vis-à-vis* statutes that have been passed, that have created expectations. And it seems to me, also, a certain restraint is called for, if precedents have created facts on the ground— because the judicial power is a retrospective, rather than a purely prospective, power, and has to take some account of reliance interests, it seems to me, and popular understandings.

PROFESSOR CALABRESI: Thank you very much. I think this panel has addressed one of the most important questions for conservatives in constitutional law.

Ten

Debate on the Original Meaning of the Commerce, Spending, and Necessary and Proper Clauses

Professor Michael Paulsen

I am about to commit an act of unmitigated blasphemy for a Federalist Society member. So, first let me establish my credentials: I am Cass Sunstein's nightmare. I am an original, public-meaning textualist. I believe that the single correct way of constitutional interpretation is to attempt faithfully to apply the meaning that the words would have had to a reasonably well-informed speaker or reader of the English language at or about the time the text was adopted. I believe further that this interpretive methodology is prescribed by the Constitution, which specifies that it is "this" Constitution which is adopted and which therefore implicitly directs textualism as the way of interpreting the Constitution. This is all set out in an elaborate article with my co-author Vasan Kesavan a couple years back in the *Georgetown Law Journal*, called "The Interpretive Force of the Constitution's Secret Drafting History." There is only one correct way to interpret the Constitution, and that is original, public-meaning textualism. Now, here is the blasphemy: I believe that applying that interpretive methodology faithfully, one must conclude that the powers conferred on the national government are generally huge, sweeping, overlapping, and very nearly comprehensive when taken together. Thus, Alexander Hamilton, whose statue I jogged by this morning, was right, and nearly every member of the Federalist Society sitting in this audience today, is probably wrong.

The Constitution's enumeration of powers, in fact, I believe, provides the national government with truly sweeping powers, if pushed to their logical limits. The fact that, for many years, those limits were never reached or even pressed does not mean that the Constitution did not, in fact, confer broad powers on the national government. The fact that, politically, the full exercise of such powers might be unpopular or constitute bad public policy does not mean that the Constitution did not, in fact, confer such broad powers. The fact that the political virtues of federalism might be eroded or altered by the full exercise of the potential national legislative powers does not mean that the Constitution did not, in fact, confer such broad powers.

Federalism, properly understood, is a term of description attached to the Constitution's allocation of powers. It is not a freestanding constitutional rule. There is no "Federalism Clause" in the Constitution. The Constitution's allocation of powers can result in many different practical arrangements, leaning more or less in favor of national predominance or state predominance in policymaking, all consistent with the federalism created by the Constitution.

My proposition is simply this: the enumerated powers of the national government are huge powers. While it is undoubtedly true that the enumeration presupposes something not enumerated, it is also true that the enumeration considered as a package fairly admits of a construction that permits the national government to act very nearly as if it were a government of general legislative power. The powers to tax, to spend, to regulate commerce, to wage war, to enforce prohibitions on state government actions abridging individual liberties, especially when combined with the sweeping power to enact laws that are necessary and proper for carrying those other powers into execution, and any other powers of the national government into execution, create a national government of truly enormous constitutional powers.

There is very little that the federal government lacks constitutional power to do, if it employs its grants of powers carefully, properly, ingeniously, and to full effect. Aside from the exceptions the Constitution creates in favor of individual rights, the primary limitation on the exercise of federal legislative power is the logical and political plausibility of the claimed relationship between the enacted policy and the constitutional powers on which it is asserted to rest.

Now, I know how deeply this position is heresy to my Federalist Society friends, and it probably means that I have forfeited, for the sixty-seventh time or so, my prospects of being appointed to the U.S. Supreme Court. Nonetheless, I am persuaded that this is the right answer. I emphasize that I do not necessarily like all of the political consequences that this constitutional position might lead to. But surely, my friends, if the Federalist Society stands for anything, it stands for the proposition that one must never let one's political impulses drive one's constitutional interpretation. Along that route lies *Dred Scott*, *Lochner*, *Roe*, *Casey*, *Lawrence*, and *McConnell v. FEC*, among hundreds of other atrocities.

So I offer here, as gently as I can, the admonition that the federalism policy-driven, narrow reading of the Constitution's grant of specific and more general enumerated powers to the national government may be a milder version of the same disease that so grotesquely afflicts our liberal, anti-constitutionalist adversaries. And that disease is of course the tendency to read the Constitution in accordance with our political preferences, rather than being guided by the objective original meaning of the words. It is a mistake to extract from the Constitution's grant of specific enumerated power a general abstract constitutional principle of federalism, and then to read that principle back into the specific enumerations as a rule of constitutional law that alters what otherwise would be the objective textual understanding of the grants of powers that the document actually gives. It is a mistake of the same type deployed by liberal activists to extract from specific constitutional provisions a general right of privacy or liberty, and then read that principle back into the Constitution, as if that is what it said.

Now, in my remaining time, I have an outline of six points, and I will try to spend only two minutes on each one. The first point is an interpretive principle. This frames everything else. Where a constitutional provision has a legitimate range of meaning—where there is ambiguity, where there is open-endedness—where there is a range of meaning and the legislature has acted pursuant to a view fairly within that range, a court may not properly invalidate what the legislature has done. I think this principle flows absolutely clearly from the very justification for judicial review set forth in *Federalist* 78 and in *Marbury v. Madison*. That justification, in a nutshell, is this: the Constitution is law, and it is supreme law. Thus, where the Constitution supplies a rule of law and a legislative act is contrary to, or inconsistent with, that rule of law, the duty of the court is to apply the rules applied by the Constitution, not the rules applied by the unconstitutional statute.

Conversely, where the Constitution does not supply a rule of law, there is no justification for a court striking down an act of the legislature as being contrary to the Constitution. It is essential, then—it is part of the core justification of judicial review—that the court must conclude that the legislative act violates a rule of law that is set forth by the text of the Constitution.

Now, I believe in what friends of mine call "naïve right-answerism." I believe that original meaning textualism yields single, correct answers to legal questions—at least sometimes. Sometimes that single right answer is a determinate point. Sometimes the right answer to a constitutional question is that a text legitimately bears a range of meaning, a number of possible applications, and it is hard to privilege one over another. In other words, sometimes you run this interpretive program and you get answer A. Sometimes you run this program and you say, "You know what? The correct reading of the text is that it could embrace A, B, C, or D." My proposition is that where the text yields "A, B, C, or D," it is not legitimate for the Judiciary to choose A, and impose that as if it is a single, correct answer. Where it yields A, B, C, or D, and the legislature has acted pursuant to option A or option C, it is the duty of the courts to accept that legislative action. The power of constitutional construction within the boundaries of a general text is for Congress, not the courts. A corollary is that the more indeterminate or, as Randy Barnett put it this morning, under determinate the range of a constitutional provision, the broader the duty of the courts to defer to what the legislature has enacted. Judge Easterbrook said much the same thing on Thursday, and, as usual, Judge Easterbrook, a sound and clearheaded thinker, is right—especially when he agrees with me.

Once you have adopted this interpretive proposition, all that remains is to recognize that the Constitution's most important grants of enumerated powers are written in broad and sometimes downright sweeping terms that bear a fairly substantial range of meaning.

My position is that, where the legislature has acted pursuant to a meaning that is within the fair range of a general text, the legislature's decision must be upheld. Note that this is not a rule of deference to the legislature in the sense of deliberately abstaining from ruling in accordance with what you think is the right answer to the constitutional question. This is *not* some notion that we should enforce the Constitution incorrectly. I think that, almost always, that sort of deference is illegitimate. Rather, what I am saying is that the right answer is that textual precision often admits a range of choice and that the right answer is that the legislature must be permitted to choose.

Now, the classic case of a broadly-worded, open-textured provision, and probably the perfect illustration of this, is the Necessary and Proper Clause, which is fairly capable of a very broad range of meanings. Congress is granted the power to pass all laws "which are necessary and proper for carrying into execution the foregoing powers and all the other powers of the government." Now, if Alexander Hamilton and James Madison were right in their description of the inevitable linguistic implications of this clause in *Federalist* 23, 33, and 41—and they were—and if John Marshall was right in following this line of reasoning, and plagiarizing Hamilton, in *McCulloch v. Maryland*—and he was—then Article I, Section 8, Clause 18 is truly the Big Lebowski of the Constitution. The Anti-Federalists were right in seeing in this clause the route to a national government of enormous powers.

The Federalist Papers soft-pedaled the argument a little bit, but actually not that much. They did not really deny the breadth of what the Anti-Federalists referred to, disparagingly, as "the sweeping clause." Rather, the *Federalist Papers* argued that the power granted by the Necessary and Proper Clause was an inevitable corollary of principles that you would have inferred from the structure of the Constitution anyway. But the Framers did not leave the matter to structural inference. They said in the *Federalist Papers* that the Necessary and Proper Clause was a sweeping power to enact laws that, within Congress's reasonable judgment, are needed and appropriate for carrying into effect all the other powers of the national government.

Now, I think that, in so-called Commerce Clause cases, it is usually the Necessary and Proper Clause that is doing the most of the work in the controversial instances. But the commerce power itself is a broad power. Congress may do anything that literally regulates interstate commerce, traffic, or "intercourse." (Think Mann Act.) It is irrelevant that the regulation of the articles or goods or means or instrumentalities of interstate commerce are being used for a non-commercial purpose. The purpose to which the commerce power is employed is not relevant to the scope of its power to do this. The power is plenary within the bounds of actual regulation of commerce.

Furthermore, the Necessary and Proper Clause, I think, is the true source of the principle that Congress may regulate intrastate activity that has a substantial effect on interstate commerce, or that is otherwise needful and requisite to a regulatory scheme of Congress' that, in fact, attempts to regulate interstate commerce or to prohibit interstate commerce. This is the position of Justice Scalia in *Raich*. It is the position of *United States v. Darby*. And I believe it is correct. A corollary of this is that Congress is, in substantial measure, the judge of what intrastate regulation is needed to accomplish the object of a legitimate interstate commerce regulation or prohibition.

Now, this is a great and fearsome power, and it can be abused. At some point, the mind rebels; we all have our squeal-points. And where it would require the court to pile inference upon inference in an essentially implausible way, a court might rightly conclude that it is unconstitutional for Congress to do what it has done. I tend to think, then, that *Lopez* is right, and *United States v. Morrison* is right, and establish kind of the limiting cases of the plausibility of the Necessary and Proper Clause rationale.

But even where you can not do something through the commerce power, there is more than one way to skin a cat. Consider the taxing power. The taxing power is the power to regulate. The power to tax is the power to destroy, and the federal government has the power to tax. Indeed, Hamilton considered the taxing power to be the most important of the enumerated powers of Congress, and it is absolutely clear from the text and history that the taxing power may be employed for regulatory purposes essentially unrelated to the collection of revenue, as long as it really does operate as a tax.

For example, the taxing power extends to duties and excises. And it is plain that one of the reasons for this empowerment was to permit the new national legislature to be protectionist, in order to advance a policy of promoting the development of domestic industries. That is a policy unrelated to the raising of revenue, and it can be accomplished by imposing a tax. The taxing power, then, is a freestanding power. The power to tax is plenary, limited only by the uniformity clause proviso that immediately follows it. The *Child Labor Tax* cases are, therefore, of course, wrongly decided.

Consider the spending power. Government has the power to spend. Just as the power to tax is the power to destroy, the power to spend—to confer or withhold the benefit—is the power to coerce or destroy. In fact, that is a paraphrase of language from the *U.S. v. Butler* case. Once again, Alexander Hamilton was right. The power to spend is a freestanding power of government that is not limited by the other specific power grants of Article I. That is what the text appears to say. It is its own separate power, and may be employed to produce results that might not be attainable under powers to regulate. A power to spend is different from a power to regulate. You may spend money even for unenumerated purposes.

Now, Hamilton was right, but he might have had the wrong reason for being right. He located the power to spend in the Taxing Clause of the Constitution. Now, if you read it carefully, you cannot possibly make the same error that Seth Waxman made in referring to this clause as the Spending Clause. There is no Spending Clause, as such, in the Constitution; there is only a power to tax for certain purposes. We have already talked about the scope of the taxing power. But, actually, there is a spending power in the Constitution. It is just located elsewhere.

Ironically, it is located in Article IV, Section 3, Clause 2, which is often known as the Property Clause. That clause says that the Congress shall have power to dispose of and make all needful rules and regulations respecting the territory or other property belonging to the United States. The spending of money is the disposing of and the making of rules with regard to the dispensation of property of the United States, however derived. It could be the taxing power, or it could be property obtained through some other means. But look at what the Clause says. If that is, as Professor David Engdahl has convincingly argued, the source of the spending power, it is a plenary power of government to spend and to make all needful rules for disposing of the government's property. It is only a power to spend. It is not also a power to directly regulate. The exercise of the spending power, therefore, does not preempt inconsistent state law. States may refuse the money. They may preserve their inconsistent policy by refusing the money in the first place.

But you might ask, can the spending power not be used *de facto* as a power to coerce, induce, bribe, and extort, even if it is not power to legally require? The answer is yes. The only limitation on what the federal government may spend money for, and the conditions it may attach, is that the condition itself not be independently unconstitutional.

Now this is the most heretical thing I have said so far. The flaw in *South Dakota v. Dole* is not that it recognizes too broad a federal government spending power but that it recognizes too *narrow* a federal government spending power. The government of the United States may spend money for any purpose for which it has money to spend.

I turn to an undervalued source of federal legislative power: the War Power. The best way to understand the different views of the Founding generation with respect to national power is to look at who fought in the Revolutionary War. Washington, Hamilton, end up with strongly nationalist views. But let us now consider what the war power adds to the analysis so far.

Remember that Congress has the Necessary and Proper power to carry into execution Congress' powers to declare war, to raise and support armies, and the president's power as commander in chief, and his duty to preserve, protect, defend the nation. The Supreme Court has said that the power to wage war is the power to wage it successfully; the power to win. It is the power, I believe, to marshal the nation's resources to the war effort and to protect the nation and its citizens from attack. Congress, I believe, has the power to pass all laws necessary and proper for carrying into execution the power of our government to win wars and protect its people. This has broad implications.

When I teach *Youngstown Sheet* and *Tube v. Sawyer*, there is this line that says, well, the president cannot do this on his own, but Congress could, pursuant to the Commerce power. Well, there is a better answer. If there is a war on, Congress clearly has the power, a dangerous power, to nationalize industries, to seize steel mills, if necessary, to effectuate the war that is being waged.

My last little point on the outline here I call *Lopez* and Beslan, and it is this. Beslan, I hope we have not forgotten, is the city in Russia where there was the siege of the elementary school. This could happen here. My proposition is that the Gun-Free School Zone Act could legitimately be adopted by the federal government as a national security defense measure. Congress could determine that prohibiting or deterring or tracking or punishing the possession of violent weapons in school zones is a power that the federal government, if it chooses, needs to exercise in order to provide for the defense of its citizens during a time of war and terrorism.

There is more yet to this theory. I can go on and on. You know how professors do. There is the treaty power and the civil rights power—

(Laughter.)

PROFESSOR PAULSEN:—but I am a lover of mercy, and so I will quit. The last point I make is that you have heard a few liberal critics on several of these panels saying that originalism tends to produce for conservatives the results they like to see. Not always; I like some but not all of the policy implications of this. I think the consequence of my position is that the federal government has a lot more power than I think I would be comfortable with, as a matter of my political preferences, as a conservative Republican. But, while I would prefer that the federal government be a government of fewer powers, we go to war with the Constitution we have, not the one we prefer. The enumeration of powers presupposes something unenumerated. True. But not very much.

Thanks.

Professor Randy Barnett

Well, I have to say that after hearing that talk, when I got up to speak, I felt a little woozy. So I have to get my wits about me. In my talk today, I am going to resist the temptation to discuss the merits and proper methods of originalism that you have heard so much about. I have written about that previously, but we have a very limited amount of time, and we are supposed to cover a lot of material. Suffice it to say that I do favor the original public-meaning version of originalism that Mike identified, and that looks to the original public-meaning of the Constitution and its amendments at the time they were enacted. In other words, I adhere to the view of originalism that says that the meaning of the Constitution must remain the same, until it is properly changed. And it cannot be properly changed unilaterally by the courts, or even in the courts acting in conjunction with other branches of government. As for my normative defense of this, Cass Sunstein reasonably accurately characterized the approach that I argue for on behalf of originalism in *Restoring the Lost Constitution*, which is based ultimately on consequences—very ultimately—mediated through rights, which themselves are based on consequences.

I am also going to resist the temptation to follow Mike down the various paths that he has just led us. I have not had the privilege of having seen his remarks prior to this. I prepared mine independently, and if I were to try to respond to Mike, I would not be able to get through my own prepared remarks. But I will say this. If Michael Paulsen had gotten up and made the speech he just made at the time of the Founding and claimed that kind of power on behalf of the national government at the time of the Founding, and if he had been seen then as being an authority on the meaning of the new Constitution and a Federalist, not only would the Constitution never been ratified, but I think he would have been tarred and feathered and run right out of town. In the process, I think he would have discovered the original public meaning of the text of the Constitution. [Laughter? Cheering?]

This panel is about three clauses that have often been used by the courts since the New Deal to expand federal power: the Commerce Clause, the Necessary and Proper Clause, and the Taxation Clause from which the spending power has (at least until today) been construed. Now, because I have not studied the matter closely, I am not going to comment on the spending power. One of the burdens of being an originalist, I have discovered since I became one, is that you have to know something about the original public meaning of each clause before you express an opinion on the subject. And I am somewhat relieved that I decided not to express much of an opinion about the scope of the spending power, now that I have heard this interesting theory that Michael has proposed, drawing on David Engdahl's work. I would have to think long and hard about this thesis to see if it is right.

I should say that I have always been attracted to Madison's view that there is no freestanding Spending Clause, but only a power to spend what is necessary and properly incident to the enumerated powers. Madison did not believe that the spending power grew out of the taxation power, but instead that all exercises of the spending power had to be incident to the other enumerated powers. I am not, however, going to make the argument for this position today.

Nor am I going to spend much time discussing the original meaning of the Commerce Clause. In my book, *Restoring the Lost Constitution*, I used the power to make electronic searches to identify every use of the word "commerce" in the Constitutional Convention, the ratification debates, and the *Federalist Papers*, along with a separate study done by—happily—research assistants and not myself, in which they examined the over fifteen hundred times the word "commerce" appeared in the *Philadelphia Gazette* between 1715 and 1800. In all of these appearances of the word "commerce," I cannot find one clear example where the term was used to apply more broadly than the meaning identified by Justice Thomas in his concurring opinion in *Lopez*, in which he maintained that the word "commerce" refers to the trade and exchange of goods, along with the process of trading and exchanging, including transportation.

I will read one quote from the January 13, 1790, issue of the *Pennsylvania Gazette,* because it is so very representative of all those uses of the word "commerce" at the Founding:

> Agriculture, manufacturers and commerce are acknowl-edged to be the three great sources of wealth in any state. By the first [agriculture], we are to understand not only tillage but whatever regards the improvement of the earth as the breeding of cattle, the raising of trees, plants and all vegetables that may contribute to the real use of man; the opening and working of mines, whether of metal, stones, or mineral drugs....By the second [manufacturers], all the arts, manual and mechanical....By the third [commerce], the whole extent of navigation with foreign countries.

So this is how this one source distinguished agriculture, manufacturing, and commerce; a very common trilogy that was repeatedly invoked.

I do, by the way, invite Dean Kramer, from whom you heard on Thursday, to "shred" all this evidence, if he can. But, for an originalist, direct evidence of the actual use of a word is the most important source of the word's meaning. It is more important than referring to the "broader context," which is the method that Professor Kramer tended to use in his book. Appealing to the "larger context" or the "underlying principles" of the text is the means by which some today are able to turn the words "black" into "white" and "up" into "down."

Now, it may come as some surprise to you to learn that even the New Deal Supreme Court never formally broadened the meaning of the term "commerce" in any of its cases. Instead, it relied on an expanded interpretation of the Necessary and Proper Clause to enlarge the powers of the national government. The New Deal Supreme Court never re-defined the word "commerce." There is no case in which it said, oh no, commerce means more today than it used to mean. The Court did not have to do that, because it expanded the use of the Necessary and Proper Clause to reach activity that it admitted was *not* commerce but which it was necessary and proper to reach anyway.

So, I am going to spend the rest of my time focusing on the Necessary and Proper Clause. Now unfortunately, because the Necessary and Proper Clause uses a term of art, you cannot find its original meaning by examining how the words "necessary" or the word "proper" was commonly used, the way you can when you are looking for a term like "commerce." You really do need to examine the context in which this phrase was introduced to the Constitution, and how it was explained to the public when it was criticized by the Anti-Federalists as conveying the kind of sweeping and unlimited powers to Congress that Mike Paulsen has just claimed for it, and that Justice Scalia claimed for it in his concurring opinion in *Raich*.

The Necessary and Proper Clause was added to the Constitution by the Committee of Detail, without any previous discussion by the Constitutional Convention. Nor was it the subject of any debate from its initial proposal to the Convention's final adoption of the Constitution. The likely reason why the Necessary and Proper Clause received no attention from the Convention became clear during the ratification convention debates, as did the Clause's public meaning. In the ratification debates, opponents of the Constitution pointed to this clause as evidence that the national government had virtually unlimited and undefined powers. It was they, the Anti-Federalists, who dubbed the Necessary and Proper Clause to be "the sweeping clause." In other words, they said, "Look, we object to this Constitution because it is going to lead to the very kind of powers that Mike Paulsen told you the federal government has." In the New York Convention, for example, Anti-Federalist John Williams contended that "it is perhaps utterly impossible to fully define this power." For this reason, "whatever they judge necessary for the proper administration of the powers lodged in them, they may execute without any check or impediment."

Although I could go on with Anti-Federalist accusations, instead I am going to switch over to the Federalist defenses of the Constitution. Federalist supporters of the Constitution repeatedly denied the charge that all discretion over the scope of its own powers effectively resided in Congress. They insisted that the Necessary and Proper Clause was not an additional freestanding grant of power but merely made explicit what was already implicit in the grant of each enumerated power. As explained by George Nicholas in the Virginia ratifying convention, "the Constitution had enumerated all the powers which the general government should have but did not say how they were to be exercised. It, therefore, in this clause tells us how they shall be exercised." Like other Federalists, Nicholas denied that this clause gave "any new power to Congress." "Suppose," he reasoned, "it had been inserted at the end of every power, that they should have power to make laws to carry that power into execution. Would this have increased their power? If, therefore, it could not have increased their powers, if placed at the end of that power, it cannot increase them if placed at the end of the list, at the end of them all." In short, "the Clause only enables them [the Congress] to carry into execution the powers given to them. It gives them no additional power."

Madison, in Virginia, added his voice to the chorus, when he said, "The sweeping clause only extended to the enumerated powers. Should Congress attempt to extend it to any power not enumerated, it would not be warranted by the clause." Also in Virginia, Edmund

Pendleton, president of the Convention, insisted that this clause did not go "a single step beyond the delegated powers." If Congress were "about to pass a law in consequence to this Clause, they must pursue some of the delegated powers but can by no means depart from them or arrogate no new powers, for the plain language of the clause is to give them power to pass laws in order to give effect to the delegated powers." The same point is made in the North Carolina Convention, while in Pennsylvania, James Wilson explained that this clause "is saying no more than that the powers we have already particularly given shall be effectually carried into execution." And Thomas McKean insisted that "it gives to Congress no further power than already enumerated."

So here, then, is the likely explanation for the lack of debate surrounding the Clause at the Philadelphia Convention. If the power to make law was already thought to be implicit in the enumerated power scheme, it is then not surprising that the Clause would provoke no discussion at the Convention. Unfortunately, today, most interpreters, including many originalists, go no farther in their investigation of the original meaning of the Necessary and Proper Clause than Marshall's opinion in *McCulloch v. Maryland*; written in 1819, some thirty years after the ratification of the Constitution.

In *McCulloch*, Marshall upheld the constitutionality of the Second National Bank of the United States. Now, as Dean Kramer correctly observed on Thursday, the bill establishing the Second Bank had been signed into law by President James Madison, a man who had, as a representative in the first Congress, strongly objected to the constitutionality of the First National Bank on the ground that it exceeded the enumerated powers of Congress. Here is what Madison said in his speech to Congress:

> Whatever meaning this clause may have, none can be admitted that would give an unlimited discretion to Congress. Its meaning must, according to the natural and obvious force of the meanings, other terms and the contexts, be limited to the means necessary to the end and incident to the nature of

the specified power. The clause is, in fact, merely declaratory of what would have resulted by unavoidable implication as the appropriate and, as it were, technical means of executing those powers. In this sense, it has been explained by the Friends of the Constitution and ratified by the big conventions. The essential characteristics of the government as composed of limited and enumerated powers would be destroyed if, instead of direct and incidental means, any means could be used which, in the language of the preamble to the bill, might be conceived to be conducive to the successful conducting of the finances or might be conceived to tend to give facility to the obtaining of loans.

He then went on to say:

Mark the validity on which the validity of this bill depends. To borrow money is the end and the accumulation of capital, implied of the means. The accumulation of capital is then the end, and the bank implied as the means. The bank has been the end, and a charter of incorporation, a monopoly, capital punishments, etc., applied as the means. If implications, thus remote and thus multiplied, can be linked together, a chain will form that will reach every object of legislation, every object within the whole compass of political economy.

This is Madison's reason for opposing the first Bank. Yet decades later, as president he signed the bill approving the second Bank. How do we explain that? Well, there is a larger context that Dean Kramer did not mention. While Madison did eventually come to be persuaded, by practice, that a bank was incident enough to the enumerated powers to be constitutional, he nevertheless strongly objected to the opinion in *McCulloch* in which Marshall famously equated the term "necessary" with mere convenience. Here is Madison's objection to *McCulloch v. Maryland*:

> Of utmost importance is the high sanction given to a lati-
> tude in expounding the Constitution, which seems to break
> down the landmarks intended by a specification of the
> powers of Congress and to substitute for a definite con-
> nection between the end and ends, a legislative discretion
> as to the former to which no practical limit can be
> assigned.

Madison, then, both acknowledged the supposedly modern insight
that the national economy is interconnected and rejected this as a
basis for a latitudinarian interpretation of "necessary":

> In the great system of political economy, having for its gen-
> eral object the national welfare, everything is related imme-
> diately or remotely to every other thing. And consequently
> a power over any one thing, if not limited by some obvious
> and precise affinity, may amount to a power over every-
> thing. Ends and means may shift in character at the will
> and according to the ingenuity of the legislative body.

And then he concluded what his real objection to this all was: "Is
there a legislative power in fact not expressly prohibited by the Constitution which might not, according to doctrine of the Court, be exercised as a means for carrying into effect from specified power?"

And it was not just Madison who was displeased with *McCulluch*.
The popular outcry against *McCulloch* was so great that John Marshall himself felt moved to defend his decision in an essay he published anonymously under the name "A Friend of the Constitution."
Imagine if former chief justice Rehnquist had been so vilified for a
judicial opinion he had written that he published anonymous op-eds
in the *Wall Street Journal* defending the opinion. But that is exactly
what John Marshall did.

Here is a part of what he said in defense of *McCulloch*, which
shows that even John Marshall denied that *McCulloch* means what it
later came to be interpreted to mean:

> In no single instance does the Court admit the unlimited power of Congress to adopt any law whatever, and thus to pass the limits prescribed by the Constitution. Not only is the discretion claimed for the legislature in the selection of its means always limited in terms to such as are appropriate, but the Court also expressly says that should Congress under the pretext of executing its powers pass laws for the accomplishment of objects not entrusted to the government it would become the painful duty of this Tribunal to say that such an act was not all the land.

That is John Marshall interpreting *McCulloch v. Maryland*, not me.

So, who was right about the meaning of the Necessary and Proper Clause? Madison or Marshall? In my article on the original meaning of the Necessary and Proper Clause, which appeared in the *University of Pennsylvania Journal of Constitutional Law*, I contended that the difference between Madison, Jefferson, and other Democratic-Republicans—and Hamilton, Marshall, and other Federalists—was a lot less than meets the eye today. Both sides insisted on some degree of what we today call "means-ends fit," plainly adapted. Both sides rejected the idea that "necessary" meant "indispensably requisite," the meaning urged upon the Court by the State of Maryland and properly rejected by Marshall. Madison had much earlier rejected "indispensably requisite" as the proper interpretation of "necessary" on the ground that it would make federal governance nearly impossible.

The primary problem with reading *McCulloch* and other Marshall opinions, like *Gibbons v. Ogden*, today is to look past the reinterpretations of these two decisions that were used during the New Deal to defend the Supreme Court's expansive interpretation of national powers. The reinterpretation of these Marshall Court opinions was used to characterize the New Deal Court as a "restoration" of original meeting, rather than the constitutional revolution that it actually was, as most progressive scholars today will readily admit. The challenge for members of the Federalist Society coalition who accept originalism is to distinguish between the Madisonian and the Rooseveltian interpretations of federal power, especially when the government invokes the Necessary and Proper Clause.

Consider the medical cannabis case of *Gonzalez v. Raich* that I argued last term in the Supreme Court. In his dissenting opinion, Justice Thomas adopted a Madisonian interpretation:

> The Necessary and Proper Clause is not a warrant to Congress to enact any law that bears some conceivable connection to the exercise of an enumerated power. Nor is it, however, a command to Congress to enact only laws which are absolutely indispensable to the exercise of an enumerated power. To act under the Necessary and Proper Clause, then, Congress must select a means that is appropriate and plainly adapt it to executing an enumerated power. The means cannot be otherwise prohibited by the Constitution. The means cannot be inconsistent with the letter and the spirit of the Constitution. In sum, neither in enacting the Controlled Substance Act nor in defending its application to Respondents has the government offered any obvious reason why banning medical marijuana use is necessary to stem the tide of interstate drug trafficking. Congress's goal of curtailing interstate drug trade would not plainly be thwarted if it could not apply the CSA to patients like Monson and Raich. That is, unless Congress's aim is really to exercise the police power of the sort reserved to the states in order to eliminate even the intrastate possession and use of marijuana [and I think we all know that is exactly what Congress is trying to accomplish; they are not trying just to limit intrastate commerce. They are trying to use their interstate commerce power to exert a police power of a sort that is reserved to the states.] Even assuming that the CSA's ban on locally cultivated and consumed marijuana is necessary, it does not mean it is also proper. Even if Congress may regulate

purely intrastate activity when essential to exercising some enumerated power, Congress may not use its incidental authority to subvert basic principles of Federalism and dual sovereignty.

In *Raich,* we did not deny that the enumerated powers of Congress are supreme where they are inconsistent with the exercise of the state police power. Rather, we claimed that, under the Necessary and Proper Clause, it is an improper extension of those enumerated powers to imply other powers that interfere with the fundamental principles of federalism and dual sovereignty. In *Raich*, an implied power to reach wholly intrastate, non-economic activity was upheld that severely interfered with the police power of states to promote the health of its citizens (and also to regulate the practice of medicine).

Now, contrast Justice Thomas's dissent with Justice Scalia's concurring opinion in *Raich*, in which he adopts a Rooseveltian interpretation of the Necessary and Proper Clause:

> Lopez and *Morrison* affirm that Congress may not regulate certain purely local activities within the states based solely on the attenuated effect that such activity may have in the interstate market. But those decisions did not declare non-economic intrastate activity to be categorically beyond the reach of federal government. Neither case involved the power of Congress to exert control over intrastate activities in connection with a more comprehensive scheme of regulation. To dismiss this distinction as superficial and formalistic is to misunderstand the nature of the Necessary and Proper Clause, which empowers Congress to enact laws in effectuation of its enumerated powers that are not within its authority to enact in isolation.

What renders Justice Scalia's interpretation of the Necessary and Proper Clause as "Rooseveltian" is his extreme deference to the decision of Congress as to whether it really is essential to a larger regulatory scheme to reach wholly intrastate, non-economic activities that, traditionally, have been included within the police power of states. Like Madison, the dissenters in *Raich* require some showing of means-ends fit. Like the New Deal Court, Justice Scalia leaves the question of means-ends fit entirely up to Congress. And also like the New Deal Court, he denies that this interference with the traditional police powers of states is an improper construction of implied federal power.

Let me conclude now by observing that I see the remarkably successful coalition that is the Federalist Society today standing at a crossroad. In one direction is a continued Madisonian commitment to originalism, according to which the powers of the national government are limited, and these textual limits are enforceable by courts. Just as the courts are restrained from changing the meaning of the Constitution, so too is Congress.

In the other direction is a Rooseveltian commitment to judicial restraint above all else, a restraint that is justified by distorting original meaning, by creating some insurmountable burden of proof before legislation can be overturned, or by claiming that is too late to revisit New Deal era "super-precedents."[1] Take your pick. Perhaps a jurisprudence of judicial restraint, complete and total judicial restraint, and unlimited national power, provides a better world than a jurisprudence of a written constitution with limited and enumerated national powers. But if that is the road that the Federalists choose to take, then I suggest we change the silhouette in our banner from that of James Madison to that of FDR.

Thank you.

Discussion on the Original Meaning of the Commerce, Spending and Necessary and Proper Clauses
Moderated by Barrington D. Parker, Jr.

JUDGE PARKER: I know there are a lot of you out in the audience, and you have questions for our two speakers. While you are queuing up at the microphone, let me take the first crack at asking a question of Michael Paulsen.

PROFESSOR PAULSEN: Well, I was just going to take thirty seconds to say that, you know, I love this debate with Randy. I think it shows that running an originalist method does not necessarily predetermine the answers, but that these are the grounds on which the argument should be fairly waged. I would love for this to be the basis on which the Supreme Court decides these kinds of cases.

And just one point. Let us not change the banner to Roosevelt. I see no good reason why one of our patron saints cannot be Alexander Hamilton.

We could change the....

PROFESSOR BARNETT: Same difference.

PROFESSOR PAULSEN: We will let you ask questions rather than go back and forth on that.

JUDGE PARKER: In the interest of balance, Randy, you have got one shot at Michael.

PROFESSOR BARNETT: I think it will come out in the course of the questions.

PROFESSOR PAULSEN: Bring it on.

JUDGE PARKER: Let us start. Go ahead.

AUDIENCE PARTICIPANT: The common law rule of interpretation during the Founding period was a presumption of the right to non-authority, from which follows that delegated powers are to be constructed as narrowly as possible, and rights against the actions of government as broadly as possible. That would mean also that the power to carry into execution would be only the power to make an effort and not to get a desired outcome.

PROFESSOR BARNETT: I should say that that is the rule of construction that is identified in St. George Tucker's treatise on the Constitution, which you can read on John Roland's website. It is the first learned commentary on the Constitution, published in 1802, and he describes exactly the rule of construction with respect to the enumerated powers and the rights retained by the people, and he does so in the context of interpreting the Ninth and Tenth Amendments.

PROFESSOR PAULSEN: I think it is an excellent question. It kind of distills the difference in approach between Randy and me. I think Randy adopts what I would call a substantive push in interpreting the scope of enumeration. The subtitle of his book is *The Presumption of Liberty*, and for good reason. If the lens through which you approach the reading of constitutional provisions is to adopt a substantive preference against reading it broadly, you are going to end up with some outcomes where you do not read particular clauses very broadly.

My methodology, which I think is Hamiltonian, and has substantial support in the Founding generation, is that you do not adopt a substantive push one way or another, and that the underlying common law interpretive methods might not apply in interpreting a written constitutional text. If the text is written in broad language, and the policymakers enact a view pursuant to that broad language such that it fits within that language, I would say that the baseline presumption is that courts should not interfere with democratic choices fairly falling within the range of enumerated power grants.

PROFESSOR BARNETT: Let me just clarify my position. I justify a presumption of liberty, the presumption that is the subtitle of my book. I do not claim that the presumption of liberty is an interpretation of the Constitution itself, except insofar as I think you can derive something like a presumption of liberty from the Ninth Amendment. By and large, what I say in my book is that the meaning of the Constitution is one thing, and then you do need certain interpretive presumptions in order to put that meaning into effect. Now Michael has just proposed to you the very strong presumption of constitutionality that he would use to put it into effect. That is the presumption that was adopted by the New Deal Roosevelt Court, and then qualified by footnote four. Whether or not this is the right choice, you do have to pick an interpretive presumption that is not literally in the Constitution.

The argument I make on behalf of the presumption I pick is that it is a closer fit with what the original meaning of the Constitution does say than the opposing presumption is. The presumption of liberty fits with what we know of the Ninth Amendment, which says that the enumeration in the Constitution of certain rights shall not be construed—*shall not be construed*—to deny or disparage others retained by the people. It is a closer fit with that than Michael Paulsen's opposing construction, which presumes constitutionality.

But both are constructions of the Constitution. By construction, I mean a doctrine by which you put the Constitution into effect. These presumptions are not—neither one is strictly speaking an interpretation of the original meaning of the Constitution itself, and that is what the legitimate debate is about, between Michael and me.

JUDGE PARKER: Thank you. Go ahead.

AUDIENCE PARTICIPANT: This is directed more to Professor Barnett. Professor Barnett, if we woke up, let us say a year from now, and there were nine Professor Barnetts sitting on the Supreme Court, as a practical matter....

(Applause.)

PROFESSOR BARNETT: I guess that would have meant that human cloning was possible after all.

AUDIENCE PARTICIPANT:...if we woke up at number nine Justice Barnetts on the Supreme Court, in light of some of the views you have expressed here and in other places, in the real world, what are some of the practical means by which your views could essentially be used in light of the fact that you walk down the street, and there is every imaginable government agency covering all aspects of American life. In the real world, what can be done about this, based on your constitutional views? And if you could somewhat address the significance, if any, of the Sixteenth Amendment in your response, I would appreciate that as well.

PROFESSOR BARNETT: It is an interesting question because it is counterfactual—it is a science fiction question is what it is. And what is interesting about it is that it will never happen because it is science fiction, because it is counterfactual. That is not the way constitutional change happens.

The way constitutional change happens is you have the death or resignation of justices one at a time. There is a political process by which a politically elected president selects the new justices. To become known and appreciated by the White House, you have to have a certain kind of conventional outlook, and that is going to be further tempered by a political process known as Senate confirmation. That screen is part of our system. So, therefore, you will never have an overnight conversion of the Supreme Court to any one particular point of view. And I suppose we should be grateful for this. Of course, during the New Deal, although President Roosevelt did not get the court-packing scheme through, he did manage to appoint eight of the nine justices in a very short period of time. So, you had close to the hypothetical experiment of the questioner, at point, everything got upheld as constitutional. But, other than a reoccurrence of what happened during the New Deal, that is not normally the way constitutional change happens. It happens gradually, and it should happen gradually. Whether it should or not, it is going to, let us put it that way.

The reason why we have these debates about originalism and about what original meaning of the Constitution is, and what legislation might or might not be constitutional, is because we have to decide if this is the direction in which we want to go. And you are never going to take even a single gradual step in a particular direction unless you know that the end result is something that you like and something that you want to go to. And so that is why we have all these debates about the end results. It is not because we think this is going to happen overnight, or that it necessarily should. And so, therefore, a hypothetical question like that has no real answer— except that if you are asking me what sort of constitutional order would be good. I would say that the constitutional order that was established by the Founders and by those who amended the Constitution, particularly the Thirteenth, Fourteenth, and Fifteenth Amendments, would be a better system of government than the one we have today.

AUDIENCE PARTICIPANT: I am Roger Pilon of the Cato Institute. Going back to our presumption of liberty, I take it to be implicit in the doctrine of enumerated powers, which is the very foundation of the Constitution and points to its theory of legitimacy, namely that the legitimacy of the powers is a function of the grant that was made in the original position, and by virtue of the fact that those powers are enumerated and thus limited by implication. Anything not granted remains as a right in the people. And so the presumption of liberty is there.

But as you build your argument, Michael Paulsen, on the Hamiltonian view, Hamilton was the odd man out. After all, the report on manufacturers on in 1791 was where the great debate over the so-called General Welfare Clause came from, and Hamilton's view that it granted Congress the power to tax and spend for the general welfare, and that debate took place over many years. William Drayton in 1828 offered the best explanation, namely that if that is what the Framers meant, then there was no point in enumerating Congress' other powers; they could have stopped right there with power number one, because anytime Congress wants to do something it is not authorized to do, it can do it by taxing and spending for the general welfare.

So it seems to me that you have got to address Randy's point that, at the end of the day, your Hamiltonian view amounts to granting a general police power to the federal government, which the courts have said for over two hundred years does not exist.

PROFESSOR PAULSEN: Great question. There are really two questions there. One is about enumerated powers, and one is about the scope of the spending power. Is it the monster that swallowed Cincinnati? The fact that we have a government of enumerated powers does not in and of itself tell you how to interpret a particular enumeration. You cannot extract from the fact of enumerated powers some sort of free-floating principle that you then put back in, and read the enumerations more narrowly than they otherwise would be read.

The scheme we have of liberty and limited power is a function of how broadly these enumerated powers are granted, or not. So again, I do not think you can extract—and with all due respect, Roger, it is the same trick the liberals use in inferring from penumbras and emanations of other bill of rights provisions, a general liberty clause or a substantive due process and the traditions of our nation, which they then read back into the text to create what is in essence a new text.

AUDIENCE PARTICIPANT [Roger Pilon]: There is no limit on your tricks, Mike. I think we have got a few coming from your microphone, if I am not mistaken. Yes, I mean this idea of reading the Necessary and Proper Clause as allowing Congress to expand its powers, whereas the Clause was understood at the time of the Framing as purely an instrumental power, not as a source of further new powers, and it seems to me that is the elephant you have let into the constitutional tent, which is now driving all of us out, and freedom with it.

JUDGE PARKER: Let me exercise my prerogative as the....

AUDIENCE PARTICIPANT [Roger Pilon]: Sure. Well, Mike invited me to speak.

PROFESSOR PAULSEN: No, it is a good question. I have to respond to this.

JUDGE PARKER: Well, I have decided to let you answer.

PROFESSOR PAULSEN: I forgot, this is being moderated by a federal judge.

I do not strongly disagree. I think Randy and I are actually pretty close in our understanding of the Framers' description of what the Necessary and Proper Clause entails. It is a power to effectuate other powers. The Framers often said that we would have found this power to be implicit, if we had not made it explicit, and it is a good thing to make it explicit. Congress is granted the Necessary and Proper Clause power to effectuate other powers. I do not believe that it is a freestanding power, like the spending power, to do whatever Congress thinks is necessary and proper. But that does not answer the question of the scope of the Necessary and Proper Clause power to enact legislation that is determined to be necessary to effectuate other power grants.

Now the spending power, which is part of the original question, is a little bit different. And I think there is a fair argument that if you read these powers to the full extent, many of them, taken to their full extremes, would render some of the others duplicative or overlapping. I do not see that as a textual problem. Nothing is more common in law than for multiple provisions to provide overlapping support for a common conclusion. When I used to sue school districts, I would have a free-speech claim, a free exercise claim, an equal protection claim—there would be many constitutional provisions that would support my claim of right. So, too, there could be many overlapping grants of power that might sustain particular congressional exercises of authority. The fact that the spending power, if pushed to its full extent, would render it unnecessary to justify some of these actions on other powers does not refute the idea that that might be the meaning of the spending power.

JUDGE PARKER: Thank you. Let me, since we are running out of time and the line is still there, please let us limit this to just one question per questioner.

AUDIENCE PARTICIPANT: Okay, one question, although it will seem perhaps like a variation on a question that was asked several moments ago. It is to Professor Barnett. Let us posit that you have the better of the argument, which I think you do, and Mr. Cooper did at lunch. But when you have seventy years of discontinuity from an originalist understanding, and we can posit that ninety percent of the U.S.C.A. is full of unconstitutional provisions that are not part of the enumerated powers, your answer to the questioner a moment ago that, well, everything will not get ripped up overnight because that will never happen as a matter of political reality, I think is a little bit unsatisfying. Do we not need a theory of how you go about implementing this kind of a change in understanding, and why? And don't you start introducing other considerations, other than originalism, when we come to that? It is an enormous enterprise, and you can say that you will not get five justices who believe in this view. But, I do not know that you are necessarily all that far away, or that it is that difficult to get confirmed people who would view agreeing with Randy Barnett as the correct view. But the problem is, in implementing your vision of constitutional law, Professor Barnett, you are faced with the enormity of the political disruption that doing this will cause. And I do not know what the right answer is to that, but I do wonder if you have a view on the question?

PROFESSOR BARNETT: I do not have a completely well considered view on the question you just asked. It is all I can do just to figure out what all the original meanings are and work on that, without also figuring out what might be called transition questions, as in how do you transition from an unconstitutional arrangement to a constitutional arrangement. It is a serious question.

Before I throw out any possibilities, let me just suggest what I think is not the right move to make, which is the reason why this argument is generally formulated. What is not the right move to make is to argue that because there are all these transition costs, because there is this disruption, however extreme you want to make it, therefore you should forget about the original meaning. It is too late to turn back the clock; it is gone, we are in a new world now. And we hear originalists like Judge Bork occasionally saying things like this. And so, I think that is what is not warranted.

What is warranted is more close attention to how you would gradually, or how you would not so gradually—depending on what you decide to do—transition from an unconstitutional arrangement to a constitutional arrangement. But you have to first decide (a) whether it is—we currently do have an unconstitutional arrangement, and then you have to be convinced that it is a good idea to transition to a constitutional one.

But how might we move in the right direction? We could approach this the way we do with people who are in jail, having been convicted of crimes. When a new rule of evidence of a new rule of criminal procedure becomes adopted we do not reopen their prosecutions, we do not reopen their convictions. Instead, we apply a better rule of criminal procedure prospectively. So, you could say that any agency or any organization that has already been upheld—the decision upholding that agency or organization is *res judicata*. We are not going to revisit that one.

I am not necessarily advocating this option, but merely identifying it as a possibility.

And here is the most important part of this approach to constitutional change. We now affirm that the principle, the constitutional principle on which a particular program or organization was upheld, is invalid and can no longer be used in a common-law-type way, reasoning by analogy to justify additional powers and additional agencies.

And so that is one way in which you might draw the line. You might say this ruling, which now is law, and which we may not want to unsettle, no longer has any gravitational force and cannot be extended by analogy to apply to other cases or institutions. And that would change nothing about the *status quo* and would just change things about what can and cannot be done in the future. It is not that disruptive.

PROFESSOR PAULSEN: I have got to ask a question about that because Randy and I actually agree that, on originalist grounds, it is flatly inconsistent with the principle of originalism to adhere to a decision that you are otherwise fully persuaded is wrong. *Stare decisis* in the strong sense of adhering to a wrong outcome is, I think we would agree, is on originalist grounds, unconstitutional.

He is nodding, but if he agrees with that, then why do you....

PROFESSOR BARNETT: You know, I agree with that, Michael. I have written that.

PROFESSOR PAULSEN: Why on earth would you say it could have no future generative effects, but we must acquiesce in all decisions or agencies or institutions or arrangements?

PROFESSOR BARNETT: I said it because he asked me that question. Did you not hear him? Were you not here?

PROFESSOR PAULSEN: You are being a faint-hearted originalist.

PROFESSOR BARNETT: I did not say I endorse that view. I said that was one way of responding to concerns about transition problems.

AUDIENCE PARTICIPANT: My question has to do with pretext analysis, and this may be specifically directed towards Professor Paulsen, since he has a broader view of the Necessary and Proper Clause. I am wondering about two things. First of all, if I were a legislator, and I were bound by my oath to the Constitution, could I permissibly vote for the Gun-Free Zones Act, believing that it would have the ends of helping the war on terror, but knowing that that is not my real purpose in voting for the act? I am really voting on different grounds: I like children or, you know, something like that. My objective is not the War on Terror, but I am convinced that it will in fact have that side effect.

And second, if I were a judge, would it be permissible for me, knowing that the legislature has acted on those grounds, to strike down a statute on those grounds? And if I was not certain the legislature was acting on a pretext, what degree of certainty, what kind of information would let me take that approach?

PROFESSOR PAULSEN: Great question. My view is that, whatever the scope of the constitutional power, you may then employ it for whatever purpose you want. The power does not go away just because you had some motivation in your head that you think of as being slightly impure or collateral to the primary purpose for which the power is given. That is the Court's doctrine on the Commerce Clause. You can use a commercial regulation or a regulation of interstate commerce in order to accomplish a police power objective. You have no conflict there. You have no conflict with the spending power. You can use the spending power and the taxing power for regulatory administrative purposes.

John Marshall did talk about pretext, and that is the part of the *McCulloch* analysis that I think is unsound. If you have a legitimate power, the fact that you are using it for a purpose for which it was not intended does not erase the existence of the power, and you would be granting to courts the power to probe into legislative minds to see if anything is there, and to invalidate laws based upon the subjective motivations that individuals or collections of legislators would have had in passing it. It is a type of approach that we reject in most areas of constitutional law, and where the Supreme Court does embrace that sort of analysis, like in certain Establishment Clause contexts, it is utterly foolish, which is why Justice Scalia usually tap dances all over it.

PROFESSOR BARNETT: So, notice that the one part of *McCulloch v. Maryland* that John Marshall himself used to fend off the accusation that he was granting an unlimited discretion to Congress to choose whatever means they decide on, is the part that Michael says is unsound.

PROFESSOR PAULSEN: That is right.

PROFESSOR BARNETT: And it just goes to show that that is essentially how the New Deal Court treated that passage of *McCulloch v. Maryland*, which is actually excised from some constitutional law case books. If you are a law student, you do not even read that passage. But that is how the New Deal Court interpreted *McCulloch*. They reinterpreted it. There is some great limited government language in some Marshall opinions in cases like *Marbury*, *Gibbons*, and *McCulloch*, that the New Deal Court simply interpreted out of existence, in just the same way that they were very happy to interpret out of existence explicit portions of the Constitution itself.

JUDGE PARKER: Final question.

AUDIENCE PARTICIPANT: I have a question for Professor Paulsen on the Necessary and Proper Clause. It has been argued that Necessary and Proper was a term of art that, in the eighteenth century derived from agency law, which allows one to construe or to limit the authority that agents had, the necessary authority that they had, but also that had to be constrained. And if that is so, why should courts be any more deferential to Congress' construction of what powers are necessary and proper to execute its enumerated powers than courts were to be to an agent's assertion of what powers would be necessary and proper to execute an agent's powers and fiduciary obligations?

PROFESSOR PAULSEN: Very interesting question. At various times in the *Federalist Papers*, Hamilton and Madison actually made the agency analogy, and it comes out, if memory serves, kind of tending in the opposite direction from the thrust of your question. But your question actually calls to mind how courts respond to broad delegations to all of these federal agencies, where the broad statute gives power, then the agency interprets the statute and enacts some sort of instantiating rule based upon the broad delegation.

We have the Chevron Doctrine, which basically says that if something is within the scope of the delegated authority, the agency can choose what rule it will. I think there is actually an analogous principle at work in constitutional law. If it is within the scope of a broad delegation of power to Congress, or to the national government generally, and Congress has chosen one rule, the fact that it is not the particular rule that the judiciary might have chosen in the first instance is insufficient to invalidate it. If you grant Chevron deference, as it were, to decisions of Congress as to how to apply powers, so long as Congress' enactments fall within the scope of broad language granting that power, they are constitutionally proper.

MR. PARKER: Thank you.

Eleven

DEBATE ON RADICALS IN ROBES

Professor Cass Sunstein

Thank you. It is really great to be here. I have been coming to Federalist Society meetings for twenty years, at least, and I am grateful for this particular invitation, and the multiple kindnesses, over the years, of many people here, including Lee Liberman, whom I have known since she was a toddler, and Gene Meyer and Leonard Leo.

I want to begin by telling you the story of the title of this book, *Radicals in Robes*, which I am not thrilled with. I got a telephone call pre-publication, and someone purporting to be George Will was on the other line, and indeed it was George Will. And he said, "This is not a bad book." He might have even said "this is a good book," but I think I might have dreamed that part. He said, "This is not a bad book, but the title is really horrible, *Radicals in Robes*." He said, "This is like"—and then he mentioned a person who is on television a fair bit, and has written a book called *Treason*. He said, "This title makes it sound like one of those books." And so, I thought he was right, and called my publisher and said, "George Will, who knows about these things, called and said, the title of this book is like *Treason* or *Slander*, that person's book." And my publisher—then, I lost any hope I had of changing the title.

I am going to talk about four strands of conservative thought. And if you will forgive me, some of this will be a little academic for lunchtime, but that is what Federalist Society meetings are for, after all. So, four strands of conservative thought. The first strand is bipartisan advocacy of judicial restraint. This strand is exemplified by most of the work of Oliver Wendell Holmes, who said, "If the people want to go to hell, I will help them; that is my job." Holmes had a teacher or a forerunner, and that is James Bradley Thayer, who wrote in 1893 that the job of the Supreme Court is to uphold legislation unless it is unconstitutional beyond a reasonable doubt. And many of the attacks on the Warren Court were motivated by enthusiasm for bipartisan judicial restraint, invoking Thayer and Holmes.

The second kind of conservative thought, the second strand, I am going to call conservative perfectionism. And by conservative perfectionism, I mean the view that the broad aspirations of the Constitution should be interpreted in their best light, perfected, made the best sense of. We can see conservative perfectionism in much of the work of the *Lochner* Court, in the attack on affirmative action as inconsistent with the ideal of color blindness, and in some contemporary efforts to revive property rights.

Conservative perfectionism has a theorist parallel to Thayer, and it is a little bit of a surprising one, but it is not unfair to invoke him and I hope you will not be offended. The theorist is Ronald Dworkin, who is a famous liberal thinker, but who is also a jurisprudence scholar who says that the job of legal interpreter is to cast the pre-existing materials in the best constructive light, to make them the best they can be—a bit as if the job of the interpreter is to take to the Constitution the same approach that the Marine Corps takes to young people, to perfect them. And that is an unmistakable strand in conservative constitutional thought.

The third kind of conservative thought I am going to call Burkean minimalism. It is reflected in the work of Judge Friendly, discussed eloquently yesterday, and in the work of Justice Harlan, the great conservative on the Warren Court. And it is exemplified in much of the writing of former solicitor general and Massachusetts Supreme Court Justice Charles Fried. Burkean minimalists believe that judges should not take on-board ambitious theories. They give the same sort of answer that Chief Justice Roberts gave to Senator Hatch. When asked his approach to the Constitution, he basically said, "I do not have a theory that accounts for my approach to the Constitution and law."

Burkean minimalists often tend not only to avoid ambitious theories of interpretation but also to proceed cautiously, one case at a time. So, frequently, they prefer narrow decisions to wide decisions, and frequently they prefer shallow decisions to deep decisions. And by shallow I mean decisions that do not accept a contentious theory about the meaning of the Equal Protection Clause or the Due Process Clause or the Commander in Chief Clause. The theorist of Burkean minimalism—who is not buried in Lincoln's or Washington's tomb—the theorist of Burkean minimalism is, of course, Burke. But there is another thinker worth mention, and that is Michael Oakeshott, the conservative theorist who attacked rationalism and theory-building on the ground that it was hubristic.

Okay, the fourth brand of conservative thought about law is originalism, and that is going to be my particular focus today.

What unifies these four strands? They sound different, do they not? Why do they all deserve the name "conservative"? Well, the reason is that all four are skeptical of the use of the Constitution to promote left-of-center political ideas. So, all four of them criticize *Roe v. Wade*, the rigid separation of Church and State, the use of the Due Process Clause to protect the right to physician-assisted suicide, the use of the Equal Protection Clause to proliferate the set of groups who are entitled to constitutional protection. All four put their face against this approach; but there are noteworthy differences.

Holmes was not an originalist, and the most prominent Thayerian is about to be Professor Adrian Vermeule, now of Harvard Law School, who is defending bipartisan judicial restraint as the right approach to the Constitution. Vermeule is emphatically not arguing on originalist grounds. Bipartisan judicial restraint was not defended in originalist terms by Holmes or by Thayer. It is an effort to create a kind of arms control agreement by people who might otherwise be enlisting the federal judicial power in the interest of their preferred causes.

The attack on affirmative action is not originalist in character. Justice Thomas and Justice Scalia have written eloquently against affirmative action. But neither of them has mined the original understanding of the Fourteenth Amendment. And Justice Thomas's very powerful dissent a couple of years ago in the *University of Michigan* case refers to Frederick Douglass, but it does not refer to the original understanding of the ratifiers generally. It is true that Justice Thomas's opinion in the *Kelo* case is originalist in character, and I think very possibly correct in its analysis on originalist terms. But the effort to protect against regulatory takings, to protect property rights against regulations that diminish the value of property—an effort whose high point was in the Scalia opinion in the *Lucas* case—that is not a thesis which is defended on originalist grounds. There is not a paragraph or a sentence or a footnote in the *Lucas* opinion that refers to the original understanding of the Fifth Amendment. So at least insofar as the effort to protect property rights has to do with regulatory takings it is a form of conservative perfectionism. It is not originalism.

Burkean minimalism is at the heart of many attacks on *Roe v. Wade*. I think it is the foundation, actually, for the attack on the effort to get a constitutional right to same-sex marriage. And it also underlies some of the criticisms of efforts to excise religion from the public sphere. But our leading Burkean minimalists are not originalists. In fact, they reject reliance on the original understanding, with Judge Friendly not speaking in terms of the original understanding in his most prominent constitutional opinions, and Professor Fried explicitly rejecting originalism as a kind of fantasy.

Okay, I could spend some time speaking about perfectionism, which has prominent liberal incarnations. All I am going to say about perfectionism, in both its conservative and liberal guises, is that it neglects the theory-building weaknesses of the federal judiciary. So if we think that judges are fallible as political and moral theorists, then we will be reluctant to sign on to Dworkin's program of authorizing judges to put constitutional ideals in the best possible light. And we will be skeptical, also, of efforts to deploy norms like color-blindness or aggressive property protection; at least if these norms partake of the most contentious approaches to political morality.

But originalism, I am going to suggest, raises distinctive difficulties, and I am going to try to trace them here.

The most serious problem, for getting the analysis off the ground, is that the Constitution does not set out the rules for its own interpretation. There is not an article in the Constitution or a section of the Constitution that requires or disqualifies any of the four contenders for theories of interpretation that I have mentioned. There are, by the way, liberal alternatives. One is liberal minimalism *à la* Justice Breyer, and the other is liberal perfectionism *à la* Justice Brennan and my old boss, Thurgood Marshall. Those are not ruled out, either. So, we have six possible theories of interpretation now on the table. And the Constitution does not require or forbid any of them. So, it is a big mistake to say that to respect the Constitution it is necessary to respect the original understanding of its terms. It may be that the best way of respecting the Constitution is to respect the original understanding of its terms, but it is not the case that respect for the Constitution entails, as a matter of logic, respect for the original understanding of its terms.

What I am about to do is give a set of results that, in my view, originalism might well mandate in a way that is intended to suggest that originalism is not the best approach to constitutional law, and indeed that it is radical. I was nervous about the accuracy or plausibility of my title. And, if I thought, on reflection, that the title was not true, I would have rejected it, no matter how many copies it might have sold. But I was comforted in the final stages of writing my book by reading Professor Thomas Merrill's wonderful paper in the *Harvard Journal of Law and Public Policy,* called "Bork v. Burke," in which he argues that the originalist approach to constitutional interpretation is anything but conservative. In fact, he uses the word "radical" to describe the originalist program, not once, but twice.

A couple of qualifications before I begin. One is that some originalists are, in Justice Scalia's terms, faint-hearted. That is, they believe
that precedent has its claims, and they are not going to use the original
understanding as a kind of bomb which will explode well-established
law. Fainthearted originalists are not horribly far away from conservative minimalists of the Burkean stripe, so; there is convergence
there. So, what I am going to be challenging is originalism that at least
is not terribly faint of heart.

It is also the case that some of the examples I am going to give are
contested. Professor Amar, in particular, who I know is here, will con-
test a number of them on historical grounds. What I am trying to do
with these examples is just to give illustrations that seem to me either
very hard to escape, as a matter of logic, from the originalist perspective, or, if they are escapable easily as a matter of logic, they are
ones that have been defended ably by prominent originalists. So, what
I am going to try to do is give a catalog of consequences that originalism, taken seriously, either might well or will produce, and to suggest that whether originalism produces those consequences is highly
relevant to the choice of a theory of constitutional interpretation. For
those of you who think that this claim is impermissibly results-oriented,
I respond, how can a theory of constitutional interpretation be chosen without at least some reference to the consequences that it would
produce, in light of the fact that the Constitution itself does not identify or specify a theory of interpretation that judges must follow? Any
theory of interpretation has to be defended, not asserted. And if it
would produce consequences that are intolerable, I suggest that is a
strong point against it.

The first consequence is that it is extremely hard to explain why
racial discrimination by the national government is forbidden under
the originalist understanding of interpretation. The Equal Protection
Clause does not apply to the national government. The notion that
the national government is forbidden from segregating the schools or
from engaging in egregious forms of racial profiling is extremely hard
to defend on originalist premises, just because there is no term that is
naturally or easily understood historically to ban the national gov-

ernment from discriminating. For those who think that *Bolling v. Sharpe*—that is the case that understood the Equal Protection Clause as forbidding racial discrimination—can be defended on originalist grounds, and there is an uphill battle there, it is harder still to defend the proposition that sex discrimination is banned by the federal government on originalist grounds. So, if we follow the originalist program, then it is just the case that sex discrimination by the national government poses no constitutional problem whatsoever.

The catalog quickly grows. Sex discrimination by the states, as Chief Justice Rehnquist long argued, is entirely acceptable on originalist grounds, unless we understand the originalist program in a way that turns it perfectionist by abandoning the specific understandings of the ratifiers. The notion that the Equal Protection Clause was originally understood to forbid states from discriminating against women has very, very little support. It is hard to find a specific understanding that supports that view.

With respect to racial discrimination by the states, Judge McConnell has brilliantly defended *Brown v. Board of Education* on historical grounds, arguing it fits with the original understanding. Raoul Berger, probably the engineer of originalism as a serious approach to constitutional interpretation, argued in 1979 that that position was preposterous. It is no longer preposterous after Judge McConnell's argument, but Michael Klarman and other historians find that he has made it a plausible argument, but not a convincing one. Even on Professor McConnell's view, the notion that states are forbidden from discriminating in marriage laws by banning interracial marriage, or discriminating in public facilities, such as golf courses and parks—I do not think that the constitutional ban on such discrimination is defended by Judge McConnell's view. So forms of racial discrimination that are roundly understood as unconstitutional would suddenly become acceptable, unless we are very fainthearted originalists.

Justice Scalia has argued that the "one person one vote" rule and property restrictions on voting—he has argued that the "one person one vote" rule is implausible on originalist grounds, and he has argued that property restrictions on voting are just fine on originalist grounds. I think Justice Scalia is correct, and that suggests that the effort to understand voting as a fundamental right for purposes of the Thirteenth or Fourteenth Amendment loses. It must be abandoned.

Justice Thomas has argued in two opinions that have gotten comically little attention that the Establishment Clause is not incorporated by the Fourteenth Amendment, such that, in his view, states could be permitted to establish official religions; not only to favor particular religions, but to establish official religions. I think on this one, Justice Thomas has the history exactly right, and the Establishment Clause, on originalist terms, is not incorporated as against the states. Judge Janice Rogers Brown has questioned the legitimacy of incorporation more generally. Many historians are with her. Professor Amar has argued enthusiastically and powerfully in favor of incorporation. And, at least it is the case that if there is a historical dispute within a body of nine responsible originalists, we cannot be clear who would ultimately prevail in the debate. But there is a serious school of thought that questions incorporation altogether.

Justice Scalia has suggested that the right of privacy is gone under originalism by "its inescapable terms." "It," meaning the Due Process Clause, guarantees only process. I think he is right textually, as well as on the original understanding. So, not only would *Roe v. Wade* be deemed illegitimate when decided, a position with which I actually agree, but also the right of privacy as a whole would be out the window, a position which I do not accept.

There would be no ban on regulatory takings. For those of you who are concerned about property rights, that ban would go out the window, as historian John Hart has argued at length in the *Northwestern University Law Review*. The original understanding of the Takings Clause meant to bar only physical takings of property. So, *Lucas,* and cases which expand on it, would be done for under originalism.

These are all cases in which prohibitions on national and state governments would be eliminated by the originalist program, in a way that would open up the democratic process. So, the Holmesians among us, and the Vermeulians—a term which I hope will become current, though it does not quite have a ring to it yet—the Holmesians and the Vermeulians would be okay with this because it opens up space for democratic processes. But, of course, there is much more.

Larry Alexander and Sai Prakash have argued—and I think, in the end, they are right—that the Non-Delegation Doctrine was part of the constitutional system in a way that would endanger the Occupational Safety and Health Administration and the Clean Air Act. And, as Randy May (who is present) has argued, it would mean the Federal Communications Commission's basic authorization would be constitutionally unacceptable.

I am not sure I agree with Steve Calabresi and Geoffrey Miller and others who have attacked the independent agencies on constitutional grounds. But certainly they have a plausible argument, as a matter of history, and their argument is widely regarded as more than plausible, that is as powerful. Chief Justice Roberts described the independent agencies as a constitutional anomaly. If that view is correct, then the National Labor Relations Board, the Federal Reserve Board, the Federal Communications Commission, the Federal Trade Commission, and others are in constitutional jeopardy.

Justice Thomas has argued for an understanding of the Commerce Clause, as has Randy Barnett, which would involve a much weaker Congress than we now have. This would mean the Endangered Species Act, the Clean Water Act, and many criminal statutes would be in constitutional trouble.

I hope this catalog is enough to suggest that the originalist program taken seriously would be profoundly destabilizing of both our rights and our institutions, in a way that would make *Roe v. Wade* look like trivia. It would do away with established constitutional doctrine along many dimensions, and it would serve also as an attack on the decisions of the elected branches of government.

No theory of interpretation, I emphasize, works in every imaginable world. We could imagine one in which originalism would make great sense. It is just not the case that our world is that world. There are appealing motivations that underlie originalism: the effort to reduce judicial intrusions into the political process, to discipline judicial discretion—Justice Scalia's major emphasis—and to stabilize constitutional law. But there are other and better ways to do that. Originalists have a heroic picture of judging, a little like my liberal teachers in the 1970s. They see the courts not as declaring, as the liberal teachers then wanted one, two, three, one hundred *Brown v. Board of Educations*, but instead, cutting through affirmative action programs, striking down acts of Congress, restricting the independent agencies, imposing new limits under Article III of the Constitution, striking down campaign finance regulation, and protecting commercial advertising.

Minimalism is too quiet to be heroic. It has none of this drama. My liberal teachers in the 1970s read the Constitution in a way that was uncomfortably close to the Democratic Party platform of the time. The catalog of results that I have just listed, which many modern originalists have called for, looks uncomfortably close to the political convictions of the Republican Party. It is the mirror image. That is why I say, often, originalism is conservative perfectionism in historical guise. That is the most nervous-making feature of the program.

Minimalism is too quiet to be heroic. It does not have any of this drama. It does not generate applause. It is too small. Some people even laugh at it. But it can claim a virtue, which is that it is admirably suited to the institutional strengths and weaknesses of the federal judiciary.

Thanks.

❦

Hon. Charles Cooper

Good afternoon, friends.

Back in July, one of Professor Sunstein's colleagues at the University of Chicago, Professor Geoffrey Stone, wrote that Supreme Court nominee John Roberts "has never embraced a vacuous ideology of originalism. And frankly, he seems too smart to do so. Roberts is too good a lawyer, too good a craftsman, to embrace such a disingenuous approach to constitutional interpretation. Everything about him suggests a principled, pragmatic justice who will move cautiously, will have a healthy respect, of course, for precedent." So, Professor Stone and others on the Left no doubt resigned to the reality that Roberts' appointment could not be blocked, began their patient campaign to tempt him with the pleasures known only to the liberal activists.

Roberts will approach his work, Stone continued, "in an open-minded, rigorous, intellectually honest manner, rather than as an ideologue whose constitutional principles derive more from fiction and faith than from legal reason." And Roberts will, Stone confidently predicted, "continue to learn and grow during his time on the Court," "evolv[ing] over time into a better, more compassionate justice." The choice, then, offered to the new Chief Justice by Professor Stone is the same one offered to all justices by the Left, which is to say, by the vast majority of law, political science, and history professors, as well as the editorial writers of the nation's leading newspapers.

The new Chief Justice can choose either fawning tributes as a brilliant open-minded and compassionate jurist, or relentless ridicule as an unprincipled, simple-minded ideologue. We can only speculate as to how powerfully the Left's siren song has played on the mind of any justice, but there can be no doubt that over the last thirty-five years several Republican-appointed justices have "evolved" and have "grown" in office in ways that have pleased the Left very much.

Professor Sunstein's new book is of a piece with his colleague Professor Stone's article. That it was designed to supply ordinance for the Left's war against President Bush's Supreme Court nominees is clear, to say the least, from the book's title, *Radicals in Robes*. Now actually, with all due respect, Cass, as bad as the title is, it is not as bad as the subtitle: *Why Extreme Right-Wing Courts Are Wrong for America.*

And who are these "radicals," these "extreme right-wingers" who threaten America? Well, Professor Sunstein is not talking about some kind of modern counterpart to Chief Justice Roger Taney, who professed devotion to the originalist method, and then, in his next breath, invented substantive due process to protect property rights in slaves. Nor is he talking about the narrow segment of the conservative movement, who long for a revival of a *Lochner*-style judicial activism. And he certainly is not worried about the appointment of a right-wing counterpart to Justice Brennan, who never cast a single vote, not one, that cut against his own liberal social and economic policy views. For Justice Brennan, the constitutional rule of law in every case was whatever the rule needed to be to yield the liberal result.

No, Professor Sunstein's right-wing extremists are simply *originalists*—that is, judges who believe the courts are bound, both by theory and by oath, to interpret the Constitution's provisions to mean what they were intended to mean. That is all. That is originalism in a nutshell. Madison concisely captured the originalist creed in his famous report on the Virginia Resolutions of 1799. "The compact ought to have the interpretation plainly intended by the parties to it." Indeed, Professor Sunstein himself explains that originalist judges "insist on interpreting the text of the Constitution in accordance with its original meaning." Not only are these judges, according to Professor Sunstein, "radicals in robes," "constitutional revisionists," and "fundamentalists on the bench," but their belief in originalism, he says, is "destructive," "dangerous," "pernicious," "terrible," "arrogant," "wrong," "incoherent," and "indefensible." And it "ultimately threatens both our democracy and our rights." Wow.

I think it is worth pausing here for a moment to remark on Professor Sunstein's efforts to change the terms of the debate. In much the same way that the Left has displaced the term "unborn child" with the term "fetus," Professor Sunstein seeks to replace the term "originalism," although he used it here today consistently, with the term "fundamentalism." That is the term he uses consistently in his book. I trust that his purpose is obvious to you all. But just in case it is not, he tells us: "As a constitutional creed, fundamentalism bears an obvious resemblance to religious fundamentalism.... 'Strict construction' of the Constitution finds a parallel in literal interpretation of the Koran and the Bible." And if we originalists are the religious fanatics of constitutional interpretation, you can surely guess who our snake-handling, tongue-speaking high priests are. Why, Justices Scalia and Thomas, of course, whom Professor Sunstein calls "movement judges."

Professor Sunstein also redefines the term "activist." No longer does it mean simply a judge who deliberately departs from the original meaning of the Constitution in order to reach a result that the original Constitution simply will not yield. Rather, Professor Sunstein uses it to describe judges who "strike down the actions of other parts of government, especially those of Congress." This convenient interpretation of the term "activist," or, one might say, this activist interpretation of "activist," allows liberals to claim, as Professor Sunstein does, that the Rehnquist Court's brand of "right-wing activism" made it the "all-time champion" activist court.

Ironically, and perhaps unwittingly, Professor Sunstein embraces the central tenet of originalism in redefining "activism." As he puts it, "People are free to use the term activist however they wish, so long as listeners understand what they mean." Yes, exactly. Professor Sunstein chooses his words carefully, and he takes pains to ensure that his readers understand the meaning he attaches to his words. That is because he wants his words to be interpreted to mean what he intends them to mean. That is the purpose of all language, and certainly of all written instruments, from books or law review articles to statutes and treaties, to contracts and wills, to musical scores and love letters. All agree, and have always agreed, that written texts should be interpreted to accord with the meanings intended by their authors. This is particularly true of our written Constitution.

All of the Framers of the Constitution were originalists. None of them embraced the preposterous notion that judges, or even members of the elected branches for that matter, would be free to depart from the Constitution's intended meaning and answer questions of constitutional law in accordance with their own economic, social, or moral values. This matters not to Professor Sunstein. "It is up to us," he says, "to decide whether to accept [originalism]. We can not say that [originalism] is right simply because the Framers believed that it is right." Really? If the Framers had included—and certainly it is true

that they did not, as we have heard Professor Sunstein emphasize—
but if they had included in the Constitution an express provision, akin
to the Eleventh Amendment, requiring that the words of the Constitution be construed by the courts to mean what they were originally
intended to mean, would it be up to us—that is, up to our judges—to
decide whether to obey? Professor Sunstein's answer must be yes,
which brings the lawlessness of his position into sharp focus.

Professor Sunstein's emphasis on "us"—that is, we twenty-first
century living Americans—is a key element of his attack on originalism. He acknowledges, to his credit, the anti-democratic difficulty of,
in his words, "allowing unelected judges to give meaning to the constitutional text." He also acknowledges the originalist claim that the
only *legitimate* rules of constitutional law—that is, the only rules of
law that are backed by the consent of the governed—are the actual
original rules of law negotiated and agreed upon by the framers and
the ratifiers of the Constitution.

But these difficulties cannot overcome Professor Sunstein's desire
to be governed by living liberal judges, rather than by dead conservative Framers. "Why should living people," he asks, "be governed by
the decisions of those who died many generations ago?" It is "false"
and "fanciful," according to Professor Sunstein, "to say that *we* are
bound by the Constitution because '*we*' agreed to it. None of *us* did.
The legitimacy of the Constitution does not lie in consent."

Now, when I read that line for the first time, the words of the Declaration of Independence rang in my ears, that to "secure these rights,
governments are instituted among men, *deriving their just powers
from the consent of the governed*." If a nation can have a soul, then
surely this is ours.

And if living judges are not bound by the original meaning
attached to the terms of the Constitution by its dead framers and ratifiers, then in what sense can the Constitution be considered binding
at all? By what warrant do courts engage in the essentially anti-
democratic process of reviewing, and occasionally nullifying as
unconstitutional, the work of living elected legislators and executives?
It turns out that this is no problem at all for Professor Sunstein. Here

is his answer. "Of course, the Constitution itself should be taken as binding. The Constitution is binding because it is good to take it as binding. It is good to take it as binding because it is an exceedingly good Constitution, all things considered."

So, for Professor Sunstein the original meaning of a constitutional provision is not binding on us, for, if it were, it would limit the freedom of liberal judges, or at least honest liberal judges, to negate bad legislative and executive policies. But the constitutional provision itself, divorced from its original meaning, is nonetheless binding on us, for, if it were not, liberal judges would have no constitutional warrant to negate bad legislative and executive policies. That is his argument. Professor Sunstein continues, "[A]ncient ratification is not enough to make the Constitution legitimate. We follow the Constitution because it is good for us to follow the Constitution. Is it good for us to follow the original understanding [of the Constitution]? Actually, it would be terrible."

But if a judge is not following the intended meaning of a constitutional provision, what exactly is the judge following when the judge is interpreting and enforcing the constitutional provision? The only answer is the judge's own sense of what is good and what is bad. The Constitution is then transformed from a charter for the rule of law into a license for the rule of courts. And that is precisely the mission of Professor Sunstein and every champion of judicial activism, whether they be conservative or liberal, and whether they call themselves minimalists or perfectionists.

Does the death long ago of the Constitution's framers and ratifiers really render the Constitution's original meaning irrelevant to "us," as Professor Sunstein posits? Well, every time a court strikes down a legislative policy as inconsistent with the rule of law embodied in a constitutional provision, or, for that matter, embodied in a statute or a judicial decision that is older than about thirty years, it enforces the political will of dead lawmakers over the political will of the living electorate. Lawmakers die, but their laws do not. A rule of law duly established by the people continues in force until it is amended or repealed, and later generations are free to amend or repeal laws whenever, again in the words of the Declaration, "it shall seem most likely to effect their safety and happiness."

A court that assumes responsibility for determining that the intended meaning of a constitutional provision no longer comports with society's, say for example, "evolving standards of morality," and then gives the provision a new and result-oriented meaning, serves the cause of self-government only if the people consented to be governed by the rule of judges. And this, they have never done, and never would do. Imagine an express constitutional provision that granted to the Supreme Court the interpretive power that today's liberal activists claim for it. There has never been an instant in our history in which the people would have granted that power to the Supreme Court.

So, let us return to Professor Sunstein's claim that it would be "terrible" for "us" to follow the original meaning of the Constitution. He supports this claim, as you have just heard, with the familiar and by now tiresome parade of horribles that allegedly would result if the court had five members as true and as faithful to the Constitution as Justices Scalia and Thomas. To be sure, interpreting the Constitution to mean only what it was intended to mean would permit legislative bodies to enact a lot of bad policies. In fact, every controversial enactment is bad, by definition, to those who oppose it. And while the Constitution, given its intended meaning, prohibits a lot of bad policies, it leaves legislative bodies great leeway to enact policies that will be viewed as bad by some activist judge and by those who support the judge's views.

And most of the horribles that Professor Sunstein parades are indeed horrible. A plausible originalist argument, as he has outlined, can be made for most of, I assume—I have not studied them all—but I assume most of the ones he has just shared with us. My favorite, however, is the example in which he poses this question dealing with the right of privacy. "[W]ould the nation really be better off if the Supreme Court rejected four decades of precedent and entirely eliminated privacy as a constitutional principle? Would it really be better if states could fine or imprison people who use contraceptives and engage in certain sexual acts?"

But my question is this. Is there any genuine risk that the states will do this? The point is that state laws such as this, where they still exist, even on paper, are dead, and the only people who might even theoretically be at risk of enforcement of such laws are those who flaunt their violation of them in order to provoke enforcement and set up test cases, people like Mr. Griswold and Mr. Lawrence. Indeed, Professor Sunstein acknowledges candidly that these laws have fallen into desuetude. And the other intolerable consequences predicted by Professor Sunstein to flow from an originalist interpretation are by and large of the same ilk. They are generally agreed to be intolerable, and therefore pose no genuine threat of coming to pass.

But the danger of intolerable consequences from the liberal judicial activism that gave us *Griswold*, and then *Roe*, and now *Lawrence*, is clear and present. Will the nation really be better off if the Supreme Court follows the logical path marked by four decades of right to privacy precedent and strikes down state laws prohibiting and punishing prostitution, or polygamy, or same-sex marriage? That is a real and a serious question, unlike Professor Sunstein's.

Professor Sunstein trumpets "minimalism," and he leaves no doubt about where he wants to "nudge," as he puts it, the Court with "narrow" and "shallow" minimalist decisions. The minimalist doctrine is not so much an interpretive methodology as a litigation strategy designed to bring about judicial imposition of the liberal social agenda more gradually and, therefore, more certainly than the abrupt and sweeping edicts favored by the liberal "perfectionists." But minimalism is liberal judicial activism on the installment plan.

Ed Whelan, in a recent review of Professor Sunstein's book, aptly and cleverly described his minimalism as "boil-the-frog gradualism," likening the American public to the frog in a pot of water on the stove. "If the court turns up the heat," he said—that is, imposes the Left's agenda—"too suddenly, the frog will jump out. But if it does so gradually, he will sit there in blissful ignorance until it's too late."

Well, my fellow frogs, the water is already pretty hot.

Discussion
Moderated by Steven G. Calabresi

PROFESSOR SUNSTEIN: Maybe I should say something. There is a new book out about—remember when everyone thought Paul McCartney was dead because, if you played the music a certain way, it said "I buried Paul," or "Paul is the walrus" or something? I feel a little bit like the Beatles must have felt when they heard their words interpreted that way.

Minimalism really is not an effort to impose a liberal social agenda. I did identify a form of Burkean minimalism, which is actually very hostile to the idea of a liberal social agenda being imposed through the judiciary. So, there are many, very different different brands of minimalism. Chief Justice Rehnquist was much of the time a Burkean minimalist, and he was not an originalist.

Okay, there is a lot here, so I guess I want to give a title to these remarks, which is "How Not to Defend Originalism." Let me sketch five defenses of originalism, three that I think plausible; two which I think you just heard, that just seem to me mysterious. The first is just a consequentialist argument that originalism gives us a stable, rock-hard Constitution. Now, that is a rule of law justification for originalism, which is consequentialist at its core. It is that the Constitution's meaning is changing too quickly to serve as the foundation for self-government. So that is a point.

Justice Scalia also makes the second argument, which is that originalism minimizes judicial discretion, which may be exercised in ways that are objectionable, either because they lead to bad outcomes, or because it is an imposition by an unelected set of people. That also is a consequentialist argument, though it has a democratic feature too.

The third argument, which actually Randy Barnett has made—I do not know if he thinks this is a justification for originalism, or a happy byproduct of it—but he argued in a debate with me that originalism produces better results overall. That is a meaningful argument.

Okay, there are two arguments for originalism that I think I heard made in Chuck Cooper's talk, and I really do not understand them. I think the first argument Chuck Cooper makes is that following the intended meaning just is interpretation, and anything else just is not. That is really implausible, I think. It is not an argument; it is just an exclamation point. Justice Scalia himself, and Justice Thomas, and the most sophisticated originalists, have no patience with that. They do not talk about intended meanings. They talk about original public meanings, following Holmes in saying, "We do not care what the law-maker intended; we care what the words mean." So, the notion that interpretation just is a matter of getting out subjective intentions does not even correspond to what the originalists say. They want to get at the original meaning, not at the subjective intentions.

Now, might they say that going after the original meaning just is interpretation? Is that what Justice Scalia believes? That is the fourth argument, and one that I find mysterious. I do not think Justice Scalia has ever said that, and it is just not a plausible view. If you look at law as it is made all over the world—and surely we should not, but let us do so just for a second—it is just not a convention that the words that the laws contain always mean what they originally meant, period or exclamation point. That is one optional approach to the problem of how to interpret texts, and I have given three reasons why it might be a good approach, but it is just not what interpretation means.

The second argument that Chuck Cooper makes, I think is not just an exclamation point, but I confess I do not understand it, and that is an argument involving legitimacy or contract. The argument is that it is terrible or obtuse or unpatriotic or something to say that the reason we follow the Constitution is that it is a great Constitution, and we are a lot better off with it—which is what I think. He thinks that the explanation goes deeper than that, that we agreed to it or something.

Now, I can see the view that we are bound by contract in part because we agreed to it, if we did. But then it would have to be explained why we bind people to contracts to which they agree, and that argument would not partake of their agreement. It would explain why it is good to bind people to contracts to which they agree; and there are lots of reasons for that. And I can also see the argument that, with respect to recent legislation produced by legislators for whose jobs we are responsible, there is a ground of legitimacy. I can see that. But the notion that we consented to the Constitution of the United States—I mean, you all look so young as I look around; even the baldish ones look young. We did not consent to the Constitution, so let us not make arguments like that that are mystifications.

You know, the consent argument is, I think, shorthand for other sorts of arguments that are more pragmatic and real.   The Constitution is binding, and the reason the Constitution is binding is that we should take it as binding. But any other argument is just a circle, sad to say, and for purposes of analysis let us avoid circles, shall we? The Constitution is best taken as binding, and so we take it as binding. The question is whether the root original understanding is best taken as binding.

I gave three arguments, two from Justice Scalia and one from Professor Barnett, that seem to be contenders. I do not think the other two are contenders. If you think the interest in a stable, rock-hard Constitution that minimizes judicial discretion produces better results overall, well, there are imaginable worlds in which that is an adequate argument on behalf of originalism. I do not think that is plausible in the United States of America.

MR. COOPER: Just a quick reaction—as I understand Cass Sunstein's response, it is that there are legitimate and valid arguments in defense of originalism, a.k.a. "fundamentalism," in his book. And each one of the ones that are valid flow from value-based judgments. And that is of a piece with his book. In literally every page of the book, the question of whether something is good or something is bad is the determining issue, as in whether it will lead to better consequences overall, as we have just heard. So, this vests our judiciary, our unelected judiciary, with the power to simply determine, as I said, whether a policy is good or bad overall.

My opinion, that I believe truly, was the opinion of the Framers, and the opinion I should think of the vast majority of people committed in this country, to democratic institutions, is that whether something is good or something is bad is determined in democratically elected institutions, by and large, with only narrow and shallow limits on the things they can do. And it may well be that something is bad in Massachusetts, but good in Alabama, and that is the genius— *the genius*—of our Constitution. At no time did any of the Founders or the ratifiers embrace the notion that unelected judges have the authority to police those decisions based upon their own value judgments.

And I reject the proposition that originalism versus minimalism, versus perfectionism, as a governing interpretive methodology for the Constitution, should be decided in the same way by asking does it yield good or bad decisions? Because, I assure you, Professor Sunstein, you and I will answer those questions differently, and it seems to me that if you can convince enough people, enough of our countrymen, of the wisdom of your view, then you should win on virtually whatever that issue is.

PROFESSOR CALABRESI: I would like to open the floor to questions at this point. Professor Sai Prakash.

PROFESSOR SAI PRAKASH: I have a question for Professor Sunstein, along the lines of Mr. Cooper's remarks. It seems to me that, for Professor Sunstein, originalism is only contingently bad if the Constitution to which it applies is a bad Constitution. And so, if we had a Constitution that you perhaps wrote, I am wondering if you would be willing to say that originalism does not work for that Constitution, because I think then it probably would work quite well, because it would satisfy whatever view you desire?

The second question is, I am wondering whether it makes any sense to talk about the consequentialist results of an interpretation as a means of deciding what the best means of interpretation is. No one looks at the Articles of Confederation and asks, "Let us try to make this the best Articles of Confederation it can be." People just read it, and they try to, I think, generally try to think of what it would have meant at the time, either according to the intent of the authors, or its public meaning. I think that is true of most writings, including your book. I am not going to read your book and say, "I am going to try to make Cass Sunstein's book the best it can be." Let me read it the way I would have....

PROFESSOR SUNSTEIN: No, I actually recommend that you do that.

AUDIENCE PARTICIPANT: I can do that if my point is to try to not to understand what Cass Sunstein is trying to say. But if I am trying to understand what he is trying to say, then I am not going to be doing that. And so it seems to me that, when it comes to the Constitution or statutes, we have a perverted idea of interpretation. And we think about what the consequences are. But there are lots of laws and constitutions that are bad, right? Slavery was a bad thing, and any interpretation, any interpretational device that tries to suggest that we should try to avoid that result, notwithstanding Randy and, you know, Lysander Spooner, I think is a wrong method of interpretation, because it is a fantasy where you are going to try to perfect something through the act of interpretation, when you do not normally do that with a letter from your mother or your father when they tell you something you do not like. So anyway, I have spoken too much, but those are my questions

PROFESSOR SUNSTEIN: They are very helpful questions. Let me say a little bit about constitutional perfectionism, which is an approach that many liberals have been drawn to which I reject. Constitutional perfectionism means you make the document the best it can be. Now, that does not mean that you change it or make it up. So Dworkin is very clear that there are two duties; one is fit, and the other is justification. So it is like a common law lawyer who is trying to fit the precedents and justify them. The notion that the perfectionist casts aside the words or ignores the document. That is inconsistent with the perfectionist plan. The perfectionist is trying to make the document be the best it can be. He is not trying to draw one up from scratch. So, that is just a clarification.

If I wrote the Constitution, would I want people to be bound by my understanding? No. First, I would not want for me to write it. Second, if I did, I would think people probably could do better in interpreting what I wrote than to try to permeate the text with my subjective understanding. The best case for originalism has nothing to do with the subjective understanding of Madison, Hamilton, *et al.* It is the argument from original public meaning.

With regard to the question—I do not know if I really picked this up, but you identified following the Constitution with following the original understanding. I think that is deeply at the heart of your argument, and Chuck Cooper's also; your argument just sketched now. And it is really radically different from Scalia's arguments for originalism. I think the argument you seem to be making is that a document just means what the original understanding is. Otherwise, we are not interpreting it. Now, I do not know what kind of argument that is. That seems to me not an argument. It is an exclamation point.

So, to say interpretation just is following the originally intended meaning, which Scalia and Thomas rightly reject, or to follow the original understanding, which they wrongly embrace, there is just no way of avoiding an argument having to do with what approach to interpretation produces good or ill. Some such argument is unavoidable. It is not possible to say, "We follow the Constitution's original meaning because the Framers understood things a certain way." First, that is a highly disputed historical claim. Second, even if it were a true historical claim, it is not an argument at all, as I think Justice Scalia is well aware. It just is not—it does not work as a matter of logic, if you will forgive me, to say that we follow the Constitution's original understanding because that was the original understanding. That is a vicious circle. I mean, if you wanted to define meaning as the original understanding, then you define meaning in the way you just defined it. But that is not an argument; that is a stipulation.

I want to define meaning in a different way. And with respect to literary texts, in fact, we do not always ask whether the meaning of *Hamlet* is Shakespeare's subjective intentions, or the original public meaning of *Hamlet*. I think either of those would be a preposterous suggestion about how to read *Hamlet*, which is not to say that for law it is a preposterous suggestion. It is just, this is something that has to be understood in evaluative terms.

Ten years ago, Fred Schauer—the leading academic defender of formalism, mind you—got it exactly right at the Federalist Society meeting where he said this has to be assessed in pragmatic terms. When you ask about my Constitution—I do not want the nation to follow my text or my original understanding. But what I do concede to you is that there are imaginable worlds in which originalism would make sense. We have a fantastic constitution. If the fantasticness of the Constitution was equaled by the fantasticness of the original understanding, then, by hypothesis we should follow the original understanding. But, in the context I have outlined, our constitutional order would be worse overall if we had gone the originalist route.

Now, I think some of you want to argue that that is irrelevant, and that is what I am having a hard time seeing. I think the claim that it is irrelevant is question-begging. Please, let us not argue by definitions or by asserting our conclusions.

PROFESSOR CALABRESI: I would like to ask Professor Sunstein a question about the extent of our obligation to follow rules from the past that we disapprove of as a policy matter. I have in mind, particularly, the abortion issue, where many Americans disagree very profoundly with the policy that the Court put in place with *Roe v. Wade*. This past September when Chief Justice Rehnquist died, the last member of the nine-justice court that decided *Roe v. Wade* passed away. So, in a sense, *Roe v. Wade* represents the dead hand of the past for us now. Most Americans were not old enough to vote when *Roe v. Wade* was decided. Why should Americans who disagree profoundly with *Roe*, who might be district court or circuit court judges, be bound by it? And if they are bound by that, why does not the original understanding in other things from our history bind as well?

PROFESSOR SUNSTEIN: Good. The bindingness of *Roe* is that if individual judges took it upon themselves to reject Supreme Court precedents because they thought they were profoundly wrong the whole system would collapse. We do not want that. So the bindingness of Supreme Court precedent is just a less dramatic and poignant illustration of why the Constitution as a whole is binding, because the whole system would collapse if we could not take it that way. I do not want to be misunderstood. Again—

MR. COOPER: Can I interrupt and just ask, what do you mean it would collapse? Why would it collapse?

PROFESSOR SUNSTEIN: You could not have a system of hierarchical law, if district court judges were refusing to enforce Supreme Court precedents that they did not like.

MR. COOPER: What about justices following *Roe* itself as a precedent, being bound by it?

PROFESSOR SUNSTEIN: My view of *stare decisis* is pragmatic and conventional. That is, that Supreme Court justices are not bound in any rigid sense, so too, the minimalist is perfectly comfortable with cutting back on *Roe*, as the Court did in *Casey*, and as it probably should do a bit more. And the minimalist is agnostic on the question of whether *Roe* should be overruled, because the minimalist thinks *Roe* was an abuse of the minimalist approach to Constitutional law; and because it has had a continued degree of fragility, the argument for overruling it is very much on the table.

MR. COOPER: But if I could just ask to follow up, what if the situation that Steve posits, with lower court judges free to interpret Supreme Court precedents in the same way that you say judges are free to interpret constitutional provisions in order to bring about better consequences overall, why would that not—why would your argument for bringing about better consequences overall not compel you to a different conclusion?

PROFESSOR SUNSTEIN: Good. If you have a Supreme Court holding that the lower court does not like, on the ground that it produces bad consequences, to authorize lower courts to abandon the Supreme Court holding because of the bad consequences, that authorization itself would have horrific consequences. You could not have a hierarchical system of law. To allow lower court judges to interpret, in my sense, Supreme Court holdings—so for example, to choose one example out of the hat, (not!) spousal notification requirement, to do that is perfectly compatible with what I am describing. So, I think your question assumes the conclusion. It assumes that the Constitution means the original understanding. And, if that is so, judges who do not follow it are monkeying with it. I do not want judges monkeying with it. I do not want judges monkeying with the Constitution.

MR. COOPER: Can we assume that Supreme Court decisions are the original understanding of those Supreme Court decisions? Why are not lower court judges free to look upon them the same way that you would have them be free to look upon constitutional provisions?

PROFESSOR SUNSTEIN: Okay, whether the original understanding of the Supreme Court's decision is binding is a nice question. We certainly do not want to understand Supreme Court precedents, I think, either by psychoanalyzing Justice Brennan and his intentions or by looking at the *New York Times* or the *Washington Post* and seeing what the original meaning was. We want to do neither of those things.

MR. COOPER: True.

PROFESSOR CALABRESI: Let us move to other questions from the audience. Over here. Yes.

AUDIENCE PARTICIPANT: I would like to ask, why can not we just all get along? But instead, as a non-lawyer I would like to ask a very simple question. Why was Article V put in the Constitution?

MR. COOPER: Well, that is not such a simple question, but I will give you a simple answer, which is: to allow us to change the Constitution when great occasions so required. But I take the upshot of your question to be—that is, I am going to get at the intention and not the meaning—is that why ought not constitutional change to occur through the amendment process, rather than through interpretation? And that is fine, if we assume that interpretation that abandons the original understanding is amendment. And I do not accept that. In my view, interpretation that does not follow the original understanding need not be amendment. It may be right; it may be wrong. But I would not count it as amendment.

PROFESSOR CALABRESI: Professor Lino Graglia.

PROFESSOR LINO GRAGLIA: In this discussion, two distinctions are important. The first is the distinction between constitutionalism and activism. We say, "We did not consent to the Constitution. The consenters are all dead. And so, why should we abide by it?" And you hear this same argument, "Why should we abide by the dead hand of the past?" And that is a very important and serious question. But it is a challenge to constitutionalism. It is a question of why do we have a constitution, and constitutional restrictions which are inherently undemocratic? And that is a serious question, and I think it should not be minimalized. But that is not the question we have here.

The second distinction that is important is the distinction between rulings of unconstitutionality and other rulings, of constitutionality or otherwise. It is only the rulings of unconstitutionality that present the difficulty. When should a court hold something unconstitutional? When is it considered authorized or appropriate to do so in our system? Well, when the Constitution in fact disallows that policy choice. And how are to we know when it does that? And it should only hold it unconstitutional when it clearly disallows the policy choice, most would say, because if it is debatable, the judgment of the legislature should prevail. We do not have the evidence; the historical research does not reveal their intentions memorialistically. They had no intention. Or no one can know what their intention would be in these circumstances. The answer to all of which ought to be that the law in question is not constitutional.

It is really quite simple. Unless we can say, this policy choice has clearly been precluded to the living people, it has not been precluded. Now, to know whether it has been precluded or not, we have to work on the assumption that communication is possible. Right?

PROFESSOR CALABRESI: We are short on time, so we ought to pause, maybe, and let Professor Sunstein respond quickly.

PROFESSOR SUNSTEIN: Okay, that is an honorable view that you are defending, and it is Thayer's. That is, it's Vermeulianism. That is, it is the view that the Constitution should be invoked to disable the democratic process, only when it plainly does so. So if that is true, affirmative action is fine, restrictions on commercial advertising are fine, campaign finance regulations are fine, regulatory takings are fine, and much more is fine that Justice Thomas and Justice Scalia have a lot of problems with. I think that is an honorable point of view.

LINO GRAGLIA: Cass, that is your parade of horribles, and you are right. All those things are constitutional.

PROFESSOR SUNSTEIN: I meant it as a parade of wonderfuls. I meant it to maybe make you hesitate about your Thayerism. But I do not believe that this bipartisan judicial restraint approach deserves attack. The Supreme Court adheres to it, and it is honorable. It is not originalism.

PROFESSOR CALABRESI: One final question. Back there.

AUDIENCE PARTICIPANT: Thank you. The Federalist Society is so rigorously evenhanded in its panels, I would have to say being here for a couple of days I am actually being persuaded to the Burkean minimalist approach.

I would like you to comment on something I heard Judge McConnell say at the very first session of the three days. What I understood him to suggest, perhaps incorrectly, was that if Oregon were to pass a law allowing active euthanasia with whatever safe-guards that they put in that might be considered to the people in this room a possibility, that he would consider that that should be struck down as being inconsistent with the federal Constitution, because there are no modes of due process, as originally understood, that would allow for putting someone to death in an involuntary manner. And it did strike me at the time that it is possible, one could have an originalist understanding of the Constitution that there is a right to life for an unborn child, which would make a debate not about whether that issue should go back to the states but whether there really is a federal right to life against abortion.

Now, it struck me that these attitudes really become impossible to understand without some notion of evolving standards of decency, which should be interpreted in a Burkean way. Would either of you like to comment on that?

MR. COOPER: If Judge Mike McConnell said it, it's probably right.

PROFESSOR SUNSTEIN: I second that, and I hope the president is listening.

PROFESSOR CALABRESI: Thanks to our panelists very, very much.

Twelve

ADDRESS BY THE
HON. EDWIN MEESE, III,
75TH ATTORNEY GENERAL OF
THE UNITED STATES

INTRODUCTION

My name is Ken Cribb, and it is my privilege to introduce this session. This is Veterans' Day, and we honor our many members present with us this weekend who have served in uniform, just as we honor the memory of the young men and women at arms, who in the current struggle against terrorism have given the last full measure of devotion. It is appropriate that we hear from Ed Meese on Veterans' Day, because he pursued policies under Ronald Reagan that brought the Services to peak readiness, and therefore to peak morale.

Having Ed with us also provides an opportunity to step back from the current preoccupation with the makeup of the Supreme Court—by the way, with the two religious liberty cases in Kentucky and Texas, we can now identify the two swing votes on the Supreme Court, and they are both Justice Breyer.

I sometimes wince when Ronald Reagan's successful presidency is attributed to his communication skills because this analysis falsely elevates form over substance. After all, if President Reagan had set the wrong goals for America, effective speeches would only have hastened failure. And this is just so with Ed Meese's deserved reputation as the skilled implementer of Reagan's policies. True though that is, this too elevates form over substance, and underestimates Ed's hard-fought battle for smaller government, lower taxes, deregulation, the defense buildup, the strategic moves against the Soviet Union, and, of course, the topic of this Convention.

Every one of these stands went against the recalcitrant conventional wisdom of the media and the other establishments in Washington, the career bureaucracies of government. Much of Congress, including many Republicans, and even some high officials in our own administration who manned key choke points, that could quietly stall the more revolutionary aspects of the Reagan agenda.

Against these powerful legions of the *status quo*, Ed Meese rode point for the Reagan revolution. The other side knew this and they attacked Ed with a furor that makes the DeLay episode look like a minuet. But Ed never wavered. And do you know who recognized his steadfastness? It was the foot soldiers of the Reagan revolution, the several thousand political appointments out in the Cabinet departments and the agencies. More than their own superiors, they looked to Ed Meese, to his staunchness under fire, to his refusal to split the difference of matters of fundamental principle, to his laser-like loyalty to Ronald Reagan.

Each year, we held what was in essence a rally in Constitutional Hall for the three thousand political appointees in the administration. Cabinet members would come onstage one by one, then the reception ranged from polite applause to enthusiasm, but it was always Ed Meese who brought the house down just by walking onto the stage. The grateful voices of those young Reaganites resound in my ears to this day. You see, they understood. And Ronald Reagan understood. I was back working at the White House when the second Meese Independent Counsel was appointed, and in my hearing, Ronald Reagan said, if Ed Meese is not a good man, there are no good men.

When Ronald Reagan asked Ed Meese to become attorney general, Ed used this moral leadership of the administration that I have just pictured for you to channel the course of American law toward new fidelity to the written Constitution. Republican presidents from Eisenhower forward had never managed to consistently select judges who would be faithful to the text of the Constitution, so that, by the end of the Nixon and Ford presidencies, there was only one Democrat in the liberal majorities of the Berger Court. The other Democrat voted with us. Thurgood Marshall was the only Democrat. Brennan had been appointed by Eisenhower; Blackman and Powell by Nixon; and Stevens by Ford.

President Reagan charged Attorney General Meese and his brain trust with restoring the rule of law under the written Constitution— as opposed to the rule of men and women who are judges—and a fourfold effort was undertaken. First, the process of judicial selection was elevated to the highest circles of the administration. Early on, Ed had recommended a vetting process that began at the Justice Department and ended with final recommendations made by the president's chief officers sitting around a table in the Roosevelt Room, just steps away from the Oval Office. And then Reagan himself would call after his decision, the judicial nominee as a way of underscoring his high expectations for a return to constitutional fidelity. That also was unprecedented.

Second, Ed and his allies improved the predictability of judicial selection by taking advantage of the scholarship in the 1970s of Robert Bork and others on the proper role of the judge. Instead of conclusory questions like, "Do you believe in judicial restraint?" Or, "Would you legislate from the bench?" Any prospective judicial nominee knows how to answer those questions. The Reagan judges would put cases; they would hear some facts: "How would you decide these facts, if it were a case before you?" Using analysis, rather than slogans, which is all we had before 1981, political activists of both the Left them the Right could be screened out.

Third, a farm team was created by appointing young intellectuals to critical positions at DOJ and the lower federal courts. Suffice it to say that most of the figures on the long list for the recent Supreme Court vacancies served at either the Reagan Justice Department or were Reagan appointees to the bench, or both, including the two eventual nominees.

Fourth and finally, Ed Meese sought to focus the legal culture on the question of the proper role of the judge under the Constitution by inaugurating what has been called the Great Debate. The debate eventually included Justices Brennan and Stevens, and Judge Robert Bork, and Ronald Reagan himself. The president never mentioned the word "Constitution" without also mentioning the word "text" in the same sentence. You will recall some of the most prominent assertions of that debate. The Constitution was a written document whose words were debated at length, carefully chosen, and therefore the Founders' handiwork may be presumed to convey an identifiable meaning. The Constitution contains the means of its amendment in Article V, and so we may conclude that the original meaning of its provisions control until amended, according to the Article V process. The Constitution itself, by its own terms, is the supreme law of the land and not the body of constitutional decisions which have grown up around it. (Can you believe the uproar that one caused?) The Executive and the Congress have no less a right and no less a duty to interpret the Constitution, as does the Judiciary. The role of the judge is to issue a rule of decision in a case or controversy, and that rule of decision must interpret and apply law. And finally, the division of power against itself in the structure of the Constitution is its genius, and the primary safeguard of our liberties. Therefore, the great structural doctrines of federalism and separation of powers must be revived.

These assertions about American law found hospitality at the Meese Justice Department at a time when the legal academic establishment had barred its doors. Twenty years later, we see the results all around us as the proponents of originalism have become legion, and as its opponents define themselves in contradistinction to the originalist position. Three decades from now, as the United States celebrates the first quarter millennium of the Constitution, a new generation of lovers of the law might hearken back to Ed Meese in the Great Debate that occurred in the 1980s on constitutional fidelity. They may be able to say that it was a turning point in the course of

American law. We cannot know for sure, but I believe we can already be justly proud of the Herculean effort that Ed Meese has made on behalf of those blessings of liberty that our written Constitution secures.

Ladies and gentlemen, the seventy-fifth attorney general of the United States.

GENERAL MEESE: Thank you very much, ladies and gentlemen. Ken, thank you very much for those kind words. I think most of you know that Ken has been my teammate throughout the days at the White House, and then at the Department of Justice, and, of course, then he went on to be a very important part of the administration, continuing his good work as the Assistant to the President for Domestic Policy. But I cannot tell you how much I appreciated having him as my constant teammate during that period of time. Of course, today he is one of the principal leaders of the conservative movement, both as president of the Intercollegiate Studies Institute, and as counselor to the Federalist Society here. So Ken, I will always be grateful to you for all you have done for me and for the country.

I also want to thank the Federalist Society for the honor that was given me last night, for the privilege of speaking today, for the theme of this conference, and also, so many of you, for your kind words, as I had the chance to see you, pass in the halls and talk to you briefly.

I appreciate very much this conference being devoted to the subject of originalism, and I consider it a privilege to have been able to work with the Federalist Society, and to watch this organization's extraordinary success over the past now nearly twenty-five years. I think that obviously, originalism, and I know many of you share this view, is literally the keystone of fidelity to the Constitution. The numerous and substantive aspects of originalism are being discussed in the various panels throughout this conference by a host of experts. And I have certainly been impressed by the way in which people have been brought together from all over the country to share their expertise with this audience, and, in Federalist Society fashion, to present different views and different sides and different positions on the various specific aspects of constitutionalism.

For my part, I would like to talk, then, today about, first, how and why what the Federalist society has called "the Great Debate" began, some of the things that have happened since, and why it continues to be important today. Why did the Department of Justice, during the Reagan administration, take on a major task in placing great emphasis on restoring constitutional fidelity? Well, I will put it very simply: the president wanted us to. That was the president's policy; that was his objective. One of his major goals was getting the country back on the right track, at a time when, in many ways, whether it was economic, foreign policy, military policy, or otherwise, we had strayed from the path that he felt was the right way in which the country ought to be going.

Let me talk about President Reagan, just for a moment, because he has been so instrumental in many of the things that we in this organization stand for. Last night Steve Calabresi, in his remarks, talked about Ronald Reagan's accomplishments during his two terms. We can look back in many ways on his successes: his work in revitalizing the economy and starting a period of economic growth that still continues to this day; his work in restoring our military capability in our position of world leadership; his accomplishment in terms of ending the Cold War with the forces of freedom and democracy being on the winning side; and his work, that perhaps is less known, but equally important, in reviving the spirit of the American people.

Since Ronald Reagan left office, historians, and even some journalists, have discovered that these achievements were not flukes and were not accidents but they were a result of Ronald Reagan's deep thinking, his personal wisdom, and his distinguished leadership. There were a lot of people, when he took office, who thought that he was an actor reading lines. But more and more, accurate research is revealing the man and the thinking that was behind his policies and behind his successes: the books by Martin Anderson and Annelise Anderson that have been published recently, where they put Reagan into his own words and in his own hand—they provide the radio broadcasts and the letters that showed his thinking throughout his life on some of the key issues which dominated his presidency; a book by Paul Kengor and others on his religious faith, which was so important to him, and which he did not wear on his sleeve but which was critical to the decisions that he made; and the book by Steve Hayward that talks about his governorship and how that was a prelude to what he did as president—all of these show that Ronald Reagan and his presidency were part of a long career, beginning in the 1940s, of opposing communism, as well as a pattern of his life in thinking about America and thinking about its future.

Particularly since he passed away a little over a year ago, when I have talked with people about Ronald Reagan or they have asked questions, I get a question: "What was he really like?" I would like to mention today three things that have always stood out in terms of what he did and who he was. The first was his optimism. As he said himself, "I believe that the glass is always half full, not half empty." And this stood out in all that he did because he had a belief, as he said many times, that the best days of this country are yet ahead.

The second thing was his vision, as well as the ability to communicate that vision to the American people, and indeed to the people of the world. But the two went together. As Ken said earlier, it was not just his ability to communicate, but he had something important that he wanted to communicate, that he passed on to the people. He was able to take complex subjects and make them understandable to almost everyone. As a matter of fact, that was one of the ways in which he was able, I think, to rally this country and the people of the world behind his crusade to end the Cold War, and his belief and his vision that the forces of freedom and democracy would conquer the totalitarianism that was rampant throughout the world. As he said in his speech in 1982 to the Parliament of Britain in the halls of Westminster, when he said we will transcend communism to the free peoples of the world, and we will consign Marxism-Leninism, to the ash heap of history. Well, that was Ronald Reagan.

But also, he did not talk about abstract economic doctrines when he was talking about the ultimate collapse of the Soviet Union. He could put it in simple terms, often in humorous terms.

The third characteristic I want to mention, which is perhaps most important to us today, is the thorough knowledge of the Founding of our country, and Ronald Reagan's deep respect for the Founders and for what they had produced, which was the Constitution. He believed that our country was a special place in the world, that our principles and traditions were the best hope for mankind. And he believed very firmly that our Constitution and its protection and preservation was essential to our continuing prosperity. He put his reverence for the Constitution in his own words many times. At the swearing-in ceremony of Chief Justice Rehnquist and Associate Justice Antonin Scalia in September of 1986, he used these words. He said, "With these two outstanding men taking these positions, this is a time of renewal in the great constitutional system that our forefathers gave us, a good time to reflect on the inspired wisdom we call our Constitution; a time to remember that the founding fathers gave careful thought to the role of the Supreme Court." And then he went on to say in talking about the Constitutional Convention, they settled on a judiciary that would be independent and strong but one whose power would also, they believed, be confined within the boundaries of a written constitution and laws.

He said that Hamilton and Jefferson disagreed on most of the great issues of the day, just as many disagree in ours. But, he said, for all their differences, they both agreed on the importance of judicial restraint. Our peculiar security, Jefferson warned, is in the possession of a written constitution. And then Jefferson made this appeal: "Let us not make it a blank paper by construction." He concluded by saying, Hamilton, Jefferson and all the Founding Fathers understood the words of James Madison: "If the sense in which the Constitution was accepted and ratified by the nation is not the guide to expounding it, there can be no security for a faithful exercise of its powers." He felt that the Founding Fathers, as he said, were clear on this issue. For them, the question involved in judicial restraint was not, as it is not, will we have liberal or conservative courts? They knew that the courts, like the Constitution, must not be either liberal or conservative. The question was, and is, will we have government by the people? And, in closing his talk, he quoted Felix Frankfurter, who once said, "The highest exercise of judicial duty is to subordinate one's personal polls and one's private views to the law." Well, that is really at the heart of the Great Debate that we are talking about today. And in those words, Ronald Reagan summed up the case for originalism, and that is why it was important to us in the Department of Justice to take steps to put these goals of the president into action.

It was interesting back in July of 1985, in the speech that has been talked about as the start of the Great Debate, how that came about It was the result of the work of many people, many of whom are here today—Gary McDowell; Terry Eastland; Blair Domeni; Ken Cribb; and a few others who sat around and suggested that maybe it was a good idea not just to get the usual perfunctory welcome to Washington speech of Attorney General but to say something substantive, and something that would advance the president's goals. And so we gave that speech. It surprised many of the ABA establishment, and it surprised most journalists. But I think it had kind of the core of what brings us together again today, some twenty years later.

In that speech, I talked about the intended role of the judiciary generally, and the Supreme Court in particular, as being to serve as the bulwark of the limited Constitution. The judges, the Founders believed, would not fail to regard the Constitution as fundamental law and would regulate their decisions by it. As the faithful guardians of the Constitution, the judges were expected to resist any political efforts to depart from the literal provisions of the Constitution. The text of the document, and the original intention of those who framed it, would be the judicial standard in giving effect to the Constitution. That was a reflection on how we viewed the Founders work, and how it was important at that time. In the course of that speech, I said that the Court's work for the past year, as it has said it has been in recent years, did not yield a coherent set of decisions. Rather, it seemed to produce what one commentator has called a jurisprudence of the idiosyncrasy, particularly in the areas of federalism, criminal law, and freedom of religion. Somehow, things are not much different today, are they?

Well, the same could probably be said of most of the terms before and since. In the course of that speech—and I say it because I think it still rings true today—what, then, should a constitutional jurisprudence actually be? It should be a jurisprudence of original intention. By seeking to judge policies in light of principles rather than remold principles in light of policies, the court could avoid both the charge of incoherence and the charge of being either too conservative are too liberal. A jurisprudence seriously aimed at the explication of the original intention would produce defensible principles of government that would not be tainted by ideological predilection. The permanence of the Constitution must not be viewed as only what the judges say it is. And if that were true, it would no longer be a Constitution in the true sense.

That speech concluded with this statement of the Ronald Reagan administration and the policy of the Department of Justice. And that is:

> We will pursue our agenda within the context of our written Constitution of limited yet energetic powers. Our guide in every case will be the sanctity of the rule of law and the proper limits of governmental power. It is our belief that only the sense in which the Constitution was accepted and ratified by the nation, and only the sense in which laws were drafted and passed, provide a solid foundation for adjudication. Any other standard suffers the defect of pouring new meaning into old words, thus creating new powers and new rights totally at odds with the logic of the Constitution and our commitment to the rule of law.

Well, as I said, this speech generated surprise and sporadic opposition from some of the journalists and some of the academic elite around the country. But it might have been a one-time event, except for a fortuitous occurrence. And that was, it might surprise you to learn, that I am deeply indebted to the late Justice William Brennan. He decided to reply in September of 1985 in a symposium at Georgetown University. He spoke disparagingly of "those who find legitimacy in fidelity to what they call the intentions of the Framers." And so, the battle was joined. Without Justice Brennan's response, I suspect that the continuing debate might not have materialized. Instead, my remarks might have well have been relegated to obscurity, which is the usual fate of most speeches to the ABA.

Instead, not only did Justice Brennan get in the fight, but Justice Stevens also joined, as Ken mentioned earlier, as did Bob Bork, and even President Reagan, in his speeches. So, the Great Debate continues to this the date, including the excellent presentations that are being made throughout this conference. Since the events of 1985, several things have happened. The Department of Justice convened a series of seminars to explore the subsidiary issues and the other aspects of the jurisprudence of originalism. Justice Scalia clarified the meaning of originalism and was very helpful as he talked about the doctrine of original meaning and original understanding. It combated those who tried to define originalism as related to some subjective intentions of the Framers. There were those who tried to reduce originalism to some idea of kind of having an Ouija board in front of you and saying, "What did Madison really think?" Or words to that effect. Instead, this idea of original meaning and original intentions caught on. Justice Scalia pointed out that, like any legal document, interpretations should be based on the words of the Constitution themselves, and what they were understood to mean, by those who drafted them and the people who ratified them.

The cause of constitutional fidelity was greatly advanced by the fine work of Judge Robert Bork. His book was, as you remember, *The Tempting of America: The Political Seduction of the Law*, and in it he set forth the case for originalism and defined the faulty jurisprudence of those who were perverting the actual meaning of the Constitution. And then, of course, the Federalist Society itself provided a great means of getting the word out to the law schools, to law students, and ultimately to lawyers, through the public speeches that I mentioned that were part of the Great Debate and which Ken referred to. They provided a series of fora in the law schools and in conferences like this for further explication of the doctrine of original meaning. And they provided a cadre of students, lawyers, and ultimately faculty members who believed in fidelity to the Constitution, and understood why that was important to the future of the nation. Even many law professors who did not agree with this idea felt compelled to at least recognize that there was a concept of originalism, which had not gotten much attention in common law courses prior to that time. Some believed that it might even be a legitimate doctrine, while others used that opportunity to debunk it.

I gave a speech at Tulane shortly afterward, in which I talked about something that Ken mentioned today, and that is that constitutional law, or the decisions of the Supreme Court, are not the same as the Constitution. I stated there that the constitutional law is not the supreme law of the land, and that only the Constitution itself was. That generated even, I believe, a *Washington Post* editorial wondering if I had gone mad.

But it also generated something else. I had said in that speech that, in the leading constitutional law case book, you did not come to the Constitution itself until you got to Appendix H. Shortly after that, I got a letter from a professor who will go nameless, who said, "If you were talking about the leading constitutional law case book, you must have meant mine, and I wanted you to know that in the next edition, I'm moving the Constitution up to Appendix A."

Well, there were various counterattacks over the years. There has been an attempt to redefine judicial activism and talk about conservative judicial activism as being whenever the Supreme Court or other courts strike down acts of Congress or the state legislatures. We know that it is legitimate for courts to overturn legislation or to overturn executive actions when they in fact conflict with the Constitution itself. But real judicial activism, as it is legitimately known, is when judges depart from what the Constitution or statutes actually say, and instead use whatever document it might be as a springboard to substitute their own policy preferences and their own personal beliefs in order to advance some political agenda.

Indeed, Justice Scalia has described this very well in his dissent in the case of *Board of County Commissioners v. Umbehr*, in which he said, "What secret knowledge, one must wonder, is breathed into lawyers when they become Justices of this Court that enables them to discern that a practice which the text of the Constitution does not clearly prescribe, and which our people have regarded as constitutional for 200 years, is in fact unconstitutional?" And then he wound up with this statement. "Day by day, case by case, the Supreme Court is busy designing a Constitution for a country I do not recognize." Well, that statement of Justice Scalia has formed the title of Bob Bork's most recent book that he put together, a series of outstanding essays on where the interpreters of the Constitution who have gone in a different direction from constitutional fidelity have made their mistakes.

Another attack on judicial fidelity to the Constitution has been the internationalization of constitutional interpretation and constitutional decisions. Looking to other countries for possible guidance or comparison might be okay for policymakers, and we might indeed learn something from other nations. But judges are not policymakers. This so-called international jurisprudence, as being in any way relevant to the constitutional interpretation, is both a sham and a fraud. Judges who employ this approach are not really looking for true guidance because, obviously, what foreign judges or foreign legislators or foreign populations think or decide cannot in any way be relevant to the faithful interpretation of our Constitution.

Instead, as in *Lawrence v. Texas*, and *Roper v. Simmons*, and some other decisions, when justices cannot find any basis for their decisions in our Constitution or in our own legal traditions or jurisprudence, they roam the world trying to find any support for their faulty decisions and eagerly grasp language from the European Convention on Human Rights or the judicial decisions of Zimbabwe or India. Or, if they can find it, some other foreign country. They use this to bolster their own ideas that they wish to substitute for proper and legitimate constitutional doctrine. In a way, their use of foreign law kind of reminds one of the old story about the drunk leaning against the lamp post. He was using it more for support than for light.

Well, obviously the Great Debate that we have talked about in this conference continues with the nominations that are taking place today, as Ken referred to earlier. We were happy to see Chief Justice John Roberts successfully go through what has now become trial by ordeal as a prerequisite to donning the black robes of a Supreme Court justice. And we are in the midst of another nomination process with another outstanding nominee, Sam Alito. George W. Bush, in my opinion, and, I think, in the opinion of most of us, has appointed outstanding judges both to the Supreme Court, and also to the courts of appeal. The judiciary is obviously heading in the right direction under his leadership. But in doing so, he has aroused the opposition of those who have a very different idea of the future of our country and a very different idea of protecting the Constitution. And that is why we have a situation now where judges who, in any other era in our history would be rapidly accepted by the Senate of the United States, are today victims of the stranglehold that some of the extreme left-wing special interest groups have on certain persons in leadership in the minority party in the Senate. And that is why it is important that the Federalist Society, through its members—since the Society itself does not take a position on individual nominees—but that as members of the Society dedicated to the Constitution, we do everything in our power to support the prompt and effective confirmation of these justices, as well as refuting the falsehoods, and the character assassination attempts that are taking place.

A final instance of what is happening at the present time is the most recent contribution to a jurisprudence of original meaning. And that is a book that the Heritage Foundation has currently published, coming out this week actually. It will be available, I might add, at the reception tomorrow evening, at a reduced price for Federalist members. But it is the *Heritage Guide to the Constitution*, and in it, one can find contributions of 108 authors, many of them members of the Federalist Society. Brilliantly edited by Matthew Spalding of the Heritage Foundation and Professor David Forte, they have taken each clause of the Constitution, some two hundred of them, and delineated its history from what the Founders had in mind originally, and bringing it down through the years of Court decisions and where we are today, as well as citing a number of key cases and other reference articles that can be useful in understanding these particular causes. I suggest to you it will be valuable to those who do cherish the Constitution in its original form, and who believe in the doctrine of both judicial restraint and constitutional fidelity.

Well, the need to preserve and protect the Constitution obviously continues to this day. Indeed, as we look at what is happening around us, it is very important that we recognize what President Reagan had in mind when he talked about the importance of the Constitution and its origins. We must seek to re-establish the role of the courts as protectors of the Constitution as it was written, and thus preserve the liberty of the people, and ensure that government is limited by the consent of the governed. We must engage in innovative thinking, as has been expressed here on many of the panels, if we are indeed to return the courts to their constitutional duty. We have a great Constitution, a great written Constitution. Let us be alert and active in our efforts to restore the full vitality of our founding charter.

The words of Alexander Hamilton call us to account, as he says, "A sacred respect for the constitutional law is the vital principle, the sustaining energy, of a free government and a free people." I believe and am confident that, with the leadership of organizations like the Federalist society, our nation and our lawyers will be equal to that task.

Thank you.

CONCLUDING THOUGHTS

Theodore B. Olson

When I was first approached to prepare an epilogue to this important publication, I recalled an old saying in American politics: "Everything has been said, but not everyone has said it." The expression is ordinarily employed as a cautionary note for speakers, but if anything, writers face an even greater peril. This volume catalogues the views of some of the most distinguished and preeminent judges, scholars, and practitioners of our time, on one of the most important modern developments in American law—the last quarter century of debate over originalism and our written Constitution. It is an extraordinary body of work. Rather than retread the rich terrain that has already been amply explored in the preceding pages, I shall focus my brief remarks instead on the important contribution that has been made to this debate by the sponsor of this publication, the Federalist Society.

A lot has changed over the last twenty-five years. We celebrated the historic landslide re-election of a great president in 1984 and mourned his passing twenty years later. We witnessed the nation's first impeachment of an elected president, followed by an historic contested presidential election. Months later, America suffered the worst attack on its own soil in U.S. history. There have been extraordinary developments on the American legal landscape as well. During the last quarter century, eight out of nine seats on the U.S. Supreme Court have changed hands. Altogether, Presidents Reagan, Bush, Clinton, and Bush have appointed two chief justices and seven associate justices, as well as countless numbers of federal district and court of appeals judges. Judicial nomination announcements have been followed by overheated hearings, vicious and frequently false personal attacks, and unprecedented filibusters, with increasing frequency and intensity.

Beyond changes in personnel, the federal judiciary has also been invigorated by renewed attention to and public debate over fundamental philosophical questions of jurisprudence and constitutional interpretation. These issues have been explored in depth, both in the preceding pages and through convention panel discussions and other events sponsored by the Federalist Society. What I wish to recognize here is the critical role that the Society has played over the past quarter century in reviving and enhancing the debate over originalism and the written text of the Constitution. Our country is better off, and our national commitment to the rule of law is stronger, as a result of the Society's efforts. And the Society itself has benefited and grown in influence and membership. What began as a symposium of law students and professors at Yale Law School on a memorable April weekend in 1982 has become, after twenty-five years, one of the most powerful intellectual forces in American jurisprudence today. The Federalist Society today is comprised of more than two hundred law school chapters, sixty-five lawyer chapters, and fifteen practice groups across the country. Although it is fueled by just an eight million dollar annual budget and twenty-five paid employees, 40,000 Society members donate countless hours of their time. Given the high billable rates that these volunteer lawyers command in the private sector, the aggregate force and impact of the Society's efforts is staggering.

What is especially striking about the rapid growth of the Federalist Society is the fact that its membership is not bound by any particular common political agenda. Nor would any such common calling appear possible in any event. Members of the Society disagree passionately about abortion, gay rights, immigration, and other controversial issues. Society members reach dramatically different conclusions about the meaning of numerous provisions of our written Constitution, such as the Takings Clause, the Ninth Amendment, and the Fourteenth Amendment, and hold conflicting views about the proper allocation of government power among the three branches of government as well as between the federal government and the States.

This political diversity is surprising, however, only to those who are unfamiliar with the Society or with originalism. Readers of this volume need not be told that the real power and energy behind originalism is not the desire to achieve any particular political outcome or result. What drives originalists is nothing more, and nothing less, than the noble pursuit of a coherent and principled approach to interpreting and implementing the various provisions of our written Constitution. Likewise, what drives the Federalist Society and its membership is not any particular political objective, but the common goal of establishing and maintaining a common, stable and consistent constitutional framework within which the difficult political and social issues of our day shall be decided. In short, both the cause of originalism and the driving force of the Society are one and the same—an intellectually honest process for fostering, debating, and ultimately implementing the ideas that will help form "a more perfect Union."

This commitment to intellectual process is reflected in the Society's very structure and is responsible for the Society's record of success. The Society is organized not around any political issue, litigation objective, legislative agenda, or electoral strategy, but instead on a single, simple concept—the inherent value of debate. Nothing could be more American than the Society's elevation of debate as the best way of testing ideas. And it is no wonder that the Society has attracted so many top scholars and practitioners to its conventions, panels, and indeed to these very pages. Names like Walter Dellinger, Akhil Amar, Jeffrey Rosen, David Strauss, Nadine Strossen, Cass Sunstein, and Seth Waxman do not evince images of right-wing, ideological conservatism.

They find welcome audiences in the Society nonetheless, because they too value the Society as a unique forum for testing ideas.

But the Society is not just a debating society. It is also an intellectual and social network. Through the Society, ideas are tested, arguments are strengthened, weaknesses are exposed, information is shared, and friendships are developed among tens of thousands of the nation's leading legal thinkers and practitioners. The Society is organized around debate, but its greatest value may be its network of relationships of trust and friendship amongst people dedicated to our legal system and devoted to furthering the rule of law throughout America and indeed the world.

The debate over originalism and our written Constitution has flourished and prospered over the last twenty-five years in no short measure due to the success and growth of the Federalist Society. So it is fitting that the Society would sponsor this important publication. The Society and its membership are as vibrant and energized as they have ever been. The cause of originalism is in good hands for the next quarter century.

CONTRIBUTORS

Akhil Reed Amar, Southmayd Professor, Yale Law School

Randy E. Barnett, Carmack Waterhouse Professor of Legal Theory, Georgetown University Law Center

Robert H. Bork, former Judge United States Court of Appeals for the D.C. Circuit and Co-Chairman of the Federalist Society's Board of Visitors

William J. Brennan, Jr., Associate Justice, United States Supreme Court, 1956-1990

Steven G. Calabresi, Professor of Law, Northwestern University and Chairman, Federalist Society Board of Directors

Charles J. Cooper, Cooper and Kirk, PLCC and former Assistant Attorney General for the Office of Legal Counsel

T. Kenneth Cribb, president of the Intercollegiate Studies Institute

Walter E. Dellinger, O'Melveny & Myers and former Acting Solicitor General

Frank Easterbrook, Chief Judge, United States Court of Appeals for the Seventh Circuit

Douglas H. Ginsburg, Judge, United States Court of Appeals for the District of Columbia Circuit

Lino A. Graglia, A. Dalton Cross Professor, University of Texas School of Law

John C. Harrison, David Lutton Massee, Jr. & Horace W. Goldsmith Research Professor, University of Virginia School of Law

Larry Kramer, Richard E. Lang Professor and Dean, Stanford Law School

Stephen J. Markman, Justice, Michigan Supreme Court and former Assistant Attorney General, Office of Legal Policy

Michael W. McConnell, Judge, United States Court of Appeals for the Tenth Circuit and Presidential Professor, University of Utah College of Law

John O. McGinnis, Professor, Northwestern University School of Law

Edwin Meese III, 75th Attorney General of the United States and Member, Federalist Society Board of Visitors

Thomas W. Merrill, Charles Keller Beckman Professor, Columbia Law School

Theodore B. Olson, 42nd Solicitor General of the United States and Partner, Gibson, Dunn & Crutcher LLP

Barrington Parker, Judge, United States Court of Appeals for the Second Circuit

Michael S. Paulsen, Briggs and Morgan Professor, University of Minnesota Law School

Ray Randolph, Judge, United States Court of Appeals for the D.C. Circuit

Michael Rappaport, Professor, University of San Diego Law School

Jeff Rosen, Professor, George Washington University Law School and frequent contributor to the *New York Times* and the *New Republic*

Suzanna Sherry, Herman O. Loewenstein Professor of Law, Vanderbilt University,

David A. Strauss, Harry N. Wyatt Professor, University of Chicago Law School

Cass Sunstein, Karl N. Llewellyn Distinguished Service Professor of Jurisprudence, University of Chicago Law School

Diane P. Wood, Judge, United States Court of Appeals for the Seventh Circuit

ACKNOWLEDGMENTS

Ihave received a great deal of help from a number of individuals in editing and producing this book. I would like to begin by thanking Leonard Leo, the Federalist Society's executive vice president, for his help in organizing the book project at every step along the way. Peter Aigner, the publishing director of the Federalist Society, worked exceptionally hard in helping at every stage with the production of the book and did a really superb job. Eugene Meyer, the president of the Federalist Society, and Professor Gary Lawson of Boston University School of Law helped organize the underlying conference which gave rise to the book. I am also very grateful to my dean, David Van Zandt, and to the Northwestern University School of Law for their financial support of all of my scholarship. And, most of all, I would like to thank my wife Mimi Tyler Calabresi for her love and support which makes everything I do possible.

STEVEN G. CALABRESI

Notes

Foreword

1. *Crawford v. Washington*, 541 U.S. 36 (2004).
2. *Apprendi v. New Jersey*, 530 U.S. 466 (2000).
3. See, e.g., *U.S. Term Limits, Inc. v. Thornton*, 514 U. S. 779 (1995).

One: Speech Before the American Bar Association, Washington, D.C., July 9, 1985, Attorney General Edwin Meese, III

1. *Garcia v. San Antonio Metropolitan Transit Authority*, 105 S.Ct. 1005 (1985).
2. *National League of Cities v. Usery*, 426 U.S. 833 (1976).
3. *United States v. Leon*, 468 U.S. 897 (1984).
4. *Miranda v. Arizona*, 384 U.S. 436 (1966).
5. *Oregon v. Elstad*, 105 S.Ct. 1285 (1985).
6. *Gitlow v. New York*, 268 U.S. 652 (1925).

Two: Speech to the Text and Teaching Symposium, Georgetown University, Washington, D.C., October 12, 1985, Justice William J. Brennan, Jr.

1. *West Virginia State Board of Education v. Barnette*, 319 U.S. 624, 639 (1943).
2. *Weems v United States*, 217 U.S. 349 (1910).
3. *Palko v. Connecticut*, 302 U.S. 319, 326 (1937).
4. *In re Winship,* 397 U.S. 358, 372 (1970). (concurring opinion)
5. *Whitney v. California*, 274 U.S. 357, 375 (1927). (concurring opinion)

Three: Speech before the D.C. Chapter of the Federalist Society Lawyers Division, Washington, D.C., November 15, 1985, Attorney General Edwin Meese, III
1. *McCulloch v. Maryland*, 17 U.S. 316 (1819).
2. *Brown v. Board of Education of Topeka*, 347 U.S. 483 (1954).
3. Bork, Robert H. *Traditions and Morality in Constitutional Law*, Washington, D.C.: AEI Press, 1984.
4. Brief for the United States as *Amicus curiae* at 24, *Thornburgh v. American College of Obstetricians and Gynecologists*, No. 84–495, June 11, 1986.
5. *Osborn v. Bank of U.S.*, 22 U.S. 738 (1824).

Four: United States Court of Appeals for the District of Columbia Before the University of San Diego Law School, November 18, 1985, Judge Robert H. Bork
1. *Griswold v. Conneticut*, 381 U.S. 479 (1965).

Six: "The Law of the Constitution," Tulane University, October 21, 1986, Attorney General Edwin Meese, III
1. Weekly Comp. Pres. Doc. 1272 on Sept. 26, 1986. *Letters and Other Writings of James Madison*, vol. 3, (Philadephia: J.B. Lippincott & Co.,1865), 442.
2. *Id.* (quoting Daniel Webster); *see generally* D. Webster, Fourth of July Oration at Fryeburg (1802), in 15 The Writings and Speeches of Daniel Webster 520 (E. Everett 1903).
3. Gladstone, "Kin Beyond Sea," *North American Review* 127 (1878), 185.

4. Letter from Richard Henry Lee to Edmund Randolph on Oct. 16, 1787. J. Ballagh, ed., Letters of Richard Henry Lee, vol. 2, (New York: MacMillan Company, 1914), 425.

5. Schecter, "The Early History of the Tradition of the Constitution." *American Political Science Review* 9, (1915) 707, 720.

6. Cooke, ed., *The Federalist Papers*, at 347, (Middelton, CT: Wesleyan University Press, 1961).

7. Warren, C., *The Supreme Court In The United States History*, vol. 3, (Boston; Little, Brown, and Co, 1923), 470–71.

8. Many critics focused on this sentence. In a further explanation his position, Mr. Meese said that while Supreme Court decisions interpreting the Constitution are not the "supreme law of the land" as the Constitution itself is "they are law, as I said at Tulane, and they are the law of the land in the sense that they do indeed have general applicability and deserve the greatest respect from all Americans." (Meese, "The Tulane Speech: What I Meant," *Washington Post*, Nov. 13, 1986, A21). Throughout this article and elsewhere, as in note 17, *infra*, Mr. Meese emphasizes that considerations of comity, prudence, and sound policy should cause the executive branch to give great consideration to Supreme Court precedent in making decisions with a constitutional dimension. But Mr. Meese also emphasizes that treating the prudential duty to consider precedent as equivalent to the obligation to act consistently with the Constitution would prevent the executive branch from re-litigating constitutional questions it believed the Court had decided wrongly. Elevating case law to the level of the Constitution might also logically undermine the Court's capacity to directly overrule itself.

9. *Plessy v. Ferguson*, 163 U.S. 537 (1896).

10. *Brown v. Board of Education of Topeka*, 347 U.S. 483 (1954).

11. *Batson v. Kentucky*, 476 U.S. 79 (1986).

12. *Swain v. Alabama*, 380 U.S. 202 (1965).

13. *Scott v. Sanford*, 60 U.S. (19 How.) 393 (1857).

14. Douglas's Rejoinder, Third Debate at Jonesboro on Sept. 15, 1858. *Collected Works of Abraham Lincoln*, vol. 3, (xx publisher xx, 1953),.142–43.

15. *Id.* at 243 (Douglas's Rejoinder, Fifth Debate at Galesburg (Oct. 7, 1858)).

16. 2 *Id.* at 516 (Lincoln, Speech at Springfield (July 17, 1858)).

17. 3 *Id.* at 255 (Lincoln's Opening, Sixth Debate at Quincy (Oct. 13, 1858)).

18. *Graves v. New York* ex rel. O'Keefe, 306 U.S. 446, 491-92 (1939) (Frankfurter, J., concurring).

19. 5 U.S. (1 Cranch) 137 (1803).

20. *Cooper v. Aaron*, 358 U.S. 1.

21. In *Brown v. Board of Ed.*, 347 U.S. 483 (1954), the Supreme Court held that enforced racial segregation in the public schools of a state violates the Fourteenth Amendment. In an effort to comply with *Brown*, the Little Rock, Arkansas, District School Board fashioned a desegregation plan that was approved by the federal district court. Yet other state authorities, including the Governor, sought to oppose school desegregation. On September 2, 1957, one day before nine black students were scheduled to be admitted to Central High School in Little Rock, the governor of Arkansas dispatched units of the Arkansas National Guard to the school grounds and placed the school "off limits" to black students. In subsequent proceedings, the district court granted a school board petition seeking postponement of the desegregation plan. The Court of Appeals for the Eighth Circuit reversed, however, and in *Cooper v. Aaron*, the Supreme Court affirmed the judgment of the Eighth Circuit, thus reinstating the orders of the district court enforcing the desegregation plan.

22. *Cooper*, 358 U.S. at 18. I emphasize that my criticism is aimed at the dictum of *Cooper*, not the holding, with which I am in complete accord. Furthermore, in my judgment, officials in Arkansas and other states with segregated school systems should have changed those systems to conform with *Brown*.

23. In addition to binding the parties in the case at hand, a decision is precedent in that it binds lower federal courts as well as state courts. Furthermore, Court decisions, as Abraham Lincoln once said, are "entitled to very high respect and consideration in all par-

allel cases" by the other departments of government, both federal and state. (Lincoln's First Inaugural Address on March 4, 1861.Gunther, G., *Constitutional Law*, 11th ed.,(New York: Foundation Press,1985), 23.). Arguments from prudence, the need for stability in the law, and respect for the judiciary will and should persuade officials of these other institutions to abide by a decision of the court. Supreme Court decisions thus have applicability beyond the instant case, but they are not "the supreme law of the land."

24. Speech to the Elmira Chamber of Commerce on May 3, 1907. *Addresses and Papers of Charles Evan Hughes* (New York : G.P. Putnam's Sons, 1908) 133, 139

25. Other critics of the *Cooper* dictum include University of Chicago Law Professor Philip Kurland. "The Court here was being carried away with its own sense of righteousness, if... it meant that a decision of the Supreme Court was supreme law in the way that a legislative act of Congress was supreme law." (P. Kurland, *Politics, The Constitution, And the Warren Court* (Chicago: University of Chicago Press, 1970), 116.). Kurland further noted:

> I am not quarreling with the result that the Court reached in *Cooper v. Aaron*. Indeed, I applaud it. Certainly interference with the effectuation of a decree of a federal court, whether by a governor of a state or a president of a union or a civil rights marcher, is intolerable and cannot be condoned. My question goes only to the elevation of Supreme Court decisions to inclusion in the Supremacy Clause of the Constitution.

    Id. at 185.

26. *Stone v. Graham*, 449 U.S. 39 (1980) (per curiam).

27. 5 U.S. (1 Cranch) at 179-80 (emphasis added).

28. *Id.* at 178.

29. Letter from James Madison 1834. *Letters and Other Writings of James Madison*, vol. 4, (xx publisher xx, 1865), 349.

30. Letter to Wilson Carey Nicholas on Sept. 7, 1803. P. Ford, ed., *The Writings of Thomas Jefferson*, vol. 8, (New York: G.P. Putnam's Sons, 1897), 247.

31. Lincoln's First Inaugural Address on March 4, 1861R. Basler, ed., *Collected Works for Abraham Lincoln*, vol. 4, (xx publisher xx, 1953), 262.
32. P. Kurland, *supra* note 19, at 186.
33. Cicero, *Pro Cluentio.*
34. Cf. J. Elliot, ed., *The Debates In The Several State Conventions On The Adoption Of The Federal Constitution*, vol. 4, (Washingon: Taylor & Maury, 1836) 543.

Eight: Panel on Originalism and Pragmatism

1. Breyer, Stephen, *Active Liberty,* (New York: Knopf, 2005).
2. *McCulloch v. Maryland*, 17 U.S. (4 Wheat.) 316, 406–07 (1819).
3. 5 U.S. (1 Cranch) 137 (1803).
4. I flesh out this line of argument in "Judicial Discretion in Statutory Interpretation." *Oklahoma Law Review* 57 (2004): 1. "Textualism and the Dead Hand." *George Washington Law Review* 66 (1998): 1119. "The State of Madison's Vision of the State." *Harvard Law Review* 107 (1994): 1328. and "Abstraction and Authority." *University of Chicago Law Review* 59 (1992): 349.
5. See, e.g., Posner, Richard A., "Foreword: A Political Court." *Harvard Law Review* 119 (2005): 32, 90. (stating that pragmatism "asks judges to focus on the practical consequences of their decisions").
6. See, e.g., Dorf, Michael C., "Foreword: The Limits of Socratic Deliberation." *Harvard Law Review* 112 (1998): 4, 26. Arguing that originalism seems to be characterized by its "inattention" to "future consequences."
7. Bork, Robert H., *The Tempting of America*, (New York: Free Press, 1990), 143–53. This makes the argument that originalism advances democracy—"In truth, only the approach of original understanding meets the criteria that any theory of constitutional adjudication must meet in order to possess democratic legitimacy."
8. See generally Scalia, Antonin, "Originalism: The Lesser Evil." *University of Cincinnati Law Review* 57 (1989): 849, 863–64.

9. The constraint rationale for originalism may animate *Employment Division v. Smith*, 494 U.S. 872, 872–90 (1992), in which Justice Antonin Scalia, a notable originalist, spends little time investigating the original meaning of the Free Exercise Clause, but emphasizes that his result will provide a clearer rule than other constructions.

10. See Alexander, Larry, " 'With Me, It's All or Nuthin:' Formalism in Law and Morality." *University of Chiicago Law Review* 66 (200): 530, 534. (Describes the framework for governance as requiring the elimination of "coordination problem[s]" and regarding the propriety of decisions and other "attempts by agents to undertake mutually incompatible actions.")

11. Scalia, *supra* note 4, at 863 ("It is very difficult for a person to discern a difference between those political values that he personally thinks most important, and those political values that are 'fundamental to our society.' ").

12. See infra notes 47-53 and accompanying text (discussing the exclusion of African Americans and women from a role in selecting drafters and ratifiers of the Constitution).

13. See Treanor, William Michael, "The Original Understanding of the Takings Clause and the Political Process." *Columbia Law Review* 95 (1995): 782, 856. Argues that originalism is animated by the belief that "the rule of law requires judges to follow externally imposed rules"

14. To be more exact, statutes are passed not under simple majority rule but under a tricameral process that creates the equivalent of a mild supermajority rule. See McGinnis, John O., and Michael B. Rappaport, "Our Supermajoritarian Constitution." *Texas Law Review* 80 (2002): 703, 769–774. But this process is not nearly as stringent as the supermajoritarian process for enacting and amending the Constitution and is not stringent enough to correct for the serious defects in majoritarian entrenchment.

15. The constitution does consist mainly, albeit not entirely, of rules rather than standards.

16. A good summary of the benefits can be found in Posner, Eric A., and Adrian Vermeule, "Legislative Entrenchment: A Reappraisal." *Yale Law Journal* 111 (2002): 1665, 1670–73. See also. McGinnis, John O., and Michael B. Rappaport, "Symmetric Entrenchment: A Constitutional and Normative Theory." *Virginia Law Review* 84 (2003): 385.

17. The reasons for the view that majority rule is beneficial are complex, but include both preference and epistemic arguments. See Michelman, Frank, "Why Voting." *Loyola of Los Angeles Law Review* 34 (2001): 985, 996. One important exception to the presumed beneficence of majority rule occurs if citizens have preferences of different intensity about an issue. In that case a majority that enjoys modest benefits can get a law enacted, even if the minority suffers much greater costs. Elsewhere we suggest that entrenchment actually tempers this problem as well. See McGinnis, John O., and Michael B. Rappaport, "Majority and Supermajority Rule: Three Views of the Capitol" (paper on file).

18. See Shugerman, Jed Handelsman, "A Six-Three Rule: Reviving Consensus and Deference on the Supreme Court." *Georgia Law Review* 37 (2003): 893, 937–39. Arguing that consensus is key to democratic legitimacy.

19. Cf. Schapiro, Robert A., "Identity and Interpretation in State Constitutional Law." *Virginia Law Review* 84 (2004): 389, 394. Stating that state constitutionalism helps transcend communal identities.

20. It might be argued that parties could avoid the prisoner's dilemma created by majoritarian entrenchment simply by entrenching a prohibition on matters that the other party would entrench when it came to power. One difficulty with this strategy is that a party cannot necessarily predict the full range of measures the other party will want to entrench and thus faces far more uncertainty in determining what entrenchments to prohibit than in determining what entrenchments to make. For instance, one party may seem to be interested in entrenching health care entitlements. While that entrenchment could be prohibited, when that party comes to

power, it might desire to make a different entrenchment. Given the difficulty in blocking the other party's desired entrenchments, the majority party may decide it is more attractive to entrench an item central its own party's ideology.

21. It is well recognized, for instance, that the supermajority for the convictions required for impeachment tamps down on partisanship. See Gerhardt, Michael J., "The Special Constitutional Structure of the Federal Impeachment Process." *Law and Contemp.* 34 (2000): Probs. 245, 250.

22. The roots of this tendency lie in the "representativeness" heuristic. That heuristic tends to make people extrapolate overconfidently about predicted characteristics of a class based upon a small sample size of which they happen to be aware. See Tversky, Amos & Daniel Kahneman, "Belief in the Law of Small Numbers." *in* Judgment Under Uncertainty: Heuristics and Biases 23, 24-25 (Daniel Kahneman et al. eds., 1982). If the sample consists of events rather than objects, the heuristic should tend to make people extrapolate in a similarly irrational manner from events of which they are aware to uncertain future events. For an important present-day application, see Shiller, Robert J., *Irrational Exuberance* (Princeton: Princeton University Press, 2000),144. (Using work on the representativeness heuristic to suggest that people will think stock market patterns today will be those of tomorrow).

23. On the veil of ignorance, see Fitts, Michael A., "Can Ignorance Be Bliss? Imperfect Information as a Positive Influence in Political Institutions." *Michigan Law Review* 88 (1990): 917, 922–923.

24. Again, the one glaring defect in those supermajority rules was their exclusion of African-Americans and women from the franchise, which we discuss below. *See infra* notes 47-53 and accompanying text.

25. U.S. Constitution, art V.

26. *Id.* at art VII.

27. *See* Bowen Catherine Drinker, *Miracle at Philadelphia: The Story of the Constitutional Convention, May to September1787,* (Boston: Little, Brown, and Company, 1966), 225–28 (discussing

events that precipitated the Constitutional Convention's decision to require the approval of nine States to ratify the Constitution).

28. See, e.g., *The Federalist* 69. Discussing both four-year term for President and impeachment as check on authority of executive.

29. See Diamond, Martin, "What the Framers Meant by Federalism." *American Intergovernmental Relations* 39, 43–44 (Laurence J. O'Toole, Jr. ed., 2d ed. 1993) (seeing American federalism as a compromise between nationalists and true federalists).

30. See Levy, Leonard, Emergence of a Free Press (New York: Oxford University Press, 1985), 234–35. (describing the Bill of Rights as tactical compromise between Federalists and Anti-federalists).

31. See Rappaport, Michael B., "The Original Meaning of the Recess Appointments Clause." UCLA 52 (2005): 1487, 1494–95 n.21.

32. For an explication of the distinction between original intent and original meaning, see Barnett, Randy E., "The Original Meaning of the Commerce Clause." University of Chicago Law Review 68 (2001): 101, 105–08. See also, Scalia, Antonin *A Matter of Interpretation: Federal Courts and the Law* (Princeton: Princeton University Press, 1998).

33. For an example of an originalist who does not believe in following the interpretive conventions of the Framers, see Caleb Nelson, Originalism and Interpretive Conventions, 70 U. Chi. L. Rev. 519, 525 n.23 (2003) (citing Gregory Bassham, Original Intent and the Constitution: A Philosophical Study 70 (Rowman & Littlefield 1992)).

34. For a discussion of the enterprise of using interpretive rules to fix meaning, see Caleb Nelson, supra, note 29.

35. See McGinnis, John O. "Justice without Justices." Constitutional Commentary 16. (1999): 541, 542–43. Discusses factors that make Supreme Court Justices remote.

36. See Amar, Akhil Reed, "The Supreme Court, 1999 Term—Forward: The Document and the Doctrine." *Harvard Law Review* 114 (2000): 26, 34–48. Similar but distinct arguments for why the Constitution and its amendments should take priority over judicial doctrine.

37. See generally Strauss, David A., "Common Law Constitutional Interpretation." *University of Chicago Law Review* 63 (1996): 877. Arguing that "it is the common law approach . . . that best explains, and best justifies, American constitutional law."

38. Some might argue that since the supermajoritarian process establishes only a presumption of beneficence, judges should be able to use non-originalist methods of construing a particular provision if they independently determine that the provision is undesirable. The difficulty with this approach is that judges have no adequate process for determining either when this presumption in favor of the original constitutional norm should be overcome and what new norm it should replaced with. Moreover, judges of various ideologies cannot be expected to reach agreement on any alternative method or even apply their own chosen method consistently because of biases unchecked by others of different ideology working within the same methodology. As a result, the norms selected would tend to unpredictable and partisan.

39. Some may argue that our pragmatic claim for originalism is as contestable as those made in the usual pragmatic theories of justice. But our claim is based on a procedural theory demonstrating the virtues of supermajoritarian entrenchments. In contrast, arguments about the beneficence of particular decisions generally must rest on substantive theories based on thicker notions of the good. Procedural arguments can command greater consensus than substantive ones. In addition, we need only defend a single claim, whereas case by case pragmatism must predict and defend the consequences of an endless series of discrete decisions.

40. See, e.g., Amar, supra note 32, at 35.

41. See Bernstein, David E., "Philip Sober Controlling Philip Drunk: Buchanan v. Warley in Historical Perspective." *Vanderbilt Law Review* 51 (1998): 797, 815 .Discussing this Progressive attack.

42. See McConnell, Michael W., "Textualism and the Dead Hand of the Past." *George Washington Law Review* 66 (1998): 1128, 1128–29.

43. Id. at 1130.

44. See Sangree, Suzanne, "Title IX and the Contact Sports Exemption: Gender Stereotypes in a Civil Rights Statute." *Connecticut Law Review* 32 (2000): 381, 412.

45. See, e.g, Lessig, Lawrence, "Fidelity in Translation." *Texas Law Review* 71 (1993): 1165, 1170–74.

46. With the exception of the 13th Amendment, the Constitution does not regulate private conduct at all. Nor does it prescribe many substantive regulations for the government. Instead it largely sets out decision-making rules for governmental institutions to regulate both private and governmental conduct.

47. Cf. McCulloch v. Maryland, 17 U.S. (4 Wheat.) 316, 407–08 (1819)

48. See Hamburger, Philip A., "The Constitution's Accommodation of Social Change." *Michigan Law Review* 88 (1989): 239, 306–09.

49. The original Constitution contained a quite modest set of restrictions on states. See U.S. Const. art.I, § 10 (containing certain limits on states such as forbidding states from coining money or entering into compacts with other states). The restrictions of the Fourteenth Amendment are more extensive, particularly if one believes that the Fourteenth Amendment incorporates the Bill of Rights. But even the provisions of the Bill of Rights construed according to their original meaning do not impose draconian restrictions on the states.

50. See Lund, Nelson and John O. McGinnis, "Lawrence v. Texas and Judicial Hubris." *Michigan Law Review* 102 (2004): 1555, 1599–1607. Discussing competitive federalism as an engine of social change.

51. See, e.g., Marshall, Thurgood, "Reflections on the Bicentennial of the United States Constitution." *Harvard Law Review* 101 (1987): 1, 2.

52. See U.S. Const. amends. XIII, XIV, & XV.

53. See, e.g., Marshall, supra note 37, at 3–5 (discussing how treatment of African Americans constituted an "inherent defect" of the original Constitution).

54. See Kull, Andrew, *The Color-Blind Constitution* (Cambridge, MA: Harvard University Press, 1992), 7–9 (noting that the original Constitution was used to argue for abolition and equality).
55. See U.S. Const. art. XIX.
56. Mansbridge, J., Why We Lost the ERA (Chicago: University of Chicago Press, 1986), 46. Suggesting that the Supreme Court's innovations in applying the 14th amendment as a principle of gender equality undermined the case for ratification of the Equal Rights Amendment.
57. While here we have addressed the most obvious defects arising from the exclusion of women and African-Americans from the framing, it might be argued that their absence caused subtler, more wide ranging problems. Under this view, these groups would have not only sought equality provisions, but also had a different substantive agenda. We do not, however, believe that one can make a strong case that the Constitution would have been systematically different had these excluded groups been included. In the absence of strong evidence that the Constitution would have been transformed by these other voters, the original Constitution's rules should be followed, because they still offer the best evidence of what good entrenchments would have resembled.
58. U.S. Const. art. II, § 1, cl. 5.

Ten: Debate on the Original Meaning of the Commerce, Spending, and Necessary and Proper Clauses

1. See Randy E. Barnett, "It's a Bird, It's a Plane, No, It's Super-Precedent: A Reply to Farber and Gerhard," 90 *Minnesota Law Review* 1232 (2006).

INDEX